THE MALE DANCER

In this challenging and lively book Ramsay Burt examines the representation of masculinity in twentieth-century dance. Taking issue with formalist and modernist accounts of dance, which dismiss gender and sexuality as irrelevant, he argues that prejudices against male dancers are rooted in our ideas about the male body and male behaviour.

Building upon ideas about the gendered gaze developed by film and feminist theorists, Ramsay Burt provides a provocative theory of spectatorship in dance. He uses this to examine the work of choreographers like Nijinsky, Graham and Bausch, while relating their dances to the social, political and artistic contexts in which they were produced. Within these re-readings he identifies a distinction between institutionalized modernist dance which evokes an essentialist, heroic 'hypermasculinity' – one which is valorized with reference to nature, heterosexuality and religion – and radical avant-garde choreography which challenges and disrupts dominant ways of representing masculinity.

The Male Dancer will be essential reading for anyone interested in dance and the cultural construction of gender.

Ramsay Burt has taught art and design history and film studies to art students, as well as painting and exhibiting his own work. He has also taught dance history and theory and has recently completed a doctoral thesis on representations of masculinity in British new dance.

THE MALE DANCER

Bodies, Spectacle, Sexualities

Ramsay Burt

London and New York

First published 1995
by Routledge
11 New Fetter Lane, London EC4P 4EE

Simultaneously published in the USA and Canada
by Routledge
29 West 35th Street, New York, NY 10001

Reprinted 1996

Routledge is an International Thomson Publishing company

© 1995 Ramsay Burt

Typeset in Palatino by
Ponting–Green Publishing Services, Chesham, Bucks
Printed in Great Britain by
Biddles Ltd, Guildford and King's Lynn

The author asserts the moral right to be
identified as the author of this work.

British Library Cataloguing in Publication Data
A catalogue record for this book is available from
the British Library

Library of Congress Cataloguing in Publication Data
A catalogue record for this book is available from the
Library of Congress

ISBN 0–415–08899–2 (hbk)
ISBN 0–415–08900–X (pbk)

For M. K. B. 1915–1982

CONTENTS

FIGURES

ACKNOWLEDGEMENTS

No doubt everyone who researches a particular subject in order to write a book ends up with a long list of people who have contributed in a variety of ways. I owe much to Valerie Briginshaw who has cast a sharp eye and given me feedback on drafts of every chapter, to Lynn Garafola who made many detailed and useful comments and suggestions about Chapters 4 and 5 and to Christy Adair and Sarah Rubidge for reading through other chapters. Thanks to Lea Anderson, Frank Bock, Nigel Charnock, Fergus Early and Lloyd Newson, who all very generously allowed me to interview them while each was in the middle of a busy working period; also to Michael Huxley, Maggie Morris, Nick Nuttgens, Jane Pritchard at Rambert Dance Company and the Hall Carpenter Archives at the British Library of Political Economy and Science. An earlier version of Chapter 6 was presented as a paper at the Definitive Post-modern Dance summer school at West Sussex Institute of Higher Education, Chichester in 1991 where I was registered as a research student. I particularly wish to acknowledge my debt of gratitude to the two supervisors for my thesis, Valerie Briginshaw and Richard Dyer: many of the ideas in the book first found form there. Lastly, without the support of my partner, Pauline Storie, and the forbearance of our children, Brendan Hessle, Merlin and Ceridwen Ash, this book would never have got finished.

Leeds, March 1994

INTRODUCTION

I hardly knew of the existence of dance or ballet at all until I was 26 years old. By then I had a degree in painting and art history, and had read some feminist film theory. A friend persuaded me to go to a festival of experimental dance at Dartington College in the south-west of England, and virtually my first dance class was a workshop in contact improvisation with Steve Paxton. In retrospect, the experience brought about a big change in my life. Had I been younger I might have tried to become a professional dancer; I have ended up writing about dance instead. I was born and brought up in a small town in the north of England far from anywhere that ballet was performed, and at a time when modern dance was virtually unknown in England except among a few people in London. As a boy and young man I was taken to art galleries and to concerts of classical music. I don't recall any of my family's acquaintances ever going to see a ballet, nor was I aware of the existence of ballet schools. Ballet was not an area of experience considered appropriate for young men like myself, or even one in which I might be interested.

My experience is not untypical of men of my class and background. Professional dance during approximately the last hundred and fifty years has not been considered an appropriate activity for white men to engage in. Such is the strength of the prejudice against male dancers that a large proportion of the men who have pursued careers in modern dance and to a lesser extent ballet have often not discovered dancing until they were in their teens or early twenties. Far fewer men go into professional dance training than women, and it is consequently much easier for men to find employment in dance than for women. At the same time, men occupy a disproportionate number of the artistic and administrative positions at the top of the dance profession. As Christy Adair points out:

> Women do have a very strong presence in dance but a good deal of work needs to be put into equal opportunities policies and practices in dance for women to benefit. In order for women's perspectives to be clearly established and influential, women need to have access to

1

positions of power and decision-making as choreographers, adminis-
trators and directors.

(1992: 238)

It would seem desirable both to improve women's position in the dance
professions and to change negative attitudes towards the male dancer.
There shouldn't necessarily be a conflict between the two, but clearly a big
increase in the number of men entering the dance professions could
worsen women's already precarious and sometimes extremely exploited
position.

This book is not primarily concerned with the structures and politics of
the dance professions but with images of men in twentieth-century theatre
dance. Theatre dance is dance performed on stage rather than dance
activity occurring in social situations. In looking at gender representations,
my approach is inspired by the achievements of the women's movement
in redefining images of women. Issues relating to images of men, however,
are often different from those which affect images of women. There is
a key difference between re-evaluating images of women and doing the
same for images of men. Part of the feminist project has been to reclaim
and redefine femininity, and to celebrate the achievements of women
artists and thus contradict the legacy of centuries of definition and
domination by men. To what extent can men's achievements in dance be
celebrated without at the same time reasserting male dominance and
thus reinforcing the imbalance of power between men and women in
our society? In an ideal world, men should be able to find ways of
expressing their individual experiences through dance and contribute to
non-discriminatory perceptions of the differences between men and
women. The reality is of course the reverse: images of men generally
reinforce male dominance over women. But, as is argued in the first part
of this book, patriarchy is maintained through limiting the ways in which
masculinity is represented in cultural forms including theatre dance. To
become aware of the conscious and unconscious ways through which
dominant ideas are inscribed in theatre dance, is a step towards understanding how to create alternative, non-oppressive representations.

The history of theatre dance in the twentieth century has been one of
continual reform and innovation, and one in which questions of gender
and gender representation have never been far from the surface. 'Modern',
'new', 'contemporary', 'postmodern' or 'post-modern', 'new wave', 'next
wave' are all terms that have been used by dance critics and commentators
to describe particular developments in theatre dance, often to imply that
this latest style renders all previous styles outmoded. The label 'modern
dance' generally refers to the work of the pioneer dance reformers (nearly
all of whom were women) who developed styles other than ballet,
including Ruth St Denis (1879–1968), Isadora Duncan (1877–1927), Doris

Humphrey (1895–1958), Martha Graham (1894–1991), Rudolph Laban (1879–1958), Ted Shawn (1891–1972) and Mary Wigman (1886–1973) during the first half of the twentieth century. The term 'contemporary dance' is sometimes used to distinguish the work produced in the United States during the 1950s and 1960s from the work of the earlier modern dance artists; most of the younger choreographers – such as Merce Cunningham, Paul Taylor and Alvin Ailey – had started their careers dancing in companies run by the earlier pioneers. These were predominantly men. It was also under the label 'contemporary' that modern and contemporary dance from the United States were introduced to Great Britain starting in the 1960s. Throughout this book, however, the term 'contemporary' is not used and 'modern' is used instead to cover both the earlier pioneering modern dance and the later work that continues within that tradition. 'Modern' dance, in this sense, is the mainstream modernist dance tradition that made up (and still largely constitutes) the repertoires of the larger mainstream European and North American modern dance companies.

The pioneers of modern dance were predominantly women. Similarly the development of ballet in Britain in the twentieth century was initiated by two women: Marie Rambert (1888–1982) and Ninette de Valois (b. 1898). To work out why there were so few men involved in these developments one has to look into the social and institutional factors that have until very recently restricted women's access to the artistic professions. Up until the nineteenth century, most women artists in the male-dominated field of painting were able to gain access to training and to the specialist knowledge of their chosen profession only by being 'under the protection' of a male artist, often their father.[1] Bronislava Nijinska (1891–1972) is the only female choreographer of the first half of the twentieth century to make work with the resources of a major, already existing ballet company – initially the Ballets Russes. An important factor that enabled her to do this was the knowledge and experience of the sorts of artistic ideas and practices that lay behind the development of the Ballets Russes' work which she had gained through her involvement in the work of her brother Vaslav Nijinsky (1889–1950). Clearly one reason why women initially developed a new area – modern dance – was because of their restricted access to creative positions in the existing one. Furthermore the female pioneers of modern dance did not have any vested interests in upholding the specialist traditions of ballet, and were therefore freer than men to develop new and alternative forms and representations. In Rambert and de Valois' case there was no prestigious tradition of ballet dancing in Britain (though there was ballet in music halls), and they were thus not competing with men in starting their schools and companies.

There were some male choreographers active in American modern dance but their situation was the mirror image of that which had faced earlier women painters. Ted Shawn would surely never have got where he did as a dancer and choreographer without the help of Ruth St Denis. José Limón (1908–72) and Charles Weidman (1901–75), as Marcia Siegel suggests, were both dependent on Doris Humphrey for much longer than they needed to be (Siegel 1987). In Britain Marie Rambert 'discovered' and nurtured the fledgling talents of several male choreographers (and, unlike de Valois, one or two women choreographers) of whom the most celebrated were Frederick Ashton (1904–88) and Anthony Tudor (1908–87). According to her autobiography (1972), Rambert was not particularly keen to choreograph work herself and gave up doing so in the early days of her ballet company. De Valois however choreographed several substantial ballets, some of which were much admired at the time. She, however, believed that men rather than women should choreograph work and the principal choreographers and artistic directors of the Royal Ballet which she founded have all been male (see Adair 1992: 111–12).

The subsequent history of modern dance in the United States has also been one of increasing male influence and subsequent dominance. The leading modern dance artists in the 1930s are generally considered to be Martha Graham, Doris Humphrey, Helen Tamiris, Hanya Holm and Pauline Koner. By 1960 the leading modern choreographer was unquestionably Martha Graham; but, after her, most of the other important choreographers were men.

In the 1970s and 1980s male ballet dancers even eclipsed ballerinas in terms of salary, media attention and drawing power at the box office. A few recent books on the male dancer[2] have celebrated what Judith Lynne Hanna has called the big bucks of modern ballet. Some female dance writers have even expressed dismay at this male resurgence, implying that these men have unfairly taken over 'areas once securely reserved for women' (Hanna 1988: 144).

Dance is not an exclusively or innately feminine activity, and most people would surely accept that the history of twentieth-century dance would have been poorer without the contribution of male dancers and choreographers. It is surely a mistake to view the resurgence of the male ballet dancer and the entry of male choreographers into the previously feminine realm of modern dance as instances of men waiting until women have put in all the hard work and then taking over. Often what leads men to start dance training is the discovery of their own unrealized potential; this is frequently brought about by seeing an inspirational performance by another male dancer. Shawn may well have been inspired by seeing the Russian ballet dancer Mikhail Mordkin (who toured the United States with Pavlova in 1909 and with his own company in 1911–12 while Shawn took up dancing in 1911). José Limón and Erick Hawkins (1909–94) were both inspired to take up dancing after seeing a performance in New York in 1929 by the German dancer Harald Kreutzberg (1902–68). Furthermore,

4

if one accepts that star male dancers generally attract large audiences, this must be largely because women enjoy watching male dancers. Statistics show that women generally outnumber men in audiences for dance and ballet performances.[3]

This book does not present a survey of male dance in the twentieth century, nor does it set out to define or celebrate the achievements of men as professional dancers. Instead it examines a selection of significant developments in the representation of masculinity in western theatre dance during the twentieth century. A critical reading of these is proposed which grounds them in the social and political contexts within which they were created. A major assumption that underlies this selection is that it is only within work that is progressive, experimental or avant-garde that staid, old-fashioned images and ideas about gender can be challenged and alternatives imagined. I have never seen a ballet performance that has not disappointed me. Perhaps I have been unlucky in what I have chosen or been able to see, but consequently this is not the book of a ballet lover.[4] I have sought instead to characterize the conventions and criteria of mainstream and more conservative dance and ballet in quite general terms, and then to use this as a basis for evaluating the work of reformers and innovators. The last four chapters of this book therefore look at: the reintroduction of the male dancer to western theatres by the Ballets Russes; the virile image of the male dancer that developed in American modern dance during the first half of the century; and the ways in which avant-garde and postmodern choreographers have been able to adapt, react against or reject the legacy of existing ways in which masculinity is conventionally represented in theatre dance.

The theoretical framework for looking at representations of gender in theatre dance that is developed in the first part of the book attempts to take into account the social and historical conditions of production and reception of dance, including issues of class, gender, race and sexuality. The rest of the book, however, at the risk of being accused of ethnocentrism, looks at representations of masculinity only in the context of western theatre dance. It is therefore concerned only with black dance artists who have worked within or have extended the tradition of western modernist dance. Regrettably this excludes the work of dance artists whose work derives from the revival of traditional African, Caribbean and Indian dance styles, as well as recent experimental Japanese theatre dance. The reason for this is the expediency of limiting the scope of enquiry. A somewhat overused adage has it that dance is a universal language. If this is so, one shouldn't underestimate the differences between its dialects. Representations of gender in African, Caribbean, Indian, Japanese and western (European and North American) dance and theatre traditions are each grounded in different, socially constructed ideas about the body. Chapter 1 of this book relates representations of masculinity in western

5

Figure 1 Nijinsky and Karsavina in *Le Spectre de la rose*
(© The Board of Trustees of the Victoria and Albert Museum.
Reproduced with permission from the Theatre Museum, V. & A.)

theatre dance to the development in Europe during the eighteenth and nineteenth centuries of scientific ideas about the modern body. To do this for each of these other traditions in the same depth would be a sizeable undertaking, and one that is beyond the scope of this book.

The case for excluding recent Japanese dance requires further comment. There have undoubtedly been some fascinating images of masculinity produced by Japanese Butoh artists. By not including these in the present study I have not meant to imply that they are fundamentally different and 'Other'. From a Japanese point of view it might be argued that Butoh is the work of European-oriented Japanese performers who were initially influenced by German modern dance artists and then by American modern dance – particularly the movement style developed by Martha Graham. What generally strikes the European observer however is not the links with their own modernist dance traditions but the conventions that derive from Japanese theatre traditions which are themselves rooted in Japanese social conventions and traditions. It is because of the complexity of the task of locating Butoh within the terms of reference of the rest of the book that it has been left out.

The other area that unfortunately, but unavoidably, receives no attention in this book is representations of masculinity in early modern dance in Germany. There were a number of men working as dancers and choreographers in modern dance styles in Germany in the period immediately following the 1914–18 world war. These included Kurt Jooss (1901–79), Albrecht Knust (1896–1978), Harald Kreutzberg, Sigurd Leeder (1902–81) and Rudolf Laban. It would be extremely useful to be able to compare the ways in which masculinity was represented in their work with, for example, the ways in which it was represented in the work of the Ballets Russes and in modern dance in the United States. However, with the exception of Jooss, there is very little evidence or documentation available in English about the choreography and performances of any of these northern European artists and it is for this reason that they are missing from the present study. However, the images of men that Pina Bausch has created in her work are included in Chapter 7.

The subtitle of the book – bodies, spectacle, sexualities – indicates key issues in the representation of masculinity in theatre dance. First the body is the primary mode of communication in dance, and it is through our bodies that we are allocated our gender. Issues relating to the social construction of the gendered body are central to the way gender is represented in theatre dance. But theatre dance is also a spectacle. Different performances invite the spectator to look at dance in different ways – for example, consider the difference in the way a performance of a classic nineteenth-century ballet presents the audience with a clearly focused spectacle while a Cunningham event is more open, leaving it up to the spectator to choose what to watch and for how long. The way spectators derive pleasure from the spectacle of dance is also determined by their gender, social background, ethnicity, age, sexuality and other components of identity. The question of sexualities is particularly important. It is argued in Chapter 3 that the traditions and conventions of mainstream theatre dance are formed by and reinforce a normative heterosexual, male point of view, marginalizing and suppressing alternative sexualities.

Future historians may look back on the period from around 1830 until around 1980 as a curiously anomalous one during which the male body became a taboo subject for cultural representation. Until comparatively recently, surviving nineteenth-century gender ideologies have denied the possibility that women might find the male body of any interest – erotic or otherwise – while punishing attempts to create a homoerotic view of the male body. At the same time, during the twentieth century, gay men, predominantly in the field of ballet, and heterosexual women, in the field of modern dance, have been largely responsible for developing male dancing. But the conventions through which they have done this have dictated, first, that the audience look from a male point of view and are thus uninterested in the spectacle of the male dancing body, and second that masculinity is an unproblematic and unquestioned norm. This has resulted in, first, the range of male dancing being largely limited to the expression of male dominance and control over female bodies, and, second, in a tough, hard, vocabulary of macho movements and gestures. The American postmodern choreographer Mark Morris gave an interviewer an illustration of how limited he found the male dancer to be in comparison with the female performer. A woman in rehearsal, he says, can be asked to act like a 65-year-old man but 'straight' (heterosexual) men are too embarrassed to act like 13-year-old girls (Acocella 1993: 92). Morris (whose work is considered in Chapter 7) is one of a comparatively small number of recent choreographers who have set out to challenge and disrupt the ways in which gender is conventionally represented in theatre dance.

Some writers have begun to ask questions about how gender and sexuality have been represented in dance. The scope of such enquiries can sometimes be limited by formalist aesthetics and modernist approaches to dance theory that have in recent years become the dominant framework for serious writing about dance in Britain and the United States. Some formalist dance theorists have argued that dance is not a representational practice, while a prevalent modernist view proposes that modern dance and ballet are progressively purifying themselves of outmoded and extraneous representational practices. The implication of both these views is that questions of how gender is represented in theatre dance are irrelevant to what has generally been thought to be the true nature of dance as art. The second chapter of this book sets out to counteract these points of view and to develop an account of representation in dance that draws on theories of expression, phenomenology and hermeneutic philosophy, and post-structuralist theory.

The first and third chapters of this book locate masculinity and its representation in theatre dance within recent sociological debates, in the area of gender studies and film and cultural studies. Chapter 1 asks the question why the male dancer over the last hundred and fifty years has been a source of unease and suspicion. Chapter 3 is concerned with conventions that determine the way the male body is looked at in cultural forms, examining in particular the idea of the gendered gaze. Together these three chapters develop the criteria for the analysis of dance work in the rest of the book which looks at: the legacy of Nijinsky in Chapter 4; the work of Graham and other American modern dance choreographers in Chapter 5, of Merce Cunningham, Trisha Brown and Steve Paxton in Chapter 6 and of Pina Bausch and other postmodern choreographers in Chapter 7.

What is argued is that masculinity as a socially constructed identity is not a stable entity. Rather, it is made up of conflictual and contradictory aspects. Representations of masculinity in theatre dance over the last hundred and fifty years have threatened (more so in some ways than other cultural forms) to disrupt and destabilize masculine identity. This suggests specific questions and issues which underlie the analysis and interpretation in the last four chapters. What makes extreme, almost stereotypical repres-entations of violent, macho masculinity appear to support dominant conservative norms of masculinity in one ballet or modern dance piece but criticize and threaten these norms in another? Why is it that some choreographers have been able to reject and subvert the conventions and traditions through which masculinity is represented, while others' attempts have been recuperated within dominant conservative gender ideologies? How is it that some choreographers have succeeded in making visible aspects of masculine experience that are otherwise denied or rendered invisible within mainstream work? Finally, this book is concerned with identifying key issues and strategies that offer the radical dance artist potential sites at which to deconstruct the conflictual and contradictory aspects of dominant notions of masculine identity and create the possibility of representing new, alternative, non-discriminatory perceptions of the differences between men and women in theatre dance.

1

THE TROUBLE WITH THE
MALE DANCER. . .

'The unpleasant thing about a danseuse is that she sometimes brings along a male dancer.' This is the title of one of Edouard de Beaumont's lithographs of scenes at the Paris Opera in the nineteenth century.[1] It shows a male figure dancing, while behind him slightly to one side is a ballerina with little sylph wings who turns her head deferentially towards him. He wears tights, has an ugly face, solid thighs and big hands. The artist, however, has not made him look grotesque, just less attractive than the ballerina. The implication is that the viewer would rather look at her, but the male dancer wants you to look at him, and anyway he is in the way. The title appeals to a shared prejudice about these 'unpleasant things'. At the end of the twentieth century, one is tempted to read into the scene more recent prejudices against the male dancer. Nevertheless the print captures a particular historical moment with its associated attitudes towards class, gender and aesthetics, all of which have had a strong influence on the development of later attitudes. Up until the nineteenth century in Europe, prejudices against the male dancer did not exist. By the end of the twentieth century these have developed and changed in response to a variety of social and historical factors. The print takes for granted that everyone knows what is wrong with the male dancer, but more or less leaves it unstated. That which is unstated, and by implication should not be stated in polite company, can be a powerful incitement to prejudice. So what then is the trouble with the male dancer?

Today one might answer this question in a number of ways, depending upon point of view and the sort of dance with which one is familiar. One might feel distaste at macho displays of male energy on the dance stage – what are they trying to prove, etc.? Or one might feel that male dancers are generally a disappointment – they just don't look very masculine. Or again one might feel that the ways in which one has seen masculinity represented in dance do not seem very relevant to one's own experience of class, race, gender, sexuality, etc. Then there are those who do enjoy watching male dance, and wish there were more male dancers around to watch. In the area of modern and experimental dance during the twentieth

Figure 2 'The unpleasant thing about a danseuse is that she
sometimes brings along a male dancer'.
Lithograph by Edouard de Beaumont from his series
L'Opéra au XIX siècle (British Museum)

century, a large number of male dancers did not actually discover dance until their late teens or early twenties. This is undoubtedly largely the result of prejudices against the male dancer.

For much of the twentieth century, the dance world has tended to appear to be predominantly a feminine realm in terms of audiences, dancers and teachers. The fact that, for example, in Britain and the United States ballet and modern dance teachers have been predominantly women has been cited as one reason for male dancers' 'effeminacy' (e.g. Manchester 1950). But for many people, a key source of contemporary prejudice is the association between male dancers and homosexuality. It is certainly true that there are a lot of gay men involved in the dance world. Although by no means all male dancers are gay, this is what prejudice suggests. One explanation of macho male display dance is sometimes surely that dancers are trying to show that they are not effeminate, where 'effeminate' is a code word for homosexual.

There is a profound silence in the dance world on the subject of male dance and homosexuality. Commenting on the fact that the early American modern dancer Ted Shawn was gay, Judith Lynn Hanna in her book *Dance, Sex and Gender* (1988) points to the irony in the time and effort he and his company of male dancers 'spent trying to prove that they were not what Shawn and many of the company were' (1988: 141). What she doesn't seem to realize is that for gay men at that time 'coming out' was not an option. With the trial of Oscar Wilde as a terrible example, and with fear of blackmail, it is not surprising that so many in the dance world have, in order to protect individuals, taken the line of denying any knowledge of homosexuality among dancers.

By no means all male dancers are gay, and the belief that they are is not in itself an entirely satisfactory explanation of the prejudice. If one takes a historical perspective, there is as yet no firm evidence of gay involvement in ballet before the time of Diaghilev and Nijinsky at the beginning of the twentieth century, whereas the prejudice against the male dancer developed during the flowering of the Romantic ballet, in the second quarter of the nineteenth century when de Beaumont drew the lithograph discussed above. Examination of attitudes towards the male dancer during this earlier period (considered below) suggests that what is at stake is the development of modern, middle-class attitudes towards the male body and the expressive aspects of male social behaviour. Gender representations in cultural forms, including theatre dance, do not merely reflect changing social definitions of femininity and masculinity but are actively involved in the processes through which gender is constructed. What concerns us here is the way that the socially produced parameters of and limits on male behaviour are expressed in representations of masculinity in theatre dance. At stake is the appearance of the dancing male body as spectacle.

What Rosalind Coward has commented on, in relation to contemporary film, in many ways sums up a modern attitude to the gendered body:

> Under the sheer weight of attention to women's bodies we seem to have become blind to something. Nobody seems to have noticed that men's bodies have quietly absented themselves. Somewhere along the line, men have managed to keep out of the glare, escaping from the relentless activity of sexual definitions.
>
> (Coward 1984: 227)

Over the last two centuries, however, it is not that male dancers have quietly absented themselves, but that they have been nervously dismissed. When the male dancer gradually disappeared from the stages of western European theatres during the period of the Romantic ballet, his place in some cases was taken by the female dancer dressed *en travestie* (Garafola 1985–6). There is a similar disappearance of the male nude as a subject for painting and sculpture (Walters 1979), and male forms of dress underwent what J. C. Flugel (1930) has brilliantly characterized as 'the great male renunciation' – the adoption of the plain, black, bourgeois suit. What became conflictual and consequently repressed was anything that might draw attention to the spectacle of the male body. That it was the spectacle and not the activity of dancing which underlay the prejudice against the male dancer becomes clear when one compares ballet and social dance at this time. There was no evident decline in the number of men participating in and enjoying social dance. What one should therefore be looking for to explain this prejudice is the development during this period of modern attitudes to the body and gender. It was these attitudes which brought about a situation in which it seemed 'natural' not to look at the male body, and therefore problematic and conflictual for men to enjoy looking at men dancing.

Research into the historical development of gender ideologies suggests that masculinity as a socially constructed identity was rarely a stable identity. Rather than enjoying a secure autonomy, men have continually needed to adjust and redefine the meanings attributed to sexual difference in order to maintain dominance in the face of changing social circumstances. This chapter aims to reveal some of the conflictual and contradictory aspects of the construction of modern masculine identities, and the way these determine and are determined by images of men in cultural forms. In particular, therefore, it is concerned with the social and psychological construction of the male body. Dance is an area in which some of the holes in the construction of male identity can sometimes be revealed. It is argued that the unease that sometimes accompanies the idea of the male dancer is produced by structures which defend dominant male norms.

While this book is primarily concerned with the male dancer during the twentieth century, this chapter sets the context for this by looking at the nineteenth century. The fact of the male dancer's decline in the nineteenth century is the context for his subsequent revival. It is the prudishness of nineteenth-century gender ideologies that initially condemns male dancers to the problematic status they have spent much of the twentieth century trying to overcome. 'Modern' ideas towards masculine social behaviour and the male body, which developed during the eighteenth and nineteenth centuries, have exerted a residual influence on more recent social attitudes towards the creativity and expressiveness of male artists as a whole up to the present. This chapter therefore looks first at the ways in which the development of ideas about the modern male body have influenced attitudes towards male behaviour that themselves can account for prejudices against men dancing on stage. It then looks at some of the earliest manifestations of these prejudices in the writings of ballet critics in the nineteenth century. What emerges from the latter is that these writers did not criticize, or were not primarily worried by, any signs of effeminacy in the male dancer; what concerned them chiefly were questions of male bourgeois identity. It was not until the early years of the twentieth century that a connection was made between male dance and homosexuality, and the chapter concludes with a discussion of this.

THE PSYCHOLOGICAL CONSTRUCTION OF MASCULINE IDENTITY

It is generally accepted that ideology works on an unconscious as well as on a conscious level, and that the formation of identity is a psychological process. Individuals, as Sander Gilman puts it, construct many organized schemata during the course of their development that form the back-ground frame of reference to all current processes of perception, imagin-ing, remembering, feeling and thinking (Gilman 1988: 1). Salient to these are the early stages of the development of gendered identity. Nancy Chodorow, working within the tradition of object relations theory, has proposed an account of the processes through which gendered identity is formed, which stresses the linkage between the individual's psychological, social and cultural experiences.

> My investigation suggests that our own sense of differentiation, of separateness from others, as well as our psychological and cultural experience and interpretation of gender and sexual difference, are created through psychological, social and cultural processes, and through relational experiences. We can only understand gender difference, and human distinctness and separation, relationally and situationally. They are part of a system of asymmetrical social relationships embedded in inequalities of power, in which we grow

14

up as selves, and as women and men. Our experience and perception of gender are processual; they are produced developmentally and in our daily social and cultural lives.

(Chodorow 1980: 15–16)

What is particularly useful for the argument in this chapter is the way that Chodorow accounts for differences between male and female emotionality and sense of bodily separateness. In the psychoanalytic model which has its origins in Freud's work, a sense of gendered identity develops out of a process of differentiation and separation from the primary caregiver. The child is born with a 'narcissistic relation to reality', and is believed to experience itself as merged and continuous with the world, and with the caregiver in particular, in a state described as one of polymorphous perversity. Separation from the caregiver involves a sense of personal psychological division from the rest of the world. This develops along with a sense of the permanence of the babies' physical separateness and the predictable boundaries of their own body, of a distinction between inside and outside. In other words, a sense of the boundaries of the body is believed to develop along with the beginnings of individual identity. Chodorow's particular contribution to our understanding of these processes is her stress on the importance of the mother figure within differentiation and separation, and the consequences that come from the fact that mothering is, in our society, almost exclusively done by women. Thus, when the child develops a sense of separateness, this is formed in relation to a female body. Chodorow suggests that whereas female infants retain a sense of relatedness with their mother through anatomical similarity, the separation experienced by boys is underlined by their bodily difference.

> Maleness is more conflictual and more problematic. Underlying, or built into, core gender identity is an early, nonverbal, unconscious, almost somatic sense of primary oneness with the mother, an underlying sense of femaleness that continually, usually unnoticeably, but sometimes insistently, challenges and undermines the sense of maleness. A boy must learn his gender identity of being not-female, or not-mother. Subsequently, again because of the primacy of the mother in early life, and because of the absence of concrete, real, available male figures of identification and love who are as salient for him as female figures, learning what it is to be masculine comes to mean learning to be not-feminine, or not-womanly.
>
> (*ibid.*: 12)

Because the initial stages of differentiation involve the perception of bodily boundaries, the maintenance and impermeability of these is linked to the imperative of being not-feminine and the suppression of the early

15

memory of connectedness with the mother. Thus 'boys and men come to deny the feminine identification within themselves, and those feelings they experienced as feminine: feelings of dependence, relational need, emotions generally' (*ibid.*: 13). Chodorow is not saying that individuals (or at least men) are innately both feminine and masculine. Her argument is that masculinity and femininity are constructed rather than innate, and relational rather than essential. The feminine identification within boys and men is in part environmental, and its consequent significance for the individual is socially and historically contingent. Central to any under-standing of sexual difference is the imbalance of power between men and women in our society. Chodorow, having, as we have seen, pointed to certain psychological features which distinguish male and female identity, further points out that, because men have the power in our society, these male features have been defined as normal and 'men have the power to institutionalize their unconscious defences against repressed yet strongly experienced developmental conflicts' (*ibid.*: 15).

Within the orthodox Freudian model the acquisition of language is seen as the key factor initiating the process of separation and the formation of identity. The child's early experiences of merged and continuous con-nection with the caregiver are, in Freudian and Lacanian theory, thought of as 'pre-verbal'. As Ann Daly has observed, 'The term "pre-verbal" has always been a subtle way of marginalizing movement: of relegating it to the negative role of "Other" in a world supposedly constructed solely in language' (1988: 49 note 4). She cites the work of Daniel Stern (1985) who has challenged this notion of the 'pre-verbal'. Daly summarizes Stern's conclusions as follows:

(1) the infant does experience a sense of self before learning to talk, (2) the infant does relate to others through movements before learning to talk, and (3) these bodily senses of self and means of interpersonal communication persist even *after* the acquisition of language. Nonverbal communication, then is not 'pre-verbal' at all. Movement and language share in the process of creating the self and communicating with others.

(*ibid.*) (emphasis in the original)

Stern, like Chodorow, links the formation of identity with the develop-ment of awareness of the body and its boundaries. This awareness is, according to Chodorow, a problematic area for men. Because the male child finds problematic and conflictual the memory of his early connected-ness with the mother, nonverbal, physical ways of communicating are problematic for men. The marginalization in western society of theatre dance, which communicates on a nonverbal level, might therefore be seen as an example of the way that, as Chodorow proposes, men have the power to institutionalize their unconscious defences against repressed yet strongly experienced developmental conflicts.

RATIONALITY, EMOTIONALITY AND MASCULINITY

Chodorow's account of masculine identity suggests that the emotions are perceived to be gendered. It would be untrue to say that modern men are rational beings devoid of feelings – like Lieutenant Spock in the television series *Star Trek*. However, some emotions are associated with masculinity while others are seen as feminine,[2] so that men are often said to be more rational and more in control of their emotions than women.

Martin Pumphrey has identified in some of the more violent male film roles of the 1970s and 1980s an inability among male heroes to face up to and deal with personal feelings, and suggests that the consequent repression of feelings leads to violence. The violence of film characters like Sylvester Stallone's Rambo and Arnold Schwarzenegger's Terminator is, he suggests, an externalized response to the crisis of modernity. Underlying this response, he argues, is an inability and refusal to face up to internal contradictions that are related to this external crisis. Hence

> Repressing and evading any self-conscious recognition of the *internal* contradictions their identities encompass, they construct their masculinities as defensive responses to the *external* crises of modernity – crises that are taken as legitimation both for the violence that demonstrates their superiority and the unrelenting rejection of self-analysis that is their most fundamental characteristic. . . . They enact what Klaus Theweleit in *Male Fantasies* describes as 'an incapacity to experience others except through fear, deceit, mistrust or domination'.
>
> (Pumphrey 1989: 95)

Theweleit's ideas are considered in Chapter 3, which also considers the ways in which a display of violence can be an approved and unproblematic guise for male dancers. Male violence towards women may even, as some radical feminists argue, serve the function of maintaining patriarchy. At any rate, anger and hatred (which lead to violence) are two of the emotions that are associated with masculinity and thus whose expression is generally considered acceptable for men.

It is sometimes said that white middle-class heterosexual men are less able to deal with or express a full range of feelings (including the 'soft' emotions that are associated with femininity) than women, black people, gays and others often designated 'Other'. This is a point of view that has been held by many of the men involved in the men's movement. Thus writers in the British Men Against Sexism movement magazine *Achilles Heel* speak of men being emotionally illiterate[3] while other writers speak of the social pressures on boys and men to be tough and insensitive. The

17

argument is advanced that boys and men are denied opportunities to 'get in touch with their bodies', and these include social pressures for men not to dance.[4]

One of the most detailed expositions of the view that men's problems stem from their inability to handle their emotions has been made by Victor Seidler. He proposes that a dependence on rationality results in men responding to feminist criticisms by distancing themselves from masculinity altogether, and thinking that it is 'possible to abandon our masculinity' (Seidler 1990: 219). The idea that men might be able to cut out and reject their masculinity comes, he argues, from a rational, instrumental model of change that we inherit within our culture. He argues that masculinity is not something that can be rejected through rational choice but something which men can work at redefining. This redefinition involves a process of personal change that includes 'accepting the nature of our emotions and feelings'. The idea that reason takes precedence over emotions and feelings is part of the Kantian–Protestant tradition that 'assumes that our lives can be lived by reason alone and that through will and determination, as Kant has it, we can struggle against our inclinations, to live according to the pattern that we have set for ourselves through reason' (ibid.: 219). Seidler therefore argues that men should be more accepting and give greater recognition to their emotions. This was, as he acknowledges, one aim of the groups of British heterosexual anti-sexist men during the 1970s loosely associated with Achilles Heel. It gave rise to an interest in the use of self-help and other therapies. Emotional and therapeutic work is a valuable corrective for the shortcomings of a purely rational analysis of the construction of masculinity, in particular, as Theweleit suggests, body work exploring male feelings and fears about the impermeability of bodily boundaries (see Chapter 3). This also overlaps with the concerns of some involved in experimental forms of new dance at that time (see Chapter 6).

There are, however, limitations with this view of the linkage between masculinity and rationality as a framework for analysing masculinity. Criticisms of the apolitical nature of this approach and its essentialist notion of a restoration through therapy to organic oneness are considered in Chapter 6. On a theoretical level, Seidler, along with other writers in Achilles Heel, speaks of what is wrong with men as if this were a problem for all men. This clearly cannot be the case. As Kobena Mercer has pointed out, 'How could you say that black men like Miles Davies or Michael Jackson, James Brown or John Coltrane are "emotionally illiterate"?' (Mercer 1988: 122). An early editorial in Achilles Heel reveals further confusion in the use of the word 'men' to mean all men. The writers state that, in making public what they feel they have learned from men's consciousness-raising groups about being men, they feel that they are finding themselves 'personally and politically as men and aligning ourselves with women and gay men in the struggle against oppressive sexual divisions'.[5] Doubtless the editorial group did not actually mean to say that gay men were not men, but that is the literal implication. (There were gay men involved in the men's movement, and gay contributors to *Achilles Heel*.) An appeal to a 'common-sense' notion that all but insignificant minorities of men conform to dominant male norms is surely part of the rhetoric of the Enlightenment tradition which Seidler aims to dismantle. The term 'men' is a construction which has the effect of creating an ideologically motivated sense of unity among men which is nevertheless conflictual and contradictory.

These arguments about male emotional illiteracy accept unquestion-ingly that emotionality and rationality are indeed opposites, and that men are actually more rational and less emotional than women. As Jeff Hearn points out, 'a strict separation of emotionality and rationality into mutu-ally exclusive qualities is mistaken, as actions can be both emotional and non-emotional (rational) at the same time' (1987: 137–8). Furthermore, the conflation of emotionality with femininity or of masculinity with ration-ality 'ideologically obscures the contradictions of gender relations under Patriarchy' (*ibid*.: 138). For white men, the polarity between rationality and emotionality may be internalized as part of the process of construction of masculine identity. This is what Chodorow suggests in the psychoanalytic work considered earlier. What is at issue where representations are concerned is not a question of whether men may actually be 'emotionally illiterate' but the extent to which the repression of emotional expression is a norm of masculine public behaviour. What Martin Pumphrey has said about male attitudes towards dress during most of the last two centuries is applicable to male attitudes towards representations of masculinity in cultural forms during the same period. The general attitude, he says, was that men should show 'an aggressive indifference to dress and a silent avoidance of bodily display' (Pumphrey 1989: 96). It is not a matter of what is going on inside, but how this is allowed to show itself on the levels at which the body creates meanings. This is in turn contingent on modern ideas about the body.

THE MODERN BODY

The development of modern ideas about the body, and about the biology of gender difference, developed as a result of the breakdown of older notions of the body in Greek thought and its assimilation within medieval and Renaissance Christian thought. The older Christian model of the sinful flesh became recast with new, scientific features by the rational French bourgeoisie and their evangelical protestant English counterparts. By the nineteenth century, the idea that the body as an entity is execrable not only persisted but became increasingly important in new and more anxious forms. The body itself was no longer admired, and lost its status as an unproblematic symbol of society. The male nude, as Margaret Walters (1979) has shown, gradually during the early years of the nineteenth century began to seem irrelevant in modern society, and faded out as a subject for painting and sculpture. Thomas Malthus (1766–1834) pointed out that the healthy body is a body that has the potential to procreate and thus, as he saw it, to threaten the demise of society through overpopulation – his argument being that population grows at a faster rate than food production (Gallagher 1987). The body, with everything it implied, became a problem and a threat. These new social attitudes and ideas were initially developed in eighteenth-century scientific and rational thought; but, despite the fact that new discoveries discredited them, they survived as signifiers of class. Thus the new anxieties about the body related to the world-view of the new middle classes within complex hierarchies of relations within society (see Gallagher and Lacquer 1987).

The anthropologist Mary Douglas's purity rule is useful for understanding these ideas of purity and impurity in relation to the body. She proposes that when the physical body is under strong social pressure, the social system seeks progressively to disembody or etherealize the forms of expression, and social intercourse increasingly 'pretends to take place between disembodied spirits' (Douglas 1970: 100). Thus, 'physical events, defecation, urination, vomiting and their products uniformly carry a pejorative sign for formal discourse. . . . Front is more dignified and respect-worthy than back. Greater space means more formality, nearness means intimacy' (ibid.: 100). New anxieties about the body resulted, during the nineteenth century, in changes in attitudes towards bodily display including display in theatre dance. Ballet is, within Douglas's terms, a pre-eminently dignified form. In the ballet ideal, dancers aspire to the condition of disembodied spirits (see Chapter 2). It was female dancers rather than males who represented in the nineteenth century these disembodied spirits. To understand why, it is necessary to examine the way nineteenth-century ideas about the body underpinned new ideologies of gender.

It is with the increasing acceptance of a rational and scientific approach to the body that Aristotelian ideas of the metaphysical inferiority of women gradually became untenable. The idea that men and women have the same potential to be free, reasoning subjects implicitly threatened male power. Christine Battersby (1989) has shown the conflicting nature of the arguments which were put forward by philosophers at that time to maintain male dominance. Scientists and commentators sought to prove that women were physically and temperamentally unsuited to serious thinking, while at the same time they appropriated for male genius aspects that had previously been ascribed to the feminine temperament. This justification of the subordination of women was, as Thomas Lacqueur (1987) has shown, based on supposedly scientific evidence of the unsuitability of the female body (in comparison with the male body) for involvement in public life. Lacqueur has shown how, for much of the nineteenth century, female menses were thought to be equivalent to animals being on heat. The womb thus became the centre of the female psychological system with all women's nervous energy going into controlling and transcending their animal nature during menses. This transcendence of their animal natures was the grounds for claiming women's moral superiority; but the fact that it used up all their mental or physical energy was supposed to make them unfit for any 'serious' employment (hence the 'female' disease hysteria). If there was any comparable attempt to limit male behaviour by referring to anatomically grounded definitions of the male temperament, this is to be found in the notion of the healthy mind in a healthy body and its development in competitive male sports (see Mangan 1981). The male body was, of course, the norm against which female anatomical and temperamental traits were judged. Men, by default and by implication, were considered to be less capable of transcending their natural lusts and desires and thus morally inferior. Thus women had some grounds for claiming to be purer and more disembodied than men. It was more appropriate therefore for female dancers to evoke the ballet ideal than for male dancers.[6]

EMOTIONALITY, DANCE AND ARTISTIC GENIUS

This definition of gendered difference is part of the larger separation of the middle-class (male) public world of work and politics from the (female) private world of the home and family (Wolff and Seed 1987, Davidoff and Hall 1987). Artistic expression itself became gendered so that, as Paul Hoch has suggested, 'Art, as an emotional (and therefore feminine) representation of the inner life became even further estranged from science, the representative mode of thought in the cruel, emotionless masculine world "outside"' (Hoch 1979: 140). The Romantic notion of the artist as inspired genius is the obvious exception to the rule that men should appear unemotional and inexpressive. Christine Battersby points out that the (male) Romantic artist was excepted from gendered divisions of social behaviour through being allowed to have 'feminine' qualities such as sensitivity, passivity, emotionality and introspective self-consciousness. Battersby argues that artists could appropriate these 'feminine' characteristics by evoking the notion of genius, and thus without suffering the lower social status of being female. When the Romantic artist expresses the underlying forces of sublime nature, this is a male creative energy responding to the male energy of nature: according to Edmund Burke (1729–97), the grandeur of an avalanche in the Alps is sublime, as are also 'kings and commanders discharging their terrible strength and destroying all obstacles in their path' (Battersby 1989: 74). The new notion

21

of male artistic self-expression was linked to the body and physicality. A sublime muscular dynamism was identified in Michelangelo's art. On another level creativity was linked to virility and male sexuality: Battersby calls this the Virility School of creativity, and one aim of her book is to reveal the misogynistic way these ideas have been used to create a climate within which women were excluded from being considered geniuses or great artists.

The Romantic idea of male artistic self-expression clearly underlies much of the hype that has surrounded the recent popularity of the male dancer. It is paradoxical, however, that these notions should initially have been developed at the time when the male dancer was disappearing in western Europe as a result of strong social disapproval. The Romantic genius was allowed a wide range of self-expression that would have been considered unacceptable in men not considered to be gifted. The way in which the Romantic composer might pound his piano while performing his own work, or the emotionalism of the Romantic poet, or the way the brush strokes betray the painter's emotions:[7] the implicit or explicit physicality of all these seems to have been acceptable for male artists in the nineteenth century. As far as theatre dance is concerned, during the nineteenth century the dancing of ballet movements was not recognized as a reputable means of artistic self-expression, let alone a means through which male genius manifests itself. Nijinsky, however, was acclaimed as a genius and, as is argued in Chapter 4, this concept was evoked to make acceptable some of the more problematic aspects of the way his roles represented masculinity. Battersby's idea of a Virility School of male artistic creativity is taken up in Chapters 5 and 6 in relation to the highly individualistic nature of American male dancing in the mid-twentieth century. Going back to the nineteenth century, there were significant differences between the performance of the male dancer and forms of self-expression in music, literature and the visual arts. The general low status of the performing arts, and of dance as a non-verbal form within them, contributed to the exclusion of the male dancer from the realm of genius. To a certain extent denunciations of the male dancer could draw on diatribes against the immorality of actors as a whole. There is also the fact that the male dancer displayed himself, and thus was in danger of infringing the conventions which circumscribed the way men could be looked at.

HOMOPHOBIA AND THE MALE DANCER

What has been proposed so far is that, increasingly since the nineteenth century, it has been considered appropriate for men not to appear soft and not to appear emotionally expressive. An individual who does not conform to these behavioural norms, and cannot claim to be a genius, has been in danger of being considered 'not to be a proper man', a euphemistic phrase that generally means homosexual. The cluster of fears associated with homosexuality is sometimes called homophobia. Homophobia is the social mechanism which prohibits or makes fearful the idea of intimate contact or communication with members of the same sex. It is generally argued that homophobia is a mechanism for regulating the behaviour of all men rather than just self-identified homosexuals. It has been proposed that homophobia is an essential characteristic of patriarchal society. Joseph Bristow puts it thus: 'homophobia comes into operation so that men can be as close as possible – to work powerfully together in the interests of men – without ever being too (sexually) close to one another . . . homophobia actually brings men into a close homosocial relation' (Bristow 1988: 128). The mechanisms which limit the subversive potential of some representations of masculinity (which include disapproval of male dance) can be seen to serve the purpose of keeping out of sight anything which might disrupt the relations within which men work powerfully together in the interests of men.

Eve Kosofsky Sedgwick proposes that homophobia in western society is directly related to the way men relate to one another homosocially. She argues that a fundamental triangular structure in our male-dominated society is one in which a woman is situated in a subordinate and intermediary position between two men. Men use women in order to impress other men as part of a 'traffic in women'.[8] In this structure, women are the intermediaries of what Sedgwick calls male homosocial desire.

Her argument is that, in men's relationships with other men in contemporary western society, emotional and sexual expression is necessarily suppressed in the interests of maintaining male power. In a broader historical and anthropological perspective, she argues, this sort of male bonding is atypical: a similar break does not occur in female bonding in modern western society, nor did it exist, for example, for Greek men at the time of Socrates. In the latter examples, there is a continuum between social, political and sexual expression. Sedgwick argues that male homosocial relationships in our society are characterized by intense homophobia, fear and hatred of homosexuality. This repressed homosexual component of male sexuality accounts for 'correspondences and similarities between the most sanctioned forms of male homosocial bonding and the most reprobate expressions of male homosexuality' (Sedgwick 1985: 89). Men are in a double bind in that they are drawn to other men, but this acceptable attraction is not clearly distinguishable from forbidden homosexual interest. 'For a man to be a man's man is separated only by an invisible, carefully blurred, always-already crossed line from being "interested in men"' (*ibid.*: 89). The main objection to the concept of homophobia is that it doesn't actually offer an explanation of why modern western society is prejudiced against and discriminates against homosexuals. Homosexual men were subject to sometimes violent discrimination prior to the nineteenth century, at times when performances by leading male ballet dancers were greeted with considerable approval. There is no simple linkage between homosexuality, homophobia and uneasiness at professional male dancers. The usefulness of the concept of homophobia is perhaps strategic, in that to give a name to the way social restrictions function to maintain certain norms of male behaviour is to make visible aspects of male experience that are otherwise hidden. It then also becomes possible to discuss the way male–male social relationships have been represented in theatre dance in terms of homophobia. This strategy is adopted when looking at José Limón's work (in Chapter 5) and at recent work by more recent choreographers who have set out to explore consciously the anxieties surrounding male–male social and sexual relations (in Chapter 7).

It is surely these social strictures which, since the mid-nineteenth century, have caused the display of male dancing to be a source of anxiety. Male appearance signifies power and success: as John Berger has put it, a man's appearance tells you what he can do to you or for you (Berger 1972) (see Chapter 3). If, however, his appearance is also desirable, he is, from the point of view of a male spectator, drawing attention to the always-already crossed line between homosocial bonding and homosexual sexuality. His appearance therefore carries with it for the male spectator the threat of revealing the suppressed homosexual component within the links he has with other men and through which he maintains his power and status in patriarchal society.

It is the inability of the male ballet dancer to represent the power and status of men in bourgeois society which was proposed by one nineteenth-century writer as being the trouble with the male dancer.

THE MALE BALLET DANCER DURING THE NINETEENTH CENTURY: GREEN BOX TREES

As has already been stated, the male ballet dancer became an object of distaste in London, Paris and many other European cities during the first half of the nineteenth century. With ballet coming to be defined as an idealized feminine world, there was, on a material level, a decline in demand for male dancers. The fashion for the all-white female *corps de ballet* must have contributed to the disappearance of men from the *corps de ballet* in most of Europe. There were still male dancers around who were valued for their technical ability as dancers. Peter Brinson has suggested:

> The more the employment, and so the technical standards of male dancers as regular members of ballet companies declined throughout the second half of the nineteenth century, the more the practice grew of employing for particular occasions the few who could display any

sort of technical brilliance. These men moved from company to company like a circus act.

(Brinson 1966: 72)

One example of professional male dancers in Italy were the Fighting Dancers or Tramagnini who performed speciality danced combats as part of theatrical spectacles in Florence during the second half of the nineteenth century (Poesio 1990). This, however, seems to have been an isolated phenomenon. Elsewhere, male dancers increasingly performed roles that demanded acting skills and mime, such as Drosselmeyer in *The Nutcracker* (1892 Petipa/Ivanov) or Dr Coppélius in *Coppélia* (1870 Saint-Léon), parts that could be performed by dancers past their prime. Overall one must conclude that the career structure for male dancers collapsed in ballet under bourgeois patronage at this time.

When, with Nijinsky and the male dancers of the Ballets Russes, the male dancer made his comeback, critics and audiences realized that the female dancer looked better when supported by a good male dancer. Nineteenth-century ballet critics, however, seemed to find the male dancer a conflictual figure. He appeared so either through association with the degenerate style of the old aristocracy or by his resembling the rude prowess of the working classes. It is these associations which stopped male dancers representing middle-class male values. Ivor Guest in *The Romantic Ballet in Paris* quotes at length from a tirade against the male dancer written by Jules Janin in 1840. For Janin, the ballet is a feminine spectacle: 'Speak to us of a pretty dancing girl who displays the grace of her features and the elegance of her figure, who reveals so fleetingly all the treasures of her beauty. Thank God, I understand that perfectly' (Guest 1966: 21). What he can't understand is of course the male dancer. In giving reasons why men do not look right on the ballet stage, he refers to the social position of middle-class men:

> That this bewhiskered individual who is a pillar of the community, an elector, a municipal councilor, a man whose business is to make and above all unmake laws, should come before us in a tunic of sky-blue satin, his head covered with a hat with a waving plume amorously caressing his cheek. . . – this was surely impossible and we have done well to remove such great artists from our pleasures.

(*ibid.*)

The male dancer dressed in sky blue satin and wearing a feathered hat has little in common with the picture of middle-class male public life which Janin evokes. In 1840, the on-stage style and manner of male ballet dancers may have been too reminiscent of the male *danseur noble* of the pre-Romantic ballet and thus with the aristocrats who had been its patrons. These aristocratic associations surely prevented the male dancer presenting a role that mediated male middle-class values.

25

Alain Corbin (1986) argues, in a history of smells and odours, that the mid-nineteenth century middle classes regarded the use of strong-smelling animal-based perfumes by the older aristocracy as a sign of their decadence, degeneracy and lack of hygiene. Prudish attitudes towards ballet and the male dancer in particular were surely another area in which middle-class distaste for what they perceived as aristocratic degeneracy was expressed. It was in countries like Britain and France where the ballet was under bourgeois rather than royal and aristocratic patronage that the decline of the male ballet dancer mainly occurred, while it was at the courts in Copenhagen and St Petersburg that the career structure of male ballet dancing survived.[9]

Janin is also perhaps suggesting that the male dancer is effeminate, as he goes on to object to woman as queen of the ballet being 'forced to cut off half her silk petticoat to dress her partner with it' (Guest 1966: 21). He seems to have felt that the ballet dancer didn't look sufficiently manly – the mid-nineteenth century being a period, as Sedgwick has suggested, in which personal style was increasingly stressed, absolute and politically significant for bourgeois men (1985: 206); or Janin may have associated cross-dressing with homosexuality (see Meyer 1992: 69): although the word 'homosexual' did not yet exist, the behaviour and practices associated with it were taboo. For Janin, ballet was a feminine sphere within which men either did not appear manly or, if they looked too manly, did not appear ideal. 'Today the dancing man is no longer tolerated except as a useful accessory. He is the shading of the picture, the green box trees surrounding the garden flowers, the necessary foil' (Guest 1966: 21).

While on the one hand middle-class sensibilities were disgusted by the spectre of a degenerate and decadent aristocracy, they also feared and were disgusted by the vigour and fecundity of the working classes. Catherine Gallagher has suggested that for the Victorian middle classes the social body, far from representing a perfectible ideal, was imagined to be

> a chronically and incurably ill organism that could only be kept alive by constant flushing, draining, and excising of various deleterious elements. These dangerous elements, moreover, were often not themselves unhealthy but rather were overly vigorous and fecund individuals.
>
> (Gallagher 1987: 90)

These overly vigorous and fecund individuals were of course members of the working classes. For the bourgeoisie, the body with everything it implied became a problem and a threat. J. S. Bratton, discussing the hornpipe within the context of nineteenth-century British working-class entertainment, suggests that it was the sort of act through which a performer could exhibit admired qualities of dexterity, physical prowess, inventiveness and pluck, within dances which would be familiar as 'working or holiday accomplishments of the audience, carried to a pitch they had not the leisure to attain' (Bratton 1990: 68). Bratton suggests that underlying middle-class distaste for this sort of performance was a real or imagined

> fear of the mass of working-class people going out in the street, getting together, and being induced to drunken disorder by the physical excitement of singing and dancing, and, ultimately, incited to riot by shows and plays which might have radical tendencies.
>
> (1990: 74)

For the mid-nineteenth-century bourgeois ballet critic, vigorous and manly displays of dancing might sometimes have carried negative connotations of working-class entertainment. One of the better known denunciations of the male ballet dancer was written in May 1838 by Théophile Gautier: 'Nothing is more distasteful than a man who shows his red neck, his big muscular arms, his legs with the calves of a parish beadle, and all his strong massive frame shaken by leaps and pirouettes' (Gautier 1947: 24). What Gautier appears to find offensive is the spectacle of the male dancer's strength and virtuosity. The rude strength and vigour Gautier describes seems more appropriate to a description of a male performer in a working-class entertainment rather than of a ballet dancer. The social and ideological meanings underlying Gautier's expressed distaste for vigorous male dance are surely the same as those described by Bratton and Gallagher.

The context in which Gautier above likened the male dancer's legs to those of a parish beadle was a review of *La Volière* (1838) choreographed by Thérèse Elssler in which, dressed *en travestie*, she partnered her sister Fanny. In another review of Fanny Elssler, Gautier announced that 'an actress is a statue or a picture which is exhibited to you and can be freely criticized' (Gautier 1947: 20). This is a rather ambiguous statement. Gautier is remembered for advancing the idea that watching ballet is a purely aesthetic experience. Pictures and statues are works of art but, like many female dancers of the time, could also be bought and possessed. This is an example of double standards typically used by men of his class and time: it suited them to be able to claim to be involved in a disinterested evaluation of formal, aesthetic qualities and thus avoid having to admit the erotic motivation behind looking in an objectifying way at women.

The male dancer must undoubtedly have got in the way of erotic appreciation of feminine display. Lynn Garafola (1985–6) has pointed out that men were freer to enjoy this erotic spectacle when male dancers were eliminated and their roles performed by women dancers *en travestie*. Not only did the male dancer become out of place on the newly feminine ballet stage but, because male appreciation of the spectacle of the ballerina took on sexual aspects, the ways that male dancers appeared on stage became a source of anxiety to bourgeois male spectators. To enjoy the spectacle of men dancing is to be interested in men. Because there was no acknowledged distinction between ballet as aesthetic experience and ballet as erotic spectacle, let alone any understanding of the way art expresses social and political meanings, the pleasures of watching men dancing became, in the mid-nineteenth century, marred by anxieties about masculine identity. The male ballet dancer came too close for comfort to the blurred and problematic line that separates, or as Sedgwick implies fails to separate, necessary and approved homosocial male bonding from forbidden homosexual sexuality.

The contradiction which led to the decline of the male ballet dancer under bourgeois patronage during the nineteenth century was that on the one hand the male dancer was required as a necessary foil to dance with the ballerina, but on the other hand his presence provoked anxiety not only in relation to class position but also in relation to the difference between homosocial and homosexual relations. The prejudice did not therefore arise because of any actual belief that male dancers were homosexual. When, however, gay men did become involved in dance and ballet, with Shawn and Nijinsky, the homophobic structures were already there to police any infringement of heterosexual norms.

HOMOSEXUALITY AND THE MALE DANCER

There is a widespread reluctance to talk about dance and homosexuality, surely making it the dance that does not speak its name. The reference here is to Oscar Wilde who, during his trial in 1895 for homosexual offences, made a celebrated speech in defence of the love that dared not speak its name in his century. Over the years since then, a homosexual culture or subcultures have developed with diverse, shifting memberships and significant inputs from artists and intellectuals. In recent years, partly as a result of the gay rights movement, theoretical work has been done on the way homosexuality has been and is represented in the arts and mass media, and research has been done into the work of gay and lesbian artists. While Melanie Weeks (1987) and Christy Adair (1992) have written about lesbianism and dance, surprisingly little attention has been given to gay men and dance. One recent book that has considered homosexuality and dance is Judith Lynne Hanna's *Dance, Sex and Gender* (1988). Although the sections on gay men reflect the large amount of material Hanna has researched for the book, they show little sympathy or understanding of the situation in which gay people live in our society and Hanna seems to be unaware of the underlying sexual politics. She sees homosexuality as a problem for gay people, which of course it may be, but she doesn't consider what sort of a problem. There is a difference between thinking of homosexuality as a psychopathology, and seeing any neurosis suffered by a homosexual as a result of internalizing society's negative image of homosexuality. The latter way of defining the problem opens up a fruitful avenue for examining gay art, but one which Hanna does not explore. Instead her concern is with 'why male homosexuals are disproportionally attracted to dance' (1988: 130), and she suggests ways in which for gay people an involvement in the dance world can alleviate or be an escape from their 'problem'. The problem, however, is not just the result of internalizing society's negative image of homosexuality but the fact that western society is and has for hundreds of years been profoundly homophobic.

The source of much of Hanna's material on gay men in ballet is the essay 'Toeing the line: in search of the gay male image in classical ballet' written in 1976 by the Canadian writer Graham Jackson (in Jackson 1978). This considers the institutional structures and pressures that influence and limit the production of ballets that deal with gay themes or subject matter and some of the ways in which a gay sensibility is expressed or can be read into ballet. This essay stands out as one of the very few pieces to consider this subject. Written in the mid-1970s the essay has a very optimistic tone – coming out seems, for Jackson, the solution for all gay men's problems. Thus his central concern is with the fact that although a large proportion of dancers, choreographers or those holding administrative positions in the dance world are gay men, and there is a large gay audience for dance, ballet (as opposed to modern dance) companies rarely if ever produce work that directly addresses the experiences and sensibilities of gay people. They don't rock the boat.

There are obvious reasons why there has been a silence on the subject of gay male dancers and choreographers. Arnold Haskell writing in 1934 is doubtless protecting individuals when he states: 'of the outstanding male dancers that I know, and I know them all, not one is effeminate in manner, and very few indeed are not thoroughly normal' (Haskell 1934: 299). But he is surely also protecting the institution of ballet itself. With the liberalization of laws about homosexuality and substantial changes in social attitudes, the continuation of the taboo on discussions of dance and homosexuality is surely both unnecessary and unhelpful.

One possible reason why the taboo still persists is the need for dance and ballet companies to raise funding and attract sponsorship from private individuals and businesses. If this is the case, it is not a very good one, whereas the arguments for greater openness are surely compelling. Not talking about something doesn't make it go away, and may insidiously make it take on greater significance than it really deserves. All male dancers are placed under suspicion with the result that, as is widely recognized, far fewer boys and men are involved in the dance world than girls and women. Moreover homophobic prejudice can, as Jackson observes, 'paralyze talented dancers from developing a personal dancing

29

style reflective of their characters [and] limit the range of male dancing severely' (Jackson 1978: 41).

This holds true for gay and heterosexual dancers. The initial reasons for keeping quiet about gay male dancers are surely no longer valid, and silences now do more harm than good. Perhaps there are now more choreographers dealing with homosexual themes than there were when Jackson wrote 'Toeing the line', but only in the marginalized, under-funded, experimental fringes. In the mainstream, fear, prejudice and the old boy network still ensure the status quo. It is a commonplace that fear and prejudice breed on ignorance. Homophobic mechanisms channel and block our understanding and appreciation of representations of mascu-linity that are made by both gay and straight dance artists. It is through understanding the ways in which these mechanisms work that their effectiveness is undermined, and the possibility of positive change is brought about.

2

DANCE, MASCULINITY
AND REPRESENTATIONS

Much of the serious writing about dance over the last ninety years has until recently ignored the question of representations of gender. This is because dance has not been thought of as a representational practice. Consideration of what theatre dance might suggest about the nature of femininity or masculinity has appeared irrelevant to what has generally been thought to be the true nature of dance as art. One can see this idea of dance in two often-stated modernist and formalist views: that the highest standards in dance are permanent, natural and lie outside history; that dance today transcends the outmoded representational forms of the nineteenth-century and earlier European tradition.

These are conservative ways of looking at theatre dance. Part of their conservatism is their tendency to accept implicitly 'traditional' ideas about the nature of femininity and masculinity as somehow 'natural', innate and essential, a matter of self-evident common sense, a universal given. If gender is an underlying essence, there is no point in questioning its nature as there is no possibility of change. Furthermore if this is accepted as the reality of how men and women are, then there is no incentive to analyse representations of gender. Another related aspect of such approaches to dance is that they efface and deny the agency of the body in producing dance. The body is of course gendered. Thus, as dance aspires to the condition of the highest form of art, so the greatest dancers somehow transcend the body in a quest for the purely spiritual. This putative metaphysical transcendence is a transcendence of the base, physical facts of anatomy and gender.

It is from a variety of radical positions that theoretical work, some of which is considered in the next chapter, has been done on how gender, class, ethnicity, sexuality and various other aspects of identity are represented in cultural forms. This new approach to the theory of representations has been inspired largely by the example of the women's movement. Gender, in this view, is seen as socially constructed, and cultural forms are one area in which gendered norms are reinforced. Representations in dance might therefore be seen as ideologically produced, and historically and socially situated. This raises the problem of how to analyse representations in dance as art without reducing the aesthetic to no more than its ideological components. The aesthetic, in this new sociological view of the arts, becomes problematic. At its most extreme, the practice of conservative critics and theorists can appear to the radical theorist almost as a conspiracy. The feminist art historians Rosika Parker and Griselda Pollock, writing in 1981 in a combative mode, pronounced:

> Crucial questions have not been posed about *how* art history works to exclude from its field of discourse history, class, ideology, to produce an ideologically 'pure' space for something called 'art', sealed off from and impenetrable to any attempt to locate art practice within a history of production and social relations.
>
> (Parker and Pollock 1981: 57)

It is thanks to Parker, Pollock and other cultural theorists working along similar lines that these sorts of questions have subsequently been placed prominently on the agenda. Much thought has also gone into the problem of recognizing the specificity of art and the aesthetic while acknowledging that these concepts are ideologically determined (see Wolff 1982). The point to recognize is that there is much more than just questions of aesthetics at stake in different ways of looking at dance.

A thorough overview of how existing dance theory deals with the question of representations is a much-needed task; this, however, would require a book in itself and is outside the scope of the present one. This chapter therefore examines dance theories from the point of view of gender representation.[1] First it considers the particular problems that the idea of gender representation causes in formalist and modernist theories. It then proposes an account of representations in dance that draws on theories of expression, phenomenology and hermeneutic philosophy. This proposes that representations in dance are made up of discursive and affective symbols which are ideologically produced and historically and socially situated. Lastly the chapter considers some of the issues and problems for dance theory that arise from the application of ideas about the body that have been developed by structuralist and post-structuralist theorists. The conclusion drawn from this is that representation in dance is contingent upon beliefs about the body, and that the gendered body is therefore an area in which the embodiment of socially produced norms is defined and contested.

FORMALIST ACCOUNTS OF DANCE

It is around discussions of ballet that the most conservative dance theories have developed. An instance of this is Selma Jeanne Cohen's discussion of dance theory in her book *Next Week Swan Lake* (1982). Taking as an example the dance of the Sugar Plum Fairy in *The Nutcracker* (1892) she glosses most existing dance theories – Langer, Goodman, Martin, Collingwood, Arnheim, semiotics. The majority of these she finds inappropriate, irrelevant or 'claiming rather much for a dance of a simple friendly Sugar Plum Fairy' (Cohen 1982: 85). She goes on to argue that the Sugar Plum Fairy's dance 'lacks relevance to our daily lives, but aren't we entitled to a little diversion?' (*ibid.*: 101), and *Swan Lake* (1894/5), which 'offers more', is still essentially to be enjoyed. To look for representational content or intense emotional expression in it would be to miss the subtle quality of the movements themselves which seem, Cohen concludes, quoting Arthur Symons: 'to sum up in themselves the appeal of everything in the world that is passing and coloured and to be enjoyed' (*ibid.*: 102). This is all very well, but *Swan Lake* is undeniably a ballet that tells a story: it is thus a representational and expressive piece. In late-twentieth-century productions these aspects are often less pronounced than formal and aesthetic values and technical virtuosity. This allows critics like Cohen to discover in it (and in similar classics of the ballet repertoire) an idealized, spiritualized ambience. These ballets can thus be fitted into Cohen's overall view that dance is universal – 'the shapes of grief, joy, love, hate, are recognizable the world over' (*ibid.*: 96). For her, contemplation of such spiritual meaning depends solely upon a response to aesthetic forms which, proponents of this view of ballet argue, reveal metaphysical and idealist meanings. All of which serves to distract from questions such as how the traditional ballet repertoire and the vocabulary of ballet movement represent gender. Cohen's desire for 'a little diversion' is itself socially and ideologically produced.

An appeal to the metaphysical or the universal is surely mystifying. It is the sort of cultural mystification which John Berger criticized in *Ways of Seeing* (1972). When an image is presented as a work of art, he argued, the way people look at it is affected by a whole series of assumptions about art, concerning things like beauty, truth, genius, civilization, form, status, taste, etc.

> Many of these assumptions no longer accord with the world as it is. (The world-as-it-is is more than just pure objective fact, it includes consciousness.) Out of true with the present, these assumptions obscure the past. They mystify rather than clarify.
>
> (1972: 11)

What the process of mystification does is to stop individuals making their own readings of works of art, and use them to help

> to define our experiences more precisely in areas where words are inadequate. (Seeing comes before words.) Not only personal experience, but also the essential historical experience of our relation

to the past: that is to say the experience of seeking to give meaning to our lives, of trying to understand the history of which we can become the active agents.

(*ibid.*: 33)

Berger is writing about the language of visual images constituted in the European painting tradition, hence his comment that seeing comes before words. The specificity of theatre dance is the expression of embodied feelings of physical space and emotional experience that are also inadequately expressed in words. Where representations of masculinity are concerned, the history of theatre dance is a rich source of information on changing norms of masculine behaviour. Considered from this point of view, male roles in classic nineteenth-century Russian ballets have some potential for helping uncover aspects of the construction of masculinity that are hidden by the idea that these ballets are a 'symbol and an embodiment of spiritual meaning' (Cohen 1982: 101).

Cohen's approach, for all its easy-going and unacademic style of writing, is a formalist one. Formalist theories of dance see the reception of dance as the appreciation of aesthetic forms, unaffected by external or extra-aesthetic considerations such as representation. The most influential formalist account of dance theory is that proposed by the Russian writer André Levinson (1887–1933). This proposes that dance is an aesthetic form which is not representational. In Levinson's view philosophers through the ages have been blind to the formal properties of dance: 'It seems as though everyone had piled upon this art mistaken burdens in his effort to redeem – even if only in a small way – the actual movements of dance' (Levinson 1983: 48). Aristotle's 'fatal dictum'[2] that dance imitates character, emotion and action 'assigns to the dance an aim outside of itself and creates confusion between saltatory motion and expressive or descriptive gesture, using dance as a substitute for words. The dance ceases to be a thing in itself' (*ibid.*: 48). Using dance as a substitute for words means treating the making of dance as nothing more than the translation of a pre-existing verbal original. By arguing that dance is not a translation of words, Levinson is making an important claim for the specificity of dance. But Levinson also means that theories of language cannot be used as models for the manner in which dance communicates its meanings, because dance, for Levinson, is not a representational form. Théophile Gautier (1811–72), Levinson suggests, was the first to realize 'the eternal subject of ballet' when he wrote: 'The dance is nothing more than the art of displaying elegant and correct designs in positions favourable to the building up of patterns in line' (*ibid.*: 52). Levinson does not comment on the fact that Gautier was involved in the creation of two ballets, contributing the (written) scenario. In freeing dance from the 'tyranny' of words and asserting its autonomy, Levinson is repudiating the notion that dance is an imitation of the things of the world. What he is apparently proposing is that audiences should ignore all representational aspects and look only at the ballet movement itself, arguing that only this is of value. Levinson is attempting to create an ideologically 'pure' space for something called 'art'.

Levinson sees ballet as a movement form through which the dancer expresses an ideal. Ballet technique, in evolving from court etiquette to the present art, 'has gradually become exalted and transfigured until it is now called upon to express the loftiest emotions of the human soul' (Levinson 1980: 299), so that 'when a dancer rises on her pointes, she breaks away from the exigencies of everyday life, and enters into an enchanted country – that she may thereby lose herself in the ideal' (*ibid*.: 300). Levinson's view is that ballet is an art form that is in no way inferior to the other arts. He claims this by in effect denying the expressivity of the dancer's body. The body, for Levinson, is something to be transcended through the discipline of learning ballet: 'To discipline the body to this ideal function, to make a dancer of a graceful child, it is necessary to begin by dehumanizing him, or rather by overcoming the habits of ordinary life' (*ibid*.: 300). Ballet technique is thus a means by which the soul can avoid being dragged down by the body. Through ballet, the soul expresses its emotions (for Levinson these are the property of the soul and not the body) in a transparently graspable way, not clouded in any way by the obtrusive exigencies of the body. Levinson thus brackets off and dismisses extra-aesthetic factors in order to make an interpretation of aesthetic forms which seemingly discovers idealist and metaphysical meanings.

Drawing on the theories of Levinson, and on theories from the visual arts developed by Roger Fry, Clement Greenberg and Michael Fried, an influential modernist account of dance was proposed in the 1970s by Marshall Cohen, Roger Copeland and David Michael Levin. These writers all propose a similar view of modernist dance: that, as it has become more modern, dance has gradually done away with traditional theatre dance forms and conventions such as traditional scenery, costume, narrative and the dancing of character roles and with what they call theatricality. Their conclusion is that dance is now no longer representational.

According to Greenberg, modernism is the use of theoretical procedures which derive from Immanuel Kant (1724–1804). Greenberg proposes that Kant was the first modernist because he 'used logic to establish the limits of logic, and while he withdrew much from its old jurisdiction, logic was left in all the more secure possession of what remained to it' (Greenberg 1965: 5). Thus the arts under modernism have been encouraged to undergo a process of Kantian self-criticism – using art to establish the limits of art – leading to the conclusion that 'Realistic, illusionist art had dissembled the medium, using art to conceal art. Modernism used art to draw attention to art' (*ibid*.: 5). Roger Copeland applies Greenberg's thesis to dance:

twenty years ago the reigning sensibility among serious experimental artists was the quest for 'purity' of the medium, the desire to determine what each art form can do uniquely well .... Choreographers were expected to emphasise the barebones essence of their medium, the human body in motion, unembellished by theatrical trappings. Music too was regarded as eminently dispensible. Silence was golden.

(Copeland 1986: 178)

Copeland connects this notion of purity to Greenbergian modernism, to Levinson's theory of ballet and to 'American' culture, quoting H. L. Mencken: 'Formalism is the hallmark of the national culture.'

In his essay 'Primitivism, modernism and dance theory' Marshall Cohen writes:

At the present time the modernist ideals of honesty, purification of the medium and even of artistic minimalism prevail, and some of the prestige of the most gifted artists prevails from the fact that their art adheres to these principles.

(Cohen 1983: 162)

According to Cohen, the most gifted artists are Cunningham and Balanchine. This is not a logical argument but a self-certifying prescription. Cohen is saying that the best work at present is modernist (and American) because the best (American) choreographers adhere to what he says are modernist ideals. These gifted artists are also male. Now American dance historians, most of whom are female, have generally claimed that the founders of American modern dance were all women – Loie Fuller, Isadora Duncan, Ruth St Denis, Martha Graham and Doris Humphrey. It is surely significant that the account of modernism which Cohen, Copeland and others (all men) are advancing is one that privileges the formally pure, up-to-date modernist work of male artists – Cunningham and Balanchine – and excludes as 'primitive' the work of the older female modern dance artists.[3]

What they mean by 'primitive' is expressive. In 'Primitivism, modernism and dance theory', Cohen denounces as primitive the idea that dance is expressive, basing his argument on a critique of Susanne Langer's theory of dance. Copeland (1986: 178) too sees expressivity in dance as a quality which is 'now' eschewed by 'serious', experimental choreographers. Thus in a description of Merce Cunningham's choreographic style he stresses the way it eschews expressivity:

His own dancing – even at its most frantic – always exudes a slight aura of aloofness, an almost prissy stiffness which resists any sort of 'natural' Dionysian abandon. In fact, Cunningham savagely parodies

Graham's Dionysian pretensions in the hilarious *Bacchus and Cohorts* section of *Antic Meet*.

(Copeland 1983: 318)

Copeland, in referring to Dionysian pretensions in Graham's work, is thereby also evoking the work of Duncan and Humphrey. The implication is that Cunningham has superseded their older 'primitivism'. The modernist process of purification, which Copeland posits, would therefore seem to consist of a progressive elimination of expression and feeling from dance, tending towards a goal of pure form. Meanwhile, Cunningham is more 'modern' than Graham because his dancing is less expressionist, and he goes on to imply that Yvonne Rainer's *Trio A* (1966) is even more modern by reducing expressiveness even further.

There are several problems with this sort of argument. Expressivity is not quantitative but qualitative, so that, as the New York School painter Ad Reinhardt put it, less is more. Furthermore, as Noel Carroll points out, Rainer, in pursuing the intention of eradicating expression in the narrowest sense in *Trio A*, introduces expressive qualities at other levels.[4] When Copeland says that Cunningham's own dancing exudes 'a slight aura of aloofness' and 'an almost prissy stiffness', these are surely qualities which his dancing expresses. Cunningham's works may not express the sorts of angst-laden feelings that abound in Graham's work, but they are still unarguably expressive in the sense that Langer uses the term (see below). Copeland seems to be thinking about expression in only a narrow sense, or conflating expressiveness as an attribute of dance movement with expressionism as a movement or tendency within the arts in the twentieth century.

Not only has Cunningham, for Copeland, moved beyond expressivity but he has also of course moved beyond representation, because, Copeland adds, 'even when Cunningham's movement seems unmistakably "animal-like" – in *Rainforest* or the famous "cat" solo – he never appears to be representing an animal, but rather borrowing its heightened powers of sensory alertness' (Copeland 1983: 318).

This is extremely tortuous reasoning: why can't he just call it representation? (The question of representation and expression in Cunningham's work is considered in more detail in Chapter 6.) In common with other formalist and modernist theorists, Copeland is interpreting the word 'representation' in an extremely narrow way. A key concept in the arguments proposed by Copeland and his friends is theatricality. This concept comes from Michael Fried's essay on minimalist sculpture, 'Art and objecthood' (1968) in which Fried proposes: 'The success, even the survival of the arts, has come increasingly to depend upon their ability to defeat theatre.' He applies Fried's notion of a modernist anti-theatricality to the

37

work of Balanchine and Yvonne Rainer. Copeland proposes that there is a connection between Balanchine's stripped-down productions like *Agon* (1957) and the minimalism of Rainer's *Trio A* (1966). Both pieces, he argues, are an example of a modernist process of purifying the medium. Rainer's minimalism is 'reductionism of the sort that even Balanchine would have found too restrictive. And yet both Rainer and Balanchine can be said to share, in varying degrees, the same anti-theatrical prejudice' (1986: 180).[5]

Surely to isolate 'the same anti-theatrical prejudice' in the work of two artists who are so different and to link it, as Copeland does, to the idea of an 'American' tradition, is an act of mystification. It ignores the meanings that *Trio A* and *Agon* had within the very different contexts in which they were made and performed. It distracts the reader from considering the way that Rainer (like some postmodern dance artists whose work is considered in Chapter 7) was performing movement which attempted to undermine the ideas of embodiment implied in the sort of classical ballet movements which Balanchine's work used. (Incidentally, it would be difficult to choose two choreographers who presented images of women in more different ways than Rainer and Balanchine). What is at issue here is not a question of whether Balanchine and Rainer's works should be considered modernist but the methods and procedures of modernist criticism itself.

The relationship between representations of masculinity and modernism in ballet and modern dance is a theme which runs through much of the second half of this book. In developing a more sociological understanding of modernism it is necessary, as Janet Wolff points out, to be aware of the relationship between modernity and modernism and not conflate the two (Wolff 1990: 3). Thus Raymond Williams, for example, has drawn attention to the experience of metropolitan living as a factor in the development of the formal innovations of the early modernists (see Chapter 4 below). In the visual arts, the theory of modernism developed by Greenberg, Fried and others has come under attack (Frascina 1985), focusing particularly on its ahistorical nature. Thus Serge Gilbaut and others have related the development of American abstract expressionist painting to domestic American politics during the Cold War period (see Chapter 6 below). As far as this chapter is concerned, it is argued that modernist works are not ahistorical but that there are connections between their modes of expression and social experience. To claim that their abstraction is nevertheless what we will call 'representational' requires elucidation of what is meant by representation and expression.

DANCE REPRESENTATION AND EXPRESSION

Nelson Goodman in his *Languages of Art* (1976) addresses the problem of analytically defining representation and expression – words which he observes 'in everyday talk we play fast and loose with'. Goodman sees art as something which we experience cognitively through systems of symbols. He proposes that we should:

> read the painting as well as the poem and that aesthetic experience is dynamic rather than static. It involves making delicate discriminations and discerning subtle relationships, identifying symbol systems and characters within these symbols and what their characters denote and exemplify, interpreting works and reorganizing the world in terms of works and works in terms of the world.
>
> (Goodman 1976: 214)

He proposes a logical account of the ways in which symbols refer to the world using the terms resemblance, description, denotation, exemplification, representation and expression. For Goodman, representation is not just a matter of resemblance or description but of denotation, and only in relationship to a given system. What a picture looks like is not necessarily what it is of. For something to be a representation of something, it must be a symbol for it, which in some way denotes what is represented, though not necessarily through resemblance. Representation is relative and conventional and 'what we see and depict depends upon and varies with experience, practice, interests, and attitudes' (Goodman 1983: 70). Exemplification is different from denotation and involves properties in the symbols which are an example or sample of the properties in the object or experience exemplified. A small sample of coloured cloth may be shown to exemplify that material. It has some properties of the cloth to which it refers – colour, weave, texture, pattern – but not others – size, shape, or absolute weight and value (Goodman 1976: 53). Doris Humphrey's *Water Study* (1928) exemplifies through moving bodies some properties of waves such as flow and momentum, but not others such as wetness and smell. What is expressed is metaphorically exemplified, and the properties a symbol expresses are its own properties. Thus:

> The expressive symbol, with its metaphorical reach, not only partakes of the greenness of neighbouring pastures and the exotic atmosphere of farther shores, but often in consequence uncovers unnoticed affinities and antipathies among symbols of its own kind. From the nature of metaphor derives some of the characteristic capacity of expression for suggestive allusion, elusive suggestion, and intrepid transcendence of basic boundaries.
>
> (Goodman 1983: 77)

Although Goodman is very particular in clarifying the differences between different forms of reference, he allows that, in practice, reference in dance pieces (as in any work of art) is through chains 'such that each link is reference of one or another of the three elementary types' (1983: 82) by which he means representation, exemplification and expression. Differences in the way symbols refer to what they symbolize thus create different nuances and meanings. For example the Tarantella section at the end of the last act of Bournonville's *Napoli* (1842) represents Italian folk dances such as the inhabitants of Naples might have danced on a festival day, but exemplifies these dances in their rhythm and pace but not in precise detail; furthermore the qualities of joyous exuberance which these dances express metaphorically exemplify the pleasure of the leading characters in the happy resolution of the narrative tensions in the ballet.

The most influential theory of dance as expression is that which Susanne Langer develops in her book *Feeling and Form* (1953). This combines cognitive explanation with a theory of emotional expression. By expression, Langer means the logical expression of symbols: the relation between the dance and the dancer's feelings is not literal and direct but is mediated symbolically. Langer's starting point is her theory of music, in which she proposes that the tonal structures of music bear a close logical similarity to the forms of human feeling:

> forms of growth and of attenuation, flowing and stowing, conflict and resolution, speed and arrest, terrific excitement, calm or subtle activation and dreamy lapses – not joy and sorrow perhaps, but the poignancy of either and both – the greatness and brevity and eternal passing of everything vitally felt. Such is the pattern, or logical form of sentience; and the pattern of music is that same form worked out in pure measured sound and silence. Music is the tonal analogue of emotive life.
>
> (Langer 1953: 27)

Just as the significant form of music expresses the logical form of sentience, Langer proposes that the forms of other arts can be seen to do the same.

The difference between dance and other sorts of movement is that dance motion is gesture. Gesture, Langer points out, is different from verbal language: language is primarily used logically and rarely exclamatorily 'but a highly expressive gesture is usually taken to be one that reveals feelings and emotion' (*ibid.*: 181). The dancer does not express her feelings directly but uses gestures symbolically to create an illusion of spontaneous self-expression, and the basis of this is physical. It is

> an actual body-feeling, akin to that which controls the production of tones in musical performance – the final articulation of imagined feelings in its appropriate physical form. The conception of feeling disposes the dancer's body to symbolize it.
>
> (*ibid.*: 181)

Langer sees the modes of symbolization for all the arts as non-discursive; there is, she suggests, no fixed association or conventional reference for symbols in the arts, whereas such fixed reference exists for words in language, which is discursive. One understands the arts, according to Langer, intuitively – by way of spontaneous, natural and direct insight. One understands the import of an art symbol:

> in toto first . . . contemplation then gradually reveals the complexity of the piece. In discourse the meaning is synthetically construed by a succession of intuitions; but in the arts the complex whole is seen or anticipated first.
>
> (Langer 1953: 329)

Langer thus discounts both the expressive and exclamatory uses of language, and the possibility of informative and discursive meanings being construed in dance gesture. She does, however, leave room for the possibility of construing the meaning of a work of art, where she allows for a process of contemplation after the initial spontaneous intuition. As Langer describes it, the process of contemplation seems to have much in common with the process of construing discursive meanings.

Although the word intuition carries with it connotations of prescience, it strictly means immediate apprehension by the mind without or before reasoning. The process of intuition is learnt rather than 'natural' and instinctive, and what is intuited is nevertheless coded. Langer is therefore giving us a valuable insight into the difference between aesthetic appreciation and the way we understand purely informative texts when she insists on the spontaneous and intuitive nature of our response to a work of art. This insight has been further developed by Maxine Sheets in her phenomenological theory of dance. Like Langer, Sheets sees dance as an abstraction from daily life and speaks of the 'import' of form thus abstracted rather than of its content or meaning. She also, following Langer, proposes that dancers do not actually feel the feelings that are expressed in their dancing, but that:

> The dancer intuits her movement as a perpetual revelation of sheer force which is spatially unified and temporally continuous – sheer form-in-the-making. And her intuition of the import of the form is the same as that of the audience. If for example, the form is symbolically expressive of forms of love, the dancer perforce intuits this import as she creates it through the form. Just as the audience is not feeling love, neither is the dancer, because there is no love to feel. Because the movement is abstracted from the symptomatic expression of feeling in everyday life and because the sheer form of feeling is abstracted from real feeling, no actual feeling is left. Only a sheer form-in-the-making is left, a form which is symbolically expressive of feeling.
>
> (Sheets 1966: 71)

Sheets is restating Langer's proposition about the intuitive nature of aesthetic perception in terms that concur with a phenomenological account of pre-reflective experience of time and space. But Sheets also advances a phenomenological account of the meaning or import of a dance piece. For her, import is the dance itself, and any attempts to describe or label it can amount only to unhelpful approximations which reduce the specificity of the actual experience of watching or performing the choreography. Thus it is a fallacy to ascribe particular meanings to particular movements, as the import resides within and is co-extensive with form-in-the-making. This is potentially a very interesting observation about the way we perceive meanings in dance, but it is not an avenue which Sheets herself pursues. Rather she sees the experience of watching or participating in dance as aesthetic experience.

Janet Wolff (1975) criticizes this notion of aesthetic experience as isolated from and not connected with other areas of knowledge and experience. She proposes that our appreciation of a work of art may be broader than just aesthetic appreciation. It is true that one can appreciate a painting without understanding all its religious, mythological, allegorical or symbolic references, but some knowledge of these often enriches one's appreciation. She therefore rejects the notion that 'art originates in experience, and is the expression of that experience, and which has come to mean that art is aimed at aesthetic experience' (*ibid.*: 109). It is this view of dance which is implicit in the work of Langer and Sheets. Wolff points to the danger of reducing experience of a work of art to abstracted 'aesthetic experience'; in making this reduction, she argues, the work of art loses its place and the world to which it belongs.

> The aesthetic dimension must be transcended ... for the true experience of art involves the understanding of meaning. Indeed this is not merely a precept to be followed, but necessarily true since perception itself always includes meaning. . . . Thus the real aesthetic experience is the act of a historical spirit not a timeless presence.
>
> (*ibid.*: 109)

By arguing that art is not timeless and universal but historically and culturally specific, Wolff raises the problem of how one can recognize and make allowances for one's own culturally and historically specific prejudices when interpreting works from cultural or historical contexts other than one's own. She proposes that the solution to this problem is to be found in Hans-Georg Gadamer's notion of the hermeneutic circle (1975). When approaching a work of art we are conscious of our prejudices but also open to the 'Otherness' of the material. 'By controlling our anticipations we are enabled to revise them, since our openness to the subject allows distorting prejudices to be discovered' (Wolff 1975: 105). This in turn allows us to return to the work of art with greater openness and more consciousness of the nature of our prejudices, and thus to make a fresh interpretation. The process is thus circular. Within this theory, a completely unbiased interpretation of a work of art (Kant's disinterested disposition) is never possible. Wolff substantiates this claim by relating it to the phenomenological foundation of the sociology of knowledge. An extremely sceptical ontology, she argues, finds no absolutely objective base for a theory of knowledge, only a relative base. Wolff goes on to distinguish two separate problems within this relativization of knowledge:

> The first is the extent to which, and the way in which the sociologist's researches are coloured and distorted by his own social-existential position. The second is the epistemological question of the sense in which one can speak of the real, or objective world, and whether such a world is knowable.
>
> (*ibid.*: 42)

In response to the second problem, Wolff rejects metaphysical speculation about the ultimate reality of the world, turning instead to the ways in which we can criticize, expose, corroborate or in other ways test the limits of our knowledge of reality, concluding:

> But in the end we are left with appearances: epistemology involves and defines the limits of ontology, and there can be no ontology outside the critical theory of knowledge. Epistemology in its turn, is inseparable from the sociological critique of knowledge although not exhausted by it.
>
> (*ibid.*: 52)

The difference between Wolff's hermeneutic method and Sheets's phenomenological account of dance is that whereas Sheets takes the consciousness of the individual as the epistemological frame of reference, Wolff proposes that 'hermeneutic philosophy forces the interpreter to begin by grasping the place of his own consciousness in its historico-cultural context' (*ibid.*: 107). The strength of the hermeneutic approach is that, in developing a sociological reading of a work, it avoids the danger of reducing the work to no more than the sum of its social, political, historical and ideological co-ordinates. This sort of reduction is avoided through acknowledging the affective and intuitive nature of our experience of the reception of works of art, and it is these which the work of Langer and Sheets shows are crucial to our experience of theatre dance. This experience is nevertheless also ideologically determined. We relate our affective response to works of art to our affective response to our lived experience. And, as Wolff argues, the process of interpreting an art work is conditioned by the social, political and cultural context and beliefs of the person making the interpretation.

DANCE, LANGUAGE AND REPRESENTATION

Whereas much of the work on gender representation has used ideas developed from linguistics, Langer and Goodman both base their work on logical theories. Both see the connection between a symbol and what it signifies as nominal – a similarity of logical structure within a given frame of reference between the symbol and that to which it refers. The symbols which the structuralists seek to isolate are discursive and it is claimed that these are involved in the reproduction of social forms and identities. Thus, as Nelson Goodman has observed, representations are relative and conventional, so that what the individual sees depends upon and varies with experience, practice, interests and attitudes.

The question of the relation between dance and language is central to the question of how representations function in dance; as Levinson argued, dance is not a substitute for words. It has also been suggested that dance expresses embodied feelings of physical space and emotional experience that are inadequately expressed in words. One of the reasons why theatre dance has not received as much attention from theorists as other art forms is because the prioritization of verbal forms in logocentric western societies has lead to the marginalization of the body. It might even be the case that, as Ann Daly has suggested, 'movement itself has traditionally been consigned to the realm of the feminine, set in opposition to male mastery over language' (Daly 1988: 43). What representations of masculinity in dance are and how they signify is contingent upon the relationship between verbal language (the privileged mode of communication in our society, claimed by some to be masculine – see Chapter 3) and the (gendered) body.

Despite Langer and Sheets's reservations, there surely exist levels on which we appreciate dance where the symbols are structured discursively. It is on these levels that our appreciation of dance is informed by our knowledge of other dance pieces and of other cultural forms, and by our experience of the world: it is in this way that, despite what Langer suggests, conventions sometimes develop that allow references and meanings to be read in dance gestures and sequences. There are, however, other levels on which meaning in dance is, as Sheets puts it, co-extensive with form-in-the-making; dance movement communicates more than just referential information. The reason why dance should not be reduced to a translation of a verbal original is that, in that process, the body will be marginalized and the expressivity and materiality of the dancing body will be denied. Because dance mediates the social construction of the gendered body, representations of gender in dance are a site of conflict between the individual and society.

DISCOURSE, DANCE AND THE DANCER'S BODY

None of the theories of dance considered thus far has considered that the marginalization of the body might have significant consequences for the agency of the body in creating dance meanings. Susan Leigh Foster, however, states as a concern of her book *Reading Dancing* 'a vision of the body's movement as an act of writing' (Foster 1986: 237). In identifying this she acknowledges the influence of French post-structuralist theory, particularly the writings of Roland Barthes and Michel Foucault. In their work, the body is formed within discourse, and discourse allows the individual to conceive and express ideas and concepts, but at the same time what it is possible to express is defined and limited by that discourse. The individual for Barthes is no more than the subject of language, formed within discourse: 'I am obliged to posit myself first as subject before stating the action that will henceforth be no more than my attribute: what I do is merely the consequence and consecution of what I am' (Barthes 1983: 460). Whereas for some structuralist and post-structuralist theorists, following Bakhtin and Volosinov, language is seen as a site of struggle and conflict over competing meanings, for Barthes and Foucault this possibility of opposition is virtually impossible. There are some possibilities of subversion – most French post-structuralists have been elegant commentators on avant-garde art and literature – but Foucault in particular held especially pessimistic views about the way that potentially oppositional voices are recuperated within dominant discourses. In Foucault's later writings, language is a model for power. He proposes that power is a network of force relations which is not purely enforced from above but comes from everywhere. Power not only is repressive and prohibitive but incites and manipulates. The individual who is the subject of power is an embodied subject so that power acts on the body by inciting desires. Thus whereas eighteenth-century philosophers saw the individual as above all rational, Foucault draws attention to the irrational pull of desire. The body, for him, is a central but potentially irrational entity within discourses which are structured linguistically.[6]

Within this post-structuralist tradition, Foster characterizes her book *Reading Dancing* as an attempt to:

> 'denaturalize' our notions of the self and our assumptions about the body. In this study I try to show how the body and the subject are formed – how they come into being – through participation in a given discourse, in this case dance classes, rehearsals, and performances of a particular choreographer.
>
> (*ibid.*: 237)

The problem in this is whose body or subject is formed here through discourse. Foster seems to be saying that dance classes, rehearsals and performances are the means by which the choreographer as subject expresses her or himself using their own or other dancers' bodies to make representations. It is also consistent with her thesis that a dancer, through classes, rehearsals and performances, finds ways in which her or his body can realize the choreographer's intention. This raises the question of the connection between the formation of body and subject in dance, and their formation in the world off stage. In *Reading Dancing* Foster seems to suggest that choreographers create whatever relationship between subject and body suits their creative purpose, rather than mediating socially constructed norms. But in a separate essay 'The signifying body' (1985), Foster advances the argument that experimental and postmodern dance is resistive and oppositional to 'the body's placement within a system of power relations and its concomitant role as a locus of ideological commentary' (1985: 46). What is at stake for Foster is the conception of the self which determines the way the dancer's body is presented on stage. In her view of conventional dance practice, dance movement as discourse is an 'evanescent medium through which ideas and feelings are expressed' (*ibid.*: 46). In expressionist work it is 'the expressive tension of the inner self which desires to communicate' while, in formalist work, actions 'are performed with the virtuoso bravado of a self which commands the body' so that 'dancers look down at their own bodies or out at the audience, as if to direct the viewers' attention to the technical feats they have mastered' (*ibid.*: 46); this invokes the 'age-old dichotomy' between mind and body. Taking as examples the work of the Grand Union and Meredith Monk, Foster argues that postmodern work refrains from enacting the traditional relationship between the body and the act of expression.

> Not only do the Grand Union and Meredith Monk deny the body as instrument of expression and dissolve the distinction between functional and aesthetic movement, but they also situate dance as one discourse among many. The performances of both groups involve theatre and music, as well as dancing. The relationship between these media replicates the non-hierarchical, non-organic interaction between body and subject which is evident in these pieces.
>
> (*ibid.*: 46)

This view enables the development of a critique of political ideologies at work within cultural forms and suggests the possibility of destabilizing patriarchal thought. The problem with this, however, is that a post-structuralist questioning of theory falls into what Janet Wolff has called an epistemological paradox: any critique of theory is itself founded on theory (Wolff 1991: 89).

Taken to its logical conclusion within French post-structuralist thought, the idea that works of art are ideologically produced and socially and historically situated leads towards a situation which Roland Barthes called the death of the author. If the writer or artist or choreographer is destined to do no more than assemble components of always-already existing, ideologically produced discourses, she or he can no longer be thought of as the sole author or originator of the resulting cultural product.

This view of the creator of cultural products is one that disregards the traditional distinction between 'art' and other forms of cultural product, and has much in common with approaches to the analysis of gender in cultural studies. From a sociological point of view, differences between mainstream and marginal representations of gender might therefore be accounted for in terms of the ways in which social and cultural groups are situated in or take up marginal or confrontational positions in relation to the dominant social groups and interests. The spectator's point of view is a crucial aspect of how one analyses cultural forms, and this is considered further in the next chapter.

Structuralist and post-structuralist French theories, at their most pessimistic, see everything as invested (to use a word that frequently occurs in translations of the work of Michel Foucault) with power. Power, of course, works in the interests of patriarchy – men. The idea of 'men' is in itself an ideological construction which has the effect of creating an ideologically motivated sense of unity among men, allowing them to work together in the interests of men against women and those deemed 'Other'. To speak therefore not of masculinity but of masculinities is to recognize the extent to which individuals and groups of men are inhibited by the dominant gender ideologies in the process of constructing and realizing their identities. It has already been argued in the last chapter that the conventions which police and protect representations of masculinity in dance have an inhibiting effect on all male dancers in the way they develop a personal style that expresses their sense of identity through dance.

From what standpoint can I as a man consider the possibility of questioning the male order as represented in dance? It would be disingenuous to claim that I can distance myself from the benefits of being male in a society where power is unequally distributed in favour of men. Furthermore there is the problem of how to dismantle masculinity using theoretical tools that are themselves part of the means through which masculinity maintains itself: how to use a rational and scientific approach to question rational and scientific theory, and how to avoid falling into a sea of relativism. This is the same problem encountered above in relation to Foster's discussion of the relationship of subject and body in dance work. One way of questioning the male order as represented in dance is to undertake an ideological critique which denaturalizes and destabilizes the criteria, traditions and conventions of the established theatre dance practice, including conventions of gender representation. If representations are ideologically constructed, the logical thing to call opposition to them is deconstruction. But deconstruction is a highly problematic concept. A deconstructive reading of a text is one which reveals the text's internal contradictions and inconsistencies. But while deconstruction might therefore be seen as a critical tool, the deconstructive reading is one in which meaning is continually deferred, and binary oppositions dissolved. Christopher Norris has argued that by continually deferring and dissolving oppositions and distinctions, post-structuralist, postmodern and deconstructive theories are in danger of being or becoming uncritical (Norris 1992). Janet Wolff has similarly argued that an entirely dispersed and fragmented politics is both misconceived and impossible. She proposes that we have to retain a commitment to theory while recognizing its provisional nature (Wolff 1990: 8). Her provisional and pragmatic answer to this problem is that of where necessary using what methodological tools we find useful to test sceptically the limits of our knowledge. It has already been suggested that it is useful to speak of masculinities rather than masculinity, in order to dismantle the effects of the ideologically motivated sense of unity among men. If, however, this process of deconstruction defers and dissolves unitary masculinity until there are as many masculinities as there are men, the concept would surely cease to have any usefulness. The deconstructive strategies of postmodern cultural practices are useful in instances where they make visible the otherwise hidden nature of the operations of ideologies. Doing this makes a limited space for the expression of alternative or oppositional points of view. It is this theoretical approach which informs the analysis of recent dance in Chapter 7.

In dance there is no possibility of opting out entirely from dominant gender ideologies. As we negotiate daily life, we are all experts in gender studies. Individuals cannot just make or analyse choreography by pretending that gender does not exist. There is no value-free, independent position from which to make judgements of a political or aesthetic nature. Furthermore discourses may enable limited expression in dance to marginal and oppositional points of view; but at the same time they have a tendency to block and deform them, as is demonstrated more than once in the second half of this book. It is possible, however, to reveal the hidden nature of the operations of gender ideologies in dance, and thus make a space from which it is possible to imagine alternatives. Laura Mulvey has neatly summed up the positive theoretical stance of much feminist practice in film that aims to present an alternative to dominant theoretical structures: 'The alternative is the thrill that comes from leaving the past behind without rejecting it, transcending outworn or oppressive forms, or daring to break with normal pleasurable expectations in order to conceive a new language of desire' (Mulvey 1975: 8). Underlying the second half of this book is the assumption that what has motivated the development of modern dance and ballet is the attempt to conceive such new languages of desire.

3

LOOKING AT THE MALE

Some of the most interesting early observations about the representation of gender in visual images were made by John Berger in the television series *Ways of Seeing*. What was unusual about his method was that, instead of adopting a traditional art historical approach that is primarily concerned with major masterpieces by great artists, he took as his starting point the question of how individuals look at visual images. Thus he observed: 'Women are depicted in a quite different way from men – not because the feminine is different from the masculine – but because the "ideal" spectator is always assumed to be male and the image of woman is designed to flatter him' (1972: 64). This led to the idea that social behaviour is a determinant of the conventions which structure cultural forms. This underlies Berger's much-quoted observation that 'Men act and women appear. Men look at women. Women watch themselves being looked at' (*ibid.*: 47) and that the gendered look informs the criteria and conventions which govern the way women and men are depicted within the tradition of European oil painting. The connection which Berger made between the act of looking in everyday life and the structures of looking encoded in visual images is one which has subsequently received much attention in work on gender representation. The idea of the male gaze has become, in Camille Paglia's words, a 'stale cliché ... that tiresome assumption of feminist discourse' (1992: 85). But, as Ann Daly had previously observed: 'As tiresome as this term has become, it remains a fundamental concept: that, in modern western societies the one who sees and the one who is seen are gendered positions' (1989: 25). This chapter applies the idea of the gendered gaze to dance.

One criticism that has been made of earlier accounts of the male gaze is that they assume that culture is immovably and exclusively masculine, thus ruling out the possibility of any alternative or subordinate expression. The development of female audiences for dance during the twentieth century has been a factor in the development of male dance, as also has been the crucially important work of Martha Graham and other women choreographers. Any application of the idea of the gendered gaze to the reception of theatre dance must be able to deal with the way the female spectator (be she choreographer or audience member) looks at the male body. A central assumption of this book is that the spectacle of the male body in dance is protected by defensive strategies. These construct the dominant point of view as male and patriarchal while marginalizing alternative and subversive points of view. Dominant male interests are protected through reinforcing the idea of an ideologically constructed, monolithic masculinity. As has been suggested previously, a range of different masculine identities exist, differing in relation to race, class, sexuality and other components of identity. In order to express the individuality of the multiplicity of present and future identities, both masculine and feminine, it is possible and indeed necessary to challenge the patriarchal point of view and develop counter-practices.

There is no contradiction between the recognition of the importance of the dancer's embodiment to an account of dance as a representational form (discussed in the last chapter) and the idea of the gendered gaze. Spectators' responses to a dance performance are made not only in relation to their own experiences of embodiment but also in response to visual imagery and cues. The primary mode of expression in dance is the body; in the theatre, however, dance is something that a spectator watches. (In French, a dance performance is called 'un spectacle', a spectacle.) A crucial difference between the way we look at dance and the way we look at two- or three-dimensional visual art and film is the fact that dancers are alive in front of us – we are aware of their presence. As Ann Daly has observed, 'Presence is the silent yet screeching excitement of physical vibrancy, of "being there". It is one of the thrills of watching dance, to see someone radiate pure energy, whether it is in stillness or in flight' (1989: 25). The implications of the idea of the performer's presence have yet to be fully worked out (see Chaikin 1972). As Philip Auslander has observed, presence is about power, and there is sometimes collusion between political structures of authority and the persuasive power of presence (1987: 24–5). The ways in which the male dancer's presence succeeds or fails in reinforcing male power is clearly central to an understanding of representations of masculinity in theatre dance. How spectators read dancers' presence is determined partly by visual cues. Some of these cues are given by the dancers, through the way they present themselves to the audience, and in the way they themselves focus their gaze.

The question of how dancers are looked at by the audience was one of the topics discussed during a roundtable discussion on movement and gender with postmodern dance artists Johanna Boyce and Bill T. Jones (Boyce et al. 1988). Boyce and Jones both make work that deals with themes relating to gender and sexuality. In the discussion they were not primarily concerned with questions of theory but with observing and articulating perceptions about the experience of dancing which influence their work as dance makers and performers. Boyce said she imagined that being on display is a fearful thing for a man because it is a situation in which he doesn't 'have total control or empowerment' over the people watching him (*ibid*.: 89). Jones said that, as a black man on stage being watched primarily by white spectators, he felt that his state in the world was that of being 'such a marginal, "special black"'. He felt that he was a 'commodity' and that this 'must be a feeling that women have' (*ibid*.: 90–1). For Jones:

> There is something about the spectators saying, in effect 'Perform for us. Show us your body.' So it made me extremely aggressive, and maybe that was my desire to impose masculine control – I also assume it was racial . . .
>
> It was a cruel and ironic way that I saw myself. You know: you're a black man – take off your shirt. You're allowed to wiggle your hips in public. You know what they're all thinking, 'Oh, I bet you have a dick down to your knees.'
>
> (*ibid*.: 89–90)

What is striking about these comments is the way that power is linked to the act of looking. Both choreographers are aware of the convention that, in order to represent masculinity, a dancer should look powerful. Boyce connects being on display with loss of power, while Jones connects the performer's gaze with objectification (being a 'commodity'), and implies that being 'extremely aggressive' is a way of reimposing control and thus evading objectification. What is commodified by being looked at on display is his sexuality as a black man – as the 'Other' to the white male norm. Issues relating to power, the gaze, sexuality, gender and the spectacle of masculinity are central to this chapter. It assumes that who looks at whom, and how surveillance relates to power in western society, are factors which influence representation of gender in dance. What is at issue is not that men should not be looked at but how they are supposed to appear when they are the object of a spectator's gaze.

The act of looking is relevant to the study not just of the reception of spectacle but of narrative forms as well. The connection between looking and the process of identification by a reader or audience member is implied by the commonly used expression that, when one identifies with a character, one *sees from their point of view*. Some theorists in film studies have accounted for this process of identificatory looking by referring to psychoanalytic theories of the early construction of gendered identity. In the work of Freud and Lacan, the acquisition of language is taken as a key moment in the formation of identity, language being seen as male and patriarchal – as Lacan puts it, 'the law of the Father'. Thus non-verbal areas of experience are associated with the somatic stages of dependence on the mother. Everything relating to what Freud called the infantile state of

51

polymorphous perversity – the early, non-verbal, pre-linguistic and bodily experiences before the infant becomes aware of her or his separate identity and the significance of their gender – is seen as marginal to dominant discourse, but a potential site of subversion of it.

Ways of analysing gender representations in cultural forms that are developed from these psychoanalytic theories have been warmly greeted by some but treated with suspicion by others. It is now generally accepted that ideology works unconsciously as well as consciously, and therefore that the psychological and social factors that influence the construction of identity also determine the way we respond to representations of gender in cultural forms. What psychoanalytic theories of gender representation offer are ways of accounting for the connection between, on the one hand, the latent structures and conventions in mainstream work and on the other hand the dominant male point of view. Some psychoanalytic theories point to the political importance of marginal aspects of social or cultural experiences that are potentially subversive of the hidden structures which these theories identify. One criticism that is difficult to counter is the argument that psychoanalytic theories subordinate cultural and historical spheres to a trans-historical psychoanalytic framework. However, as will be seen, some of the areas and issues which some of these theories focus on coincide with similar interests in the work of radical and experimental artists. Consequently, despite the above reservations, psychoanalytic theories offer unusual insights into aspects of experimental art work, particularly in relation to representations of gender and sexuality. The popularity of psychoanalytic theories of gender representations in cultural forms suggests that, although their detractors say they are methodologically unsound and dangerous (e.g. Wolff 1990), to their fans the dangers are perhaps fascinating. It is because these theories discuss ways in which the body is marginal and subversive of dominant discourse that this chapter explores the possibility of applying the theoretical approaches developed in film studies and elsewhere to the analysis of gender representation in dance.

Because aspects of these theories are controversial, and the problems inherent in them not easily resolved, this chapter has been organized so as partially to separate an account of narrative identification from Freudian and Lacanian accounts of the construction of gendered identity. The underlying aim is to find non-reductive ways (which are sensitive to social and historical contexts) of thinking about the gendered gaze and the psychological mechanisms that defend male norms. Therefore, the chapter first considers the structures and conventions that act defensively to limit the spectacle of the male body in cultural forms. Second it examines theories of gender representation that draw on Freudian and Lacanian psychoanalytical concepts to propose a theory of spectatorship. It concludes by looking at theories of marginality and subversion, and considers ways of thinking about these which are not dependent upon some of the more problematic parts of these psychoanalytic theories.

THE MALE GAZE AND THE SPECTACLE OF MASCULINITY

John Berger, to substantiate his claim that the 'ideal' viewer is male, suggested a simple test. Take any painting of a traditional female nude and, in your imagination, turn the woman into a man; 'then notice the violence which the transformation does. Not to the image, but to the assumptions of a likely viewer' (1972: 64). Feminist painters like Sylvia Sleigh have gone one stage further and painted nude portraits of men in poses that do almost exactly what Berger suggested and draw on the conventions of the traditional European female nude. The intention is clearly to try to eroticize the spectacle of the male body for the visual pleasure of a female spectator. In some crucial ways, however, the men don't look very masculine. It is this problem, of what happens when attempts are made to present the male body as a pin-up, that Richard Dyer has addressed.

Dyer argues that images of men must appear active in some way in order to appear in line with dominant ideas of masculinity. Women in pin-ups (and in nude paintings) almost always avert their eyes from their viewers and acknowledge them, thus allowing themselves to be surveyed as erotic objects. Men in pin-ups look out actively, often upwards, barely acknow-ledging the viewer and thus resisting the attempt of the viewer's gaze to objectify them. Whereas women are usually shown in passive poses, men are generally shown caught in some sort of activity. Even if men are not in action, 'the male image still promises activity by the way the body is posed. Even in an apparently supine pose, the model tightens and taughtens his body so that the muscles are emphasised, hence drawing attention to the body's potential for action' (Dyer 1982: 67). Dyer gives as one example of this a photograph by Cecil Beaton of Johnny Weissmuller. In this Weissmuller's naked torso is placed among tropical vegetation suggesting his role as Tarzan. He is posed with his body turning, resting on his arms. He is caught in action with his body tensed, and his eyes 'look up in a characteristic pose of masculine striving' (1987: 118). It is these conventions which make images of men look masculine. Where men are presented in images without these conventions, their masculinity appears unstable, but, where the conventions are adhered to, the image resists being objectified and appreciated from an erotic point of view.

The compositional device of the raised and stressed torso that gives Weissmuller the appearance of striving is one that Michelangelo used in many of his images of the naked male body. The most famous example of this is the image of Adam in the Creation of Adam section of the Sistine

53

Figure 3 The ballerina's gaze is passive, allowing the spectator to survey her body as an erotic object. Her partner gazes at her, thus deflecting the spectator's gaze and redirecting it towards her. These devices dictate that the spectator looks from a male point of view.

(© Camera Press Ltd. Reproduced with permission from Baron/Camera Press Ltd, London)

Chapel ceiling. The way that the language of gestures in theatre dance overlaps that of visual art is clearly demonstrated by the use of this image by Balanchine in *Apollon Musagète* (1928) at the beginning of Apollo's duet with Terpsichore. Apollo's previous solo, linking this with the previous duet, ends with Apollo on his side on the floor, resting on one leg and pushing his torso up with one arm (characteristically striving). His other arm is raised in mid-air with one finger pointing. Terpsichore sidles across the floor towards him on pointe but both are looking away from each other. With her right arm she points up to the heavens, while her left arm reaches down towards his pointing hand and their two fingers touch. Just as Michelangelo's God imparts the divine spark of life to his Adam by touching his finger, so Terpsichore, the muse of dance, gives Apollo divine inspiration with the same gesture. He then turns round to face in her direction but looks past her, upwards and, during the duet, his gaze alternates between looking up and looking at his partner. Dyer comments on the function of this upwards male gaze as follows: 'In the case where the model is looking up, this always suggests spirituality: he might be there for his face and body to be gazed at, but his mind is on higher things, and it is this upwards striving that is most supposed to please' (1982: 63). When Apollo does get to his feet to dance with Terpsichore, she goes into an example of the ballet position called arabesque, balancing on one leg with the other raised behind, one arm forward and the other balanced behind. Keeping all these limbs in the same position in relation to one another, she bends forward from the waist; whereupon Apollo picks her up around the waist and lifts her right up and over his shoulder, so that she ends upside down and facing away from him.

If the gaze is one area through which masculinity is signified in ballet, then in the *pas de deux*, or duet, the appearance of strength and the ability to control women are other important signs. In an important essay on images of women in Balanchine's choreography, Ann Daly (1986) has indicated a number of ways in which Balanchine's women (as in the example of Terpsichore lifted by Apollo) appear helpless and passive through being displayed in a vulnerable and sexually demeaning way towards the audience. The question of sexual and fetishistic components in the spectator's gaze is considered later in this chapter. It would be simplistic to dismiss the *pas de deux* as no more than an exhibition in which the female dancer is an object to be manipulated. The actual practice of partnering and lifting is one which requires a high degree of co-operation between the male and female dancer, but the extent to which the spectator is made aware of this varies between one duet and another, and between different styles and traditions. Sarah Rubidge suggests that there are certain questions that one can ask about the relationship implied in the *pas de deux*:

How often does the male initiate the lifts? How often is the woman used as a passive object? How often does the male dancer, by touching a part of his partner's body, cause her to move? Does the female dancer initiate movement in the male in a similar way? How often do the partners bear each other's weight equally in a duet – or trust their weight to their partner?

(1989: 5)

Another sign which Rubidge points out can contribute to the representation of gender in the *pas de deux* is the dancer's use of space. In the *grand pas de deux* in Russian nineteenth-century ballets, each dancer has a solo *pas*. Whereas, Rubidge points out, the male dancer traverses the stage commandingly with spectacular jumps, the female dancer performs much smaller and neater steps within a more confined area.

Spectacular jumps are one way in which the male dancer can appear strong. When, Dyer argues, masculinity can be signified through the appearance of strength, a distinction should be made between the appearance of strength and actual signs of physical effort. As Dolin observed 'the good (male) partner will always try to avoid any appearance of hard work, however difficult it may be, and believe me, often is' (1969: 12). Within this gallant and chivalrous tradition the male dancer's role is almost rendered invisible. Generally, within the ballet tradition introduced to western Europe by the Ballets Russes and continued in particular in Britain by dance artists such as Dolin, the male role in the *pas de deux* tended to be inconspicuous and uncontroversial. This is far from the acrobatic and physically powerful style of male ballet dancing that was introduced to the western ballet world through the western tours of Russian ballet companies. Dolin, writing in 1969, regretfully acknowledged that since the first European performances by the Bolshoi Ballet in 1956 a new style of partnering had come into fashion: 'It is of no use to be, and remain, old fashioned, but I shall never reconcile myself to the current vogue of executing the lovely classical adagios (*pas de deux*) of *Swan Lake* and *The Sleeping Beauty* as if they were weight-lifting contests' (Dolin 1969: 12). This more assertive and powerful style of partnering introduced by the Russians is more in line with the norms of heterosexual masculinity which dictate that men should appear strong and should challenge the audience's gaze. Where the appearance of the male dancer during the duet is relatively inconspicuous and gallant rather than controlling, he looks less masculine, and this is a factor behind the unease that accompanies the idea of men dancing on stage. For most of the twentieth century, the construction of male roles in dance and ballet has generally been overshadowed by the need to counteract this negative image. This has sometimes resulted in a 'macho' overcompensation – of trying to prove that ballet is tough really, or that modern dance is not soft like ballet.

In whatever ways the male dancer's strength is signified or hidden during the *pas de deux*, the male partner's gaze is crucial in signifying his masculinity. He never acknowledges the spectator's gaze, and his own gaze is directed towards the ballerina. As Adrian Stokes put it:

> Her partner guides and holds her. And he – he then watches her *pas* with upraised hand, he shows her off. He has the air of perpetual triumph, and when the time comes for his own variation he bounds, leaps, bounces and rejoins the ballerina in the wings amid applause. Such is the abstract of the *pas de deux*, the crux of ballet.
>
> (Stokes 1942: 81)

Anton Dolin gives a similar account: 'He is there to focus attention upon her from their first entrance until the last call is finished' (Dolin 1969: 12). This applies even when he is applauded:

> following the adagio the true ballerina expects her partner to lead her on. . . . [He] should keep his whole attention on her and with obvious admiration at what she has accomplished. He knows that without him she could not have achieved such perfection, but it is gentlemanly not to show it!
>
> (*ibid.*: 12)

By himself gazing at the ballerina, he identifies himself with the males in the audience and is in turn available to be the bearer of their looks. Here, the interplay of spectator's and dancer's gazes is not just determining how the spectacle is interpreted but creating a sense of narrative.

NARRATIVE AND IDENTIFICATION

Recent work on film theory proposes that structures exist within the way a story is told that make us identify with particular characters, and, in mainstream cultural forms, this identification is regulated to reinforce dominant notions of masculinity and femininity. Drawing on Freud's theories of the development of the subconscious, this work proposes that the way a spectator identifies with a character on the screen is similar to the process Freud attributes to daydreams: that they are an ideal, invulnerable projection of the self (ego). 'Although a boy might know quite well that it is most unlikely he will go out into life, make his fortune through prowess or the assistance of helpers, and marry a princess, the stories express the male phantasy of ambition' (Mulvey 1981: 13). John Ellis has suggested that the psychological process through which a spectator (of film) makes identifications is both free and complex: 'Identification is therefore multiple and fractured, a sense of seeing the constituent parts of the spectator's own psyche paraded before her or him' (Ellis 1982: 43). Audience members may thus make quite complicated identifications, not just women with women heroines, men with male heroes. Spectators make similar identifications when watching dance theatre. However, the process of narrative effectively regulates the sort of free identifications described above, so that they are made to conform along the lines of socially defined and constructed categories of male and female. When we identify with a character in a story, we often say that we 'see their point of view', and it is literally how we see them that makes us read the story from their point of view. Laura Mulvey, in her essay 'Visual pleasure and narrative cinema' (1975), proposes that audiences have two different types of ways of looking at narrative film (and, it is argued, at theatre dance): a look with which the spectator, caught up in the story, identifies with the protagonist, and a more detached look of pleasure at visual display; this latter is structured by the way characters within the narrative look at each other.

Looking, as we have seen, is also gendered. It is Mulvey's contention that film stories recount what men are seen to do (thus advancing the narrative), but the (visual) presence of women provides a spectacle that freezes the flow of action. Women may be the cause of things that happen, or they may be the reward which the film hero tries to win (the film ending with the two of them living happily ever after). But, Mulvey argues, the function of women in narrative is to be an 'erotic object for the characters within the screen, and [an] erotic object for the spectator within the auditorium' (Mulvey 1975: 8). As such, shots of women stop the flow of narrative. The film audience looks from the male point of view, and thus looks at the women in the film through the way the men in the film look at them. The male hero or protagonist is the bearer of the audience's gaze.

The narratives of ballets and modern dance do not generally grip their audiences in the way that films do. Theatre dance generally consists of sections of display or spectacle interspersed with little bits of narrative. In late-nineteenth-century Russian ballets, the story line is advanced through mime sections between the set dances, so that the story temporarily interrupts the spectacle. In twentieth-century narrative choreography (e.g. Fokine, Tudor, Graham, Limón), characterization has become more integrated into the dance movement itself; narrative tensions are largely expressed, worked out and resolved within choreographed material. As has just been demonstrated, the *pas de deux* is a key area in which the narrative themes in the ballet are worked out.

Mulvey (1981) has related narrative structure in film to V. A. Propp's work on the structural analysis of folk tales in which 'princess' represents a desired reward for a prince (unmarried) and thus a resolution of the narrative. This narrative structure in which an unmarried prince (or equivalent) is seen to be in need of a wife can be usefully applied to ballet stories. Eric Aschengreen (1974) has pointed out that the stories of *Giselle* and *La Sylphide* are told and resolved not from the point of view of the eponymous ballerina's role but from the point of view of James and

Albrecht. *La Sylphide*, *Giselle*, *La Peri* and *Swan Lake* are each about a man for whom there are two women, one with whom he ought to settle down and marry, and another, who is more romantic and unattainable, and for whom he yearns – a sylphide, a wili, a peri or an enchanted swan queen. The male heroes generally learn by the end of the ballet that they cannot get what they want when the object of their desire dies, and they end up older but wiser. Albrecht, in the original version of *Giselle*, ends up back with the woman he was initially meant to marry; according to Théophile Gautier, Albrecht ends the ballet 'with his head resting on the shoulder of the beautiful Bathilde who forgives and consoles him' (Gautier 1983: 199).

There are also, of course, narratives which have at their centre a strong female character. In the Romantic melodrama, a common device is for such a central female character to be faced with a choice between two men. Mulvey suggests that these deal with the dilemma of the central female character torn between the socially acceptable role of femininity and her desire to have an unacceptable but more exciting lifestyle. She gives as an example the cowboy film *Duel in the Sun* (1946), in which the main two male characters represent the different sides of the leading female character's desires and aspirations. Examples in ballet and modern dance of similar melodramatic triangles with a strong central female lead include Antony Tudor's *Pillar of Fire* (1942) and to a lesser extent his *Lilac Garden* (1936), Cranko's *Onegin* (1965), and a number of Martha Graham's pieces from the early 1940s (considered in Chapter 5) including *Appalachian Spring* (1944).

Even though the male character here is seen from the point of view of the central female character, narrative conventions nevertheless dictate that the way he appears must still assume that the spectator watching the ballet is male. Problems arise where a male dancer is viewed in an erotic way by the female character, or by a male one. As Steve Neale has suggested, 'in a heterosexual and patriarchal society, the male body cannot be marked explicitly as the erotic object of another male look: that look must be motivated in some way, its erotic component repressed' (Neale 1983: 14). He argues that the problem lies within and must be resolved through the narrative, usually through some sort of punishment. Punishment generally must be seen to follow in narratives where the central character goes against social convention, and this applies also in the few mainstream gay narratives in ballets. Women or men are not supposed to look erotically at men. In the film *Duel in the Sun* Pearl, the leading character, comes to a tragic end, although Scarlett O'Hara in the book and film of *Gone with the Wind* gets off more lightly for not repressing her desire for Rhett Butler. Jocasta, in Graham's *Night Journey* (1947), comes to a bad end for having desired Oedipus, as does he himself for having been the erotic subject of her gaze. As Graham Jackson (1978: 38–9) points out, gay ballets (in which men are the erotic object of the male gaze) such as

Undertow (Tudor 1945) and *Monument for a Dead Boy* (Van Manen 1965) are acceptable only if they end tragically.

Neale proposes that the spectator's look is an investigative one, but that, whereas women are constantly under investigation, men rarely are: 'women are a problem, a source of anxiety, of obsessive enquiry; men are not. Whereas women are investigated, men are tested. Masculinity, as an ideal, at least, is implicitly known. Femininity is, by contrast, a mystery' (1983: 15–16).[1] The spectator looks at the male and female dancer in the *pas de deux* in a similar way. The ballerina is a mystery, and her display *en pointe* and in lifts facilitates her investigation by the spectator's gaze. Male vigour in general is known: it is how a particular male dancer measures up that is tested in his solo *pas*.

One of the most extreme forms of testing masculinity within a narrative is a fight. Neale points out that one moment when the film audience are allowed to look at men – and specifically at male bodies – as spectacle is in the shoot-out of a western film. These are 'moments of spectacle, points at which the narrative hesitates, comes to a momentary halt, but they are also points at which the drama is finally resolved, a suspense in the culmination of the narrative drive' (Neale 1983: 8). Male sexuality is commonly associated with aggression and violence, and Neale suggests that within the shoot-out there are structures that stop or punish erotic display. Following Paul Willemen, he argues that, in the films of Anthony Mann, erotic looks by a male protagonist at another man 'seem structurally linked to a narrative content marked by sado-masochistic phantasies and scenes' (Neale 1983: 12).

Neale further suggests that in Serge Leone's Spaghetti westerns, the erotic component of the way the protagonists exchange aggressive looks in gun duels is also recuperated. This convention of exchanged looks is parodied through the use of extreme and repetitive close-ups, and thus the way that the film is edited makes the narrative start to freeze, and spectacle take over: 'by stopping the narrative in order to recognize the pleasure of display, but displacing it from the male body as such and locating it more generally in the overall components of a highly ritualized scene' (Neale 1983: 12). Neale accounts for the more violent and sado-masochistic elements of this display in psychoanalytical terms, and this will be considered shortly. (Pumphrey's comments on male violence and the crisis of modernity considered in Chapter 1 offer an alternative account.) Neale's suggestion that the fight is generalized and becomes a ritual has immediate application to the way fighting is portrayed in theatre dance.

There are choreographed fights in twentieth-century Russian ballets – e.g. various versions of *Romeo and Juliet*, and *The Stone Flower* – and in American modern dance – e.g. Jacob's struggle with Esau and with the angel in Robert Cohan's *Hunter of Angels* (1967), and in José Limón's pieces including *The Moor's Pavane* (1949) (see Chapter 5). Indeed the exchange of looks between male protagonists in Limón's work seems to lead inevitably to fights between them. Men as fighters have also been standard fare in American modern dance since Ted Shawn's early pieces (see Chapter 5) and the more recent *Troy Game* (1974) by Robert North. There are many more instances of male dancers as warriors. For the seventeenth-century courtier fencing and dancing had much in common with one another. Examples from the nineteenth century include the Fighting Dancers or Tramagnini who have already been mentioned (in Chapter 1). In twentieth-century ballet there are warrior dances in Fokine's *Polovtsian Dances* (1909), and *Spartacus* (Jacobson 1956; and Grigorovich 1968). What is important to the current discussion is the way that the theme of male violence can be used as a guise for presenting a spectacle of the male dancer's body. Display of fighting movement clearly uses movement qualities which are appropriately masculine and thus unproblematic for the male dancer. Formalized fighting movements evoke a ritualized or ceremonial re-enactment of fighting against a generalized and non-specific ill. Where the resulting abstracted image is not fixed in any historical period, its modernity can suggest the future, or some ideal, mythical beings out of time. This suggests beings who are more intense, more energetic and more physically aware than ordinary people – such as the audience. This rarefied abundance makes them appear more masculine than ordinary men. Furthermore, the ponderous seriousness with which the potentially erotic power of the male dancers' bodies are displayed may not always stop them from becoming an object for pleasurable (sexual) consumption, especially for female spectators, but it at least maintains the appearance that these are tough, heterosexual men. Because, as Steve Neale has suggested, 'the male body cannot be marked explicitly as the erotic object of another male look'. It is the ritualized nature of the fight as dance that represses the erotic component.

By 1983 when Neale wrote this, changes were taking place in the ways images of masculinity were being presented in cultural forms; since the mid-1970s there has been more and more exposure and eroticization of the male body. This can be related to new consumerist attitudes towards the body. Michel Foucault has proposed that there are ways in which industrial production since the eighteenth century has depended on manual labour and thus necessitated the imposition of strict disciplines and controls on the working body. With the decline of the need for these sorts of disciplines (with the decline by the 1970s of traditional heavy and manufacturing industries in the West) the body, Foucault's argument continues, became available as a site for new sorts of consumerist ex-ploitation ('Body/power' in Foucault 1980). This view offers interesting insights into the dance and exercise booms in Europe and North America in the late 1970s and 1980s.

The film *Saturday Night Fever* (1978) cashed in on the new popularity of dance and male concern for bodily appearance. Early in the film, the importance for Travolta of clothes is established; in one section the camera dwells on John Travolta's body as he dresses in front of a mirror. Spectators are made to look at a male body in a way in which they would previously only have investigated a female star. Changes in the way the male body is displayed in the mass media have accompanied changes in patterns of male consumerism. A much-commented-on example of this was an advertising campaign in Britain and the United States during 1986 for Levi 501 jeans which unashamedly eroticized the male body. In one television commercial, a man (James Mardle) gets into a bath wearing only his jeans; in another, a man in a launderette (Nick Kamen) strips off down to his shorts, putting all his clothes into a washing machine. As Frank Mort points out:

> Though Kamen stripped to his boxer shorts and white socks and the 'bath' began with a naked torso, it was the display of the body *through the product* that was sexy. Belt, button-flies, jeaned thighs, bottoms sliding into baths was what made the ads erotic, less the flesh beneath. And so the sexual meanings in play are less to do with macho images of strength and virility (though these are certainly still present) than with the fetishised and narcissistic display – a visual erotica. These are bodies to be looked at (by oneself and other men?) through fashion codes and the culture of style.
>
> (Mort 1988: 201, emphasis in original)

Suzanne Moore has argued that 'the new breed of images of masculinity would not have been possible without two decades of gay and feminist politics which advocated the idea that sexuality is socially constructed rather than god-given and immutable' (1988: 45) and that these new images allow women to look pleasurably at images of men: 'the codification of men via male gay discourse enables a female erotic gaze' (*ibid.*: 53).

Both Mort and Martin Pumphrey relate these changes in visual conventions to changes in consumer patterns. During the nineteenth and through most of the twentieth centuries, women were 'urged to conceive of themselves as active consumers' (Pumphrey 1989: 92). Barbara Ehrenreich (1983) discusses ways in which, since 1945, men have gradually become more active consumers. The generation of men coming of age in the late 1970s and 1980s proved increasingly responsive to commercial pressures to become active consumers of fashion, thus throwing off older attitudes that men should be aggressively indifferent about what they wear and silently avoid any bodily display (Pumphrey 1989: 96). Neale says that the male body is feminized when it is the object of an erotic look. Pumphrey doesn't see this as feminization but as a sign of shifts in social definitions of masculinity, qualifying this by the fact that these changes are 'unevenly and erratically spread across generational, class, economic, professional, ethnic and regional divisions' (1989: 93). Nevertheless Pumphrey suggests that changes in the codes that govern display of the male body are signs of acceptance that masculinity, like femininity is 'a thing of surfaces, not essentials' (1989: 97), and as such a threat to patriarchy's 'natural' right to dominance. But when one examines these images, the signifiers of male power in the male gaze and in the appearance of male strength and dominance are unchanged. Perhaps the only thing that has gone is the prudish Victorian attitude that women could not possibly be interested in the male body. The impact of these recent changes in attitude towards male display are taken up in Chapter 7 in relation to some recent choreography.

PSYCHOANALYTICAL THEORIES OF THE CONSTRUCTION OF GENDER

So far, an account of the structural analysis of narrative in film has been considered in relation to its applicability to the analysis of dance. It is, however, an important part of the approach developed by Mulvey, Neale and others that both film and social practice are constructed within psychic mechanisms that form the patriarchal subconscious. Mulvey's thesis, as we have seen, is that film is read from a male point of view, and that, while male protagonists are actively involved in the narrative, women slow up the narrative by presenting an erotic spectacle. She further proposes that mainstream narrative film is structured so as to satisfy male fetishistic desires as these are described in Freud's theories of the development of gender and sexuality through the Oedipal stage.

Mulvey uses psychoanalytic theory to distinguish between the look of identification and the look of objectification, basing her thesis on Freud's theories and their development by Lacan. She accounts for the look of identification by referring to 'the mirror stage' of the constitution of the ego: here the infant first recognizes her or his image in the mirror and thinks it is more complete, more perfect than her or his own body. This is supposed to structure future identification with a hero as ego-ideal – a process, as we have seen, that Freud ascribed to daydreaming. From this, Mulvey extrapolates a theory of narcissistic looking in film.

Mulvey connects the look of objectification with what Freud called scopophilia. According to Freud, scopophilia is one of the component instincts of sexuality 'which exist as drives quite independent of the erotogenic zones' (Mulvey 1975: 8). This is an eroticized look motivated by a psychic need to avoid reliving the moment when the male child first realizes that the mother does not have a penis. The fact of having seen that the mother lacks a penis, according to Freud, evokes in the male child a castration complex. For the adult male, eroticizing the act of looking at woman serves the function of turning her into a fetish or penis substitute. This makes up for her symbolic lack, and thus the adult male avoids the trauma that her lack would otherwise provoke. For Mulvey, scopophilia is linked to fetishism.

Rose English (1980) sees the ballerina as a male fetish without following up all the implications of Mulvey's idea of scopophilia. What she does take from Mulvey is the idea that women's bodies cannot be portrayed other than through modes of representation which produce them as objects for the male gaze, and as the projection of male desires. English draws our attention to the well-known painting of a scene in *La Sylphide* in which the sylphide appears beside James who is dozing in a chair. In this, English suggests, the way James's hands are resting on his crotch, in the fur of his sporran, signifies that this is in fact a masturbatory fantasy. This, she argues, is the hidden structure underlying the narratives of Romantic ballets. In these, English suggests, the ballerina is a 'giant dancing phallus, crowned with a tiara' (English 1980: 19) and the *pas de deux* signifies male masturbation. The ballerina's use of *pointe* work turns her into a phallic fetish: her leg is stiff, her feet end in firm pink points, and the muscles in the whole leg are expanded, hard and firm. The male partner holds and moves her lovingly as if she were a penis. Thus, English argues, the death of the ballerina in so many Romantic stories is 'the point when she at last goes limp, being the orgasm of the phallus that she represents in the fantasy of the hero' (*ibid.*: 19). English's thesis is therefore that the image and performance of the ballerina has been tailored to fit the pattern of male genital stimulation and sexual desire.[2]

English's account does not entirely follow Mulvey's theory of fetishistic looking. Whereas English is concerned with fantasy, Mulvey, following Freud, sees the motivation behind the male gaze as a drive; this raises the question whether it is innate or learnt. If a drive is taken to be innate, then Mulvey's theory is in danger of falling into ahistorical essentialism. A drive can be seen as an appetite (such as an appetite for food) which needs to be satisfied: but whereas an appetite may be instinctual, as Ethel Spector Person (1980) points out, it has been argued that the method of satisfying it is learned. The idea that sexual desire is purely natural and instinctual, and not culturally conditioned, would lead to the naturalization of sexuality as normal. Person has pointed to the result of appetitional and other theories of sexual motivation which propose a social and cultural analysis of sexual motivation, and suggests that 'the burden of proof must fall on proponents of instinctual theory' (Person 1980: 611). The implication of Mulvey's essay is that scopophilia is innate, and consequently her theory takes on a trans-historical character. Overall she betrays a tendency to subordinate social and cultural spheres to a rigid account of psychological processes.

Stephen Neale's work on images of men has already been considered. Where Neale's work differs most significantly from Mulvey's theories is in the way he attempts to make a psychoanalytical account of a female as well as a male gaze (which Mulvey (1981 and 1989) herself attempted). He suggests that men and women can both identify with a hero, and thus wish to be in a position of assuming control of the narrative. He also argues that images of both men and women can be the subject of a spectator's look which can alternate between narcissism and fetishistic looking. He supports this by referring to Lacan's account of the child's entry into language.

In Lacan's work, the child's realization of the significance of his possession of a penis or her lack of it is taken to be the moment when the child becomes bound within the symbolic order of patriarchy – the world of patriarchal law and language. In this approach the unconscious is understood to be structured like a language. Prior to this, the pre-Oedipal child exists in a state of polymorphous perversity which is outside and beyond language. Neale argues that:

> The acquisition of language is a process profoundly challenging to the narcissism of early childhood. It is productive of what has been called 'symbolic castration'. Language is a process (or set of processes) involving absence and lack, and these are what threaten any image of the self as totally enclosed, self-sufficient, omnipotent.
>
> (Neale 1986: 130)

By wishing to identify narcissistically with an omnipotent hero (of either sex) the spectator makes an identification which will cause her or himself to be aware of their own inadequacy in comparison with this omnipotent position. This will recall the memory of their infantile narcissistic state and the challenge to this caused by their entry into the Symbolic. The resulting anxiety about their own present inadequacy causes them to be subject to 'symbolic castration'. This can then be compensated for through fetishistic looking – a fetishistic attachment to an object imbued with sexual meaning. This disavows or makes up for the lack implicit in castration. Thus Neale proposes:

> the male body can signify castration and lack, can hence function as the object of voyeuristic looking, in so far as it is marked as such – an arm, a leg or an eye may be missing, the body may be disfigured in some way, or it may be specified as racially or culturally 'Other'. The male body can be fetishised inasmuch as it figures within a fetishistic image or inasmuch as it signifies masculinity, and, hence, possession of the phallus, the absence of lack.
>
> (ibid.: 130)

So what then is the difference, at this level of significance, between the male and female body? For Neale it is that the male body can be fetishised because it has a penis, while the female body is fetishised 'against the threat of castration it represents' (ibid.: 130). Like Mulvey's use of the concept of scopophilia, the problem here is that Neale's theory is seemingly trans-historical. It also depends (as does Mulvey's theory and the French feminist uses of Lacanian theory considered next) upon a problematic account of psychological development. Stern's research, which has already been mentioned in Chapter 1, challenges the idea that the formation of identity comes with the acquisition of language. This doesn't invalidate the premise that the way the body is looked at in cultural forms is determined by the social and psychological construction of individual identity. The problem is how to account for the psychological aspects of this construction, and what use such an account might be for analysing representations of gender.

MARGINALITY, LANGUAGE AND THE FEMALE BODY

Lacan's theories about the pre-Oedipal state have also been used by Julia Kristeva, Catherine Clément, Hélène Cixous, Luce Irigaray (and others working along similar lines in France and the United States)[3] to propose a view of femininity as that which is marginal to law, language and the patriarchal order. For these French feminists, language is male, and femininity therefore can not exist in language. It can be identified only through that which is subversive of, or resistant to, language – the Symbolic – and is a memory of the pre-social, pre-linguistic, bodily experience of polymorphous perversity – the pre-Symbolic.

Hélène Cixous thus proposes that there is an 'écriture féminine', a female/feminine sensibility within women's writing which acknowledges physical and bodily qualities that are denied in male writing (Moi 1985: 102–26). Kristeva proposes a semiotic chora which is similarly a residue of memories of somatic stages, and is hence a site of opposition to language, and the law of the Father. Thus psychoanalysis is invoked to set desire and sexuality against rational, intellectual discourse and, in the work of these French feminists, to define a feminine desire and sexual pleasure or 'jouissance' (Moi 1985: 120–1). This female sensibility is marginal, breaks free from the bounds of language and disrupts and exposes the patriarchal order. It is this marginal aesthetic sensibility which is to be identified within the work of feminist artists.

One problem with these French feminist theories is their emphasis on the female body as marginal to, but subversive of, patriarchy; this runs the danger of essentializing femininity and the body, whereas, as was argued in Chapter 2, our experience of the body is a social and psychological construction. Christine Battersby (1989: 136 and 165–6) has pointed out that the French word 'féminin' does not distinguish between female and feminine, and argues that a major flaw in Lacanian and French feminist thought is the resulting conflation of the biological and culturally acquired characteristics associated with womanhood. Whereas Kristeva has argued that Mallarmé or Artaud may write 'like a woman', that is not the same thing as writing 'as a woman'. The female/feminine is expressed in 'écriture féminine' by emphasizing the irrational and pre-linguistic, and thus refers to the state before the development of the ego. But this could be given a negative interpretation as a state of incoherence and madness. As Battersby points out,

> A male creator credited with an *oeuvre* that is *féminin* might retain his cultural significance while celebrating non-entity; but a female viewed as hysterical and ecstatic has to fight off a much more mundane kind of cultural nonentity.
>
> (*ibid.*: 145)

Some radical feminists and lesbian artists however might argue that they would expect to be dismissed in this way by mainstream audiences; the British choreographer Emilyn Claid has made this point and said that she finds the ideas about the female body developed by Cixous inspirational for her own practice.[4]

The other substantial problem is that, for any communication to be possible, the communicator and receiver must necessarily have developed beyond the pre-Symbolic into the Symbolic. To what extent can any *écriture féminine* or semiotic chora that is grounded in the pre-Symbolic therefore be possible? Thus, as Janet Wolff points out, the pre-Symbolic state remains untheorizable, although Wolff nevertheless agrees with the French feminist proposition of 'the crucial link between language and patriarchy, and of the linguistic constitution of the patriarchal regime' (1990: 74). The idea of the body as a marginal site of opposition to language is one that is potentially useful in understanding how gender representations work in theatre dance. While not resolving the epistemological problems concerning the untheorizable nature of somatic experiences, Ann Daly's observations (see Chapter 1) about the way the concept of the pre-verbal marginalizes movement and dance are useful here. Following Stern, she argues that the infant develops a sense of self through non-verbal bodily communication before she or he develops any awareness of language. This means that some of the sorts of bodily expression and experience, to which French feminists refer, can still be thought of as marginal without needing to be considered grounded in the somatic. These early stages of infantile development are also, following Chodorow (again from Chapter 1), ones in which awareness of the body and its boundaries differs for the male and female child. This view of infantile development departs radically from Freudian and Lacanian theories. Within the latter, the Mother can sometimes become a castrating 'monstrous female' – in Freud's essay on Leonardo (1963) and Kristeva's on Bellini ('Motherhood according to Bellini' in 1980), both artists suffered psychic harm at the hands of their mothers. Chodorow implies that we should look for the source of the problem in the structure of society as a whole rather than blaming individual mothers.

ABJECTION AND THE MALE BODY

Klaus Theweleit's account of the violence of male sexual fantasy is based on the idea that men fear and hate the repressed memory of the monstrous-feminine. In *Male Fantasies* (1987) he sets out to analyse the connections between fascism and the violent and misogynist fantasies of a particular group of German soldiers (members of the Freikorps) in the 1920s. He identifies in the fictional and autobiographical writings of the Freikorps a fear of women's sexuality. Women are associated with floods and inundation. Theweleit argues that the boundary-less floods of the blood of the communist women these soldiers kill is associated with the soldiers' original polymorphously perverse relation with their mothers. Sexual desire is traumatic for men as it recalls the pre-Oedipal state which was boundary-less, because, Theweleit argues, white western heterosexual masculinity is structured by oppressive (Oedipal) boundaries. He thus repudiates the orthodox Freudian model of infantile development, taking up instead the more libertarian 'anti-Oedipal' theory of Deleuze and Guattari (1983). Theweleit, in rejecting Freudian orthodoxy, cites several psychoanalysts (such as Melanie Klein and Margaret Mahler) concerned with object relations theory whose work has also influenced Chodorow (Theweleit 1987: 211, 214, 265–6). His account of the violence of male sexual fantasy is thus based on a similar view of infantile development to that of Chodorow. Both believe that men disavow the repressed memory of their infantile dependence on their mother. Men's fear of women, and of aspects of their identity which might be described as feminine, is derived from the conflictual and problematic nature of male embodiment within patriarchal culture.

Theweleit identifies, in the writings of the Freikorps soldiers, a parallel between radical left-wing political ideas which represent a dissolving and removal of capitalist political structures (which contain and maintain patriarchal society), and sexual pleasures that threaten to overwhelm and dissolve the boundaries of the male body. The soldier's protective psychological 'body armour' functions as a dam to stop the flow of pleasurable sensation from 'a (female) interior and a (male) exterior' (*ibid.*: 434).

> For the soldier-male dam, none of the streams we've mentioned can be allowed to flow. . . . not a single drop can be allowed to seep through the shell of the body. One little drop of pleasure – a minute flyspeck on the wall of a house, or a single escapee from a concentration camp – threatens to undermine the whole system [the system of dams]. Those drops are more than mere metaphors; they are harbingers of imminent defeat ('we're going under').
>
> (*ibid.*: 266)

Thus personal sexual fears and public political ones are linked by the same fear of boundary-lessness. Theweleit names these fears fascist, the politics of fascism and violent male heterosexual fantasy both being dependent upon the maintenance of tight physical boundaries. For Theweleit, radical therapies suggest the most suitable way of treating fascist soldiers.

Theweleit sees fascism not merely as something restricted to German people during the Nazi era but as a tendency in all men, even in up-tight, left-wing intellectuals like Bertold Brecht (*ibid.*: 55). The only male individuals whom Theweleit considers free from fascist tendencies are schizophrenics. His thesis thus builds on the work of radical psychotherapists like Willhelm Reich who have sought to identify the psychology of fascism (*ibid.*: 222–5). As might therefore be expected, he goes on to use theories developed by Reich and later radical therapists to criticize the embodiment of 'normal' male sexuality. As Alice Kaplan (1989) has suggested, Theweleit's writing evokes the idea of a 1970s-style therapy group with Theweleit as leader to which 'he has gathered together from outside time a few fascist terrorists, uptight left-wing intellectuals, and boundaryless psychotics' (1989: 161).

Both Kaplan (1989) and Turner and Carter (1986) locate the social context of Theweleit's work in the emergent political counter-culture of the 1970s and 1980s. Turner and Carter broadly characterize this as a series of loose alliances, or shared concerns and responses to ecological issues, passivism and non-violent protest, gay politics, feminism and new age mysticism, along with beliefs in the efficacy of consciousness-raising, therapy and meditation. Theweleit's emphasis on the body and therapy is one which can also be found in some of the fringes of experimental dance at that time. It is in this context that various forms of experimental movement research including contact improvisation developed. The question of whether new, radical and subversive ways of representing gender developed within these experimental fringes is considered in Chapters 6 and 7 below.

Theweleit's unpalatable idea that men hate women offers a possible explanation for the objectification of women in helpless and demeaning positions in some *pas de deux*. Whereas for Mulvey and Neale, the female body is fetishised to disavow lack, the implication of Theweleit's work is that the violence implicit in this kind of display is motivated by fear and hatred of feminine softness and boundary-lessness. These qualities are hated by men because they are unwilling to face up to their developmental insecurities about the body. This idea suggests an alternative way of explaining the studied dullness of male appearance since the mid-nineteenth century – what J. C. Flugel called 'the great male renunciation'. If an aspect of male identity is sometimes a need to resist and not give in to the threat posed by women, then men's indifference to and avoidance of bodily display is a way of denying women the possibility of pleasurably gazing at men.

Theweleit's view of masculinity is an abject one. The idea of abjection relates what is disturbing about extreme and violent representations of masculinity to developmental insecurities derived from separation from the primary caregiver. Julia Kristeva calls abject that which threatens the subject as a 'clean and proper' body. It is neither subject nor object, but dangerously indeterminate. Following Mary Douglas (1966), Kristeva proposes that these threats operate in the margins and boundaries of the socially and psychologically constructed body. The idea of abjection is useful for analysing representations of masculinity that are problematically extreme or that transgress the limits of social convention. What is disturbing about the violent fantasies which Theweleit analyses is that they are so extreme and are presented as so grotesque as to be beneath humanity. The same could be said of the men in *Sacre du printemps* (discussed in Chapter 4), or in DV8's *Dead Dreams of Monochrome Men* and Pina Bausch's *Bluebeard* (in Chapter 7). The spectre of male failure is also abject: for example as presented in *Blues Suite* (in Chapter 5).

Here, as in the other accounts considered in this chapter, the body is seen as a site of potential subversion. Because abjection is always ambiguous, referring to a transitional stage of development, what is being subverted through representations of abject masculinity is the idea that masculinity is an unproblematic, unquestioned norm.

MARGINALITY AND MOVEMENT RESEARCH

Whether one accepts the French feminist view or that derived from Chodorow, Daly, Theweleit and Stern, three things follow. First, the sorts of non-verbal, bodily communication that are the primary means of expression in theatre dance are marginal to verbal language. Second, verbal language is associated with patriarchy, and is the privileged mode of communication in our society. Third, non-verbal bodily experiences are associated with femininity and the mother's body, and are problematic for the male child (either because of the repressed memory of the Freudian 'monstrous female' or, following Chodorow, because of the conflictual and problematic nature of the male child's early separation from the mother).

As was argued in Chapter 2, the relationship between the (gendered) body and language determines how representations function in theatre dance. It is for this reason that it is worth exploring the common ground between the French feminist view of knowledge about the body, the phenomenological theory about the reception of dance proposed by Sheets (see Chapter 2), and the theories underlying the work of dancer teachers Mary Fulkerson, Steve Paxton and others involved in new dance research (see Chapter 6).

For the French feminists, considered above, the experiences of embodiment are resistant to and indefinable in language, and subversive of dominant forms of social knowledge. For Sheets it will be recalled, the import of dance is the dance itself, and attempts to describe or label it can amount only to unhelpful approximations which reduce the specificity of the actual experience of watching or performing the choreography. Fulkerson (1982) has written that the knowledge of the body that comes from lying down and being still is different from the way the body is conventionally conceptualized and discussed in the modern western world. Fulkerson sees bodily experience as being beyond verbal description, and even subversive of it. She suggests that 'thoughts that arise genuinely from stillness are not explainable in words' (1982: 9) although they can be remembered by verbal 'images' that describe particular starting points for movement work. She points out also that anatomy is 'traditionally taught by examining structures such as bones, muscles, ligaments, nerves'. Naming body parts restricts bodily awareness to those parts, and fragments the body as a whole, whereas 'When the body functions, however, these separations do not exist and it is more productive to allow feeling and sensation to attend an image that crosses these categories and directs attention to involve the whole body' (1982: 9). Where theatre dance is concerned, Fulkerson distinguishes between work that is 'trying to be like' something else and work which is 'just trying to be'. Although work that is 'trying to be like' can be pleasing through being familiar, it doesn't interest Fulkerson: 'It is the work that tries "to be" which puzzles, angers, moves, challenges me and keeps my attention' (1982: 25) and 'It is difficult to accept a thought that is unrecognizable because one does not know when one has such a thought' (*ibid.*). Hence Fulkerson is advocating a radical approach that tries to break through the limitations of verbal language into the area of non-verbal bodily expression. In her teaching she is concerned with types of movement research that see bodily expression as beyond verbal description and subversive of it. For her, experimental dance is an area in which dancers uncover ideas which are not restricted by words, nor by a logocentric tendency in our society which makes us unaware of our bodily potential. As Cynthia Novack (1990: 63) has pointed out, Fulkerson's ideas were an important early input in the development of contact improvisation, and there are similarities between Fulkerson's ideas on movement research and training and those of Steve Paxton (considered in Chapter 6). What is therefore relevant to analysis of representations in dance is the view all the above share of the potential of the body as a marginal site of opposition to language.

CONCLUSIONS

Many of the theories examined in this chapter have drawn on a variety of psychoanalytic accounts of the formation of identity. These argue that the dominance of language and its connections with a dominant patriarchal world-view leads to the marginalization of cultural expressions from points of view which are oppositional to heterosexual male norms. Because the body is marginal to verbal discourse, its expressiveness is one such potential site of opposition. The problematic status of the male body, discussed in Chapter 1, therefore gives the presentation of the male body in dance the potential for undermining and threatening the maintenance of male power.

Some aspects of psychoanalytic theory, such as Mulvey's concept of scopophilia and fetishism and Lacan's concept of the Symbolic and the pre-Symbolic are not used to analyse dance in the rest of this book, although references are made to Chodorow and Theweleit's work. By separating the structural analysis of looking, developed in these theories, from their psychoanalytic aspects, what is proposed is a view of spectatorship in dance based on the gendered nature of the gaze, on identificatory looking and the pleasure of surveying the spectacle. It has been argued that conventions defend and protect men's dominant position in patriarchal society by enforcing particular normative images of masculinity in cultural forms. Given that masculinity is not, and has never been, a stable entity, the particular areas in which these defences operate are sites of instability for masculine identity.

Conventions generally dictate that no spectator should be shown the male body as if he were the object of a pleasurable gaze. This is because the spectator is presumed to be male and his dominant male gaze a heterosexual one. For a man to look in an erotic way at a man's body is to look in a homosexual way, and homosexuality is a threat to the continuity of homosocial relations, the latter being an essential element in the ways in which men work closely together in the interests of men (this being the account of homophobia given in Chapter 1). Where theatre dance is concerned, conventions have developed about the ways in which male dancers look actively and refuse to acknowledge or be controlled by the challenge of the audience's gaze. Serious male dance in the theatre has been developed in the twentieth century largely by heterosexual women and homosexual men. The ways in which they have been able to present the male body have been limited and policed by visual and narrative conventions which enforce the male gaze. The following chapters look at some of the problems that have faced female and homosexual male choreographers in expressing their marginal points of view. Since the late 1970s, the conventions surrounding the male gaze seem to have shifted somewhat, so that it has become acceptable for the male body to be seen to be the object of a female erotic gaze as long as this acknowledges the power of the male body. But the ways in which masculine power itself is represented have remained largely unchanged – a man's appearance still, as John Berger puts it, 'suggests what he is capable of doing to you or for you' (1972: 46).

In theatre dance, the acceptable male dancer is, following this line of argument, one who, when looked at by the audience, proves that he measures up to supposedly unproblematic male ideals: he looks actively at his female partner or upwards in an uplifting way; he appears powerful, uses large, expansive movements; he controls and displays women dancers in duets. Some or all of these conservative qualities are identified, in later chapters, in the work of Graham, Limón, Ailey, Cunningham and in the legendary bravura aspects of Nijinsky's performances. It is argued, however, that choreographers may in some instances be able to take advantage of their marginal position to produce works which challenge dominant norms of gendered behaviour. The qualities that make a male dancer appear acceptable can sometimes be used in a denaturalizing and destabilizing way; for example in Nijinsky and Nijinska's choreography, and in the work of Pina Bausch and Lloyd Newson and of other choreographers considered in Chapter 7. Other choreographers, discussed in the last two chapters of the book, have intentionally refused to use these qualities at all in creating material for the male dancer. Instead, material has been performed which rejects the expansive spatial and dynamic qualities associated with bravura male dancing. Choreographers have also undermined the conventions of partnering by disrupting expectations of who lifts whom in male–female duets, or, in male–male duets, by challenging or making visible the homophobic fears that underlie male bonding.

This oppositional theatre dance has emphasized, in a radical way, the materiality of the body so as to contradict metaphysical notions that dance mediates transcendent and idealist meanings (the formalist view of dance discussed in Chapter 2). An assertion of the physicality of the masculine body that challenges the normative conventions, described above, has the potential to present otherwise invisible aspects of male experiences of embodiment. These can sometimes be made visible in performances of work influenced by contact improvisation and other forms of new dance research. The presentation of these sorts of male experiences can draw attention to repressed aspects of the construction of masculine identity which, as Chodorow and Theweleit propose, are conflictual and contradictory for modern western men.

To dismantle the concept of the dominant male point of view, and to consider how representations of masculinity in theatre dance appear to spectators who look from other points of view, is to read dance against the grain of the generally accepted account of dance history. It is this revisionist view of dance history that underpins the analyses offered in the rest of this book.

4

NIJINSKY: MODERNISM AND HETERODOX REPRESENTATIONS OF MASCULINITY

Vaslav Nijinsky (1889–1950) is a key figure in the reintroduction of the male ballet to the stages of European theatres at the beginning of the twentieth century, and for initiating and developing representations of masculinity that have dominated ballet and even to some extent modern dance throughout the century. From reminiscences of the first perform-ance of Diaghilev's Ballets Russes in Paris in 1909, it is clear that Nijinsky became a star overnight, and he went on to become probably the most famous dancer of the twentieth century. With this has come the inevitable processes of mythologization, making it difficult to establish precisely what his contribution was to the development of representations of masculinity in dance.

What the Ballets Russes as a phenomenon contributed to this develop-ment is easier to map out. The tradition of male partnering in the *pas de deux* was reintroduced to the West: the first programme in Paris in 1909 included the Blue Bird *pas de deux* from *Sleeping Beauty*, showing Petipa's development of the supported adagio (i.e. a duet with lifts);[1] in 1910 Diaghilev included *Giselle* (in the Moscow version) in his pro-gramme of ballets. European ballet audiences realized that the *pas de deux* had not looked right without a good male partner, and Nijinsky was certainly that (though some might have argued that Mikhail Mordkin (1880–1944) also with the Ballets Russes that season was better). In addition, the *Polovtsian Dances* in the opera *Prince Igor* similarly showed western audiences what they had been missing since the male *corps de ballet*s in western European theatres had been disbanded in the mid-nineteenth century.

But all this is probably not what comes to mind when the pre-1914 Ballets Russes is mentioned. This is the period of exotic ballets, with the 'new' choreography by Fokine (1880–1942) and costumes and sets by Bakst (1866–1924) and Benois (1870–1960), that showcased Nijinsky's talents. There was no precedent in European theatre dance history for a piece like Fokine's *Le Spectre de la rose* in which the male role (Nijinsky's) is clearly

74

the central one and the female dancer (initially Karsavina) plays a supporting role. Lynn Garafola has called these new male roles 'heterodox' (Garafola 1985–6: 39), meaning that they transgressed rigid categories of masculine behaviour. Clearly Diaghilev (1872–1929) brought about the creation of these ballets to show off his lover's talents. While Diaghilev and Nijinsky's sexual orientations were a factor in developing male dance, Nijinsky's dancing didn't appeal just to homosexual spectators. He was a star.

Nijinsky the star was not 'the real' Nijinsky (whatever that might mean) but a construction that helped towards the success of the Ballets Russes project as a whole. Diaghilev, as Garafola (1989) points out in her study of the Ballets Russes, was a brilliant publicist. What the public took to be 'Nijinsky' should therefore be thought of as a mask or persona, a continuum between his on-stage roles and his interpretation of them, the style of the pieces he himself choreographed and the image of him generated for publicity purposes. Fokine, who choreographed most of Nijinsky's new roles, appears to have left artists a very free hand in interpreting and fleshing out the bare skeleton of the choreography that he had indicated to them.[2] While Fokine enjoyed a certain autonomy, he would have been working to a scenario and within the constraints of commissioned or arranged music. Diaghilev and his associates would already have indicated very specific ideas about the piece before Fokine actually got to the rehearsal room, and they would have taken an active interest in the ballet's progress. The visual artists themselves contributed to the way Nijinsky's roles mediated his gender. There is the jewelled male brassière designed by Bakst which Nijinsky wore in *Schéhérazade* (1910), or the Bakst costumes in *Narcisse* and *Le Dieu bleu*, which, as Garafola suggests, with their 'abbreviated skirt, sharply demarcated waist, exposed collarbones and shoulders teased conventions of masculinity' (Garafola 1989: 39).

Nijinsky clearly played a key part both in reintroducing traditional roles and in creating new ones in Fokine's choreography. In addition to this, there is his own choreography and its contribution towards the development of modernism and neoclassicism in ballet. Through the choreographic innovations which he introduced and his sister Bronislava Nijinska (1891–1972) developed, ways of representing gender were developed which were much more radical and critical than those of Fokine. This chapter therefore looks first at Fokine's ballets, and then at the modernist choreography developed by Nijinsky and continued by Nijinska. It considers the extent to which these new ways of representing masculinity constituted a challenge to the ballet tradition and to contemporary, conservative views of masculinity, and to what extent the new representations could be accommodated within them.

HETERODOXY AND HOMOSEXUALITY

The reintroduction of the male dancer to the European theatre stage in 1909 in new and sometimes heterodox images appears paradoxical. The period 1890–1920 was a time when there was much discussion and widespread insecurity about the nature of male identity, giving rise to reactionary anti-feminist and anti-homosexual ideas and a related re-assertion of traditional male values. It was also a time when the feminist and homosexual movements were emerging, thus making it possible to create these new and heterodox male images. It appears paradoxical therefore that male dancing, predominantly developed and promoted by homosexual men, should at this moment have made a widely acclaimed comeback among both elite and popular audiences.[3] The explanation for this lies in two areas.

First, the audiences that saw the Ballets Russes in those years were very different from those which in the middle years of the nineteenth century had rejected the male dancer. The latter were almost exclusively male. In nineteenth-century Paris, these were the young men about town, members of the Paris Jockey Club, for whom an *entrée* to the loges and meeting spaces at the Opera House was a means of meeting available females (Guest 1966: 28; Garafola 1985–6: 36; see also Nochlin 1991: 75–94). Diaghilev's audiences up until 1914, as Lynn Garafola (1989) points out, were the elite of society, artists and those who, by supporting his enterprise, gained entry to that elite. Chief among his supporters were women: Misia Edwards (later Sert), the Marchioness of Ripon, Lady Ottoline Morrell, Lady Juliet Duff, Margot Asquith and Lady Cunard, and later Coco Chanel. The very high quality of the Ballets Russes productions and the technical accomplishments of individual dancers, together with Diaghilev's legendary skills as publicist, lent respectability to the hetero-dox new representations of masculinity. In addition to this the increasingly significant female constituency in the audience clearly enjoyed watching male dancers and Nijinsky in particular.[4] Suzanne Moore has argued in relation to the female gaze that 'the codification of men via gay discourse enables a female erotic gaze' (1988: 53), and Nijinsky's dancing would seem a clear example of this. The many prominent homosexuals in the audience, for example Cocteau, Compte Robert de Montesquiou, Proust, Lytton Strachey, Keynes and Cecil Beaton, would also have been appreci-ative of Nijinsky's performance.

The second factor which permitted the creation by the Ballets Russes of heterodox representations of masculinity was the Russianness of those involved. In Britain, the prevalent concerns about the decline in masculine norms were concerns about *English* or *western* men. Nijinsky and the male dancers in the Ballets Russes were neither. One English magazine com-mented thus on the popularity in London society of the Ballets Russes:

> We want to know the truth about these semi-Asiatic and semi-European people . . . Of this [Victorian] disease of super-civilization these Russians are emphatically free . . . they are pagan with the pure untroubled paganism of the healthy child.[5]

The Victorian disease was degeneracy and decadence, from which the Russians, as only half-European and from a less industrially developed country, were imagined to be free. There was at the time a widespread debate about fears that this 'super-civilization' was causing modern European men to lose touch with their 'essential', 'natural' masculinity (Kimmel 1987). One participant in this was Lord Baden-Powell. In his book *Rovering to Success: A Guide for Young Manhood* (1922), he states, 'God made men to be men. On the other hand civilization, with its town life, buses, hot-and-cold water laid on, everything done for you, tends to make men soft and feckless beings. That is what we want to get out of' (Baden-Powell 1922: 24). He goes on to praise English public schools for forming character and 'licking' upper- and upper-middle-class boys into shape, and compares this with the manhood initiation rites of Zulus, Swazis and Matabeles.

> Unfortunately, for the ordinary boy in civilized countries there is nothing of this kind. We badly need some such training for our lads if we are to keep up manliness in our race, instead of lapsing into a nation of soft, sloppy, cigarette suckers.
>
> (*ibid*.: 25)

It was these 'ordinary' boys lower down the social scale who were attracted to the boy scout movement. Baden-Powell goes on to connect traditional male values with notions of nation and race, proposing that, by preparing for success '"you'll be a MAN, my son" and you will thus be making one more man for the nation' (his emphasis, and the reference is to Kipling's poem 'If'). The semi-Asiatic and semi-European Russians were thus closer to the Zulus and Matabeles than the average English man, and thus male Russian dancers were exempted from some of the restrictions of Victorian gender norms.

This offers a way of accounting for English reactions towards the Ballets Russes, but it was on the strength of their reception in Paris rather than London that their reputation was founded. Under the Code Napoleon, homosexuality was not illegal in France from 1792 until 1942. Many literary figures in France during the nineteenth and early twentieth centuries were homosexual and the arts and artists generally enjoy a greater prestige in France than in Britain. Attitudes towards sexual mores were more relaxed in France than in England at the time, and there was a little more tolerance of homosexuality – it was for example to France that Oscar Wilde went for refuge after his release from Reading Gaol. There were nevertheless concerns expressed at this time by the younger generation of middle-class Parisian youth about degeneracy and declining standards of masculine behaviour. For example, in 1911, under the joint pseudonymn Agathon, Henri Massis and Alfred de Tarde wrote two influential newspaper surveys or 'enquêtes', 'L'Esprit de la nouvelle Sorbonne' [Spirit of the new Sorbonne] and 'Les Jeunes Gens d'aujourd'hui' [The young people today]. Their conclusions about the anti-intellectual, athletically minded cast of young people are not dissimilar to the concerns about degeneracy being expressed around this time in Britain and, as we shall see, the United States (see Wohl 1979). Overall, then, the exotic, Russian and 'oriental' settings of so many of the Ballets Russes productions accentuated the fact that the dancers were not entirely European, but in touch with the 'primitive' and 'oriental'.

One great, but largely unmentioned, source of fear about masculinity during this period was homosexuality. Jeffrey Weeks has argued that the strong homosocial relationships between men during the nineteenth century were deeply ambivalent and became increasingly dangerous for the respectable as awareness of homosexuality grew (see Weeks 1977 and Richards 1987). The Oscar Wilde trials had brought about a new and widespread public awareness of homosexuality, and the period 1890–1920 was one in which extensive legislative and medical attempts were made to define and control homosexuality (Weeks 1986). This brought about a new awareness among homosexual men of a sense of identity, and of the existence and vulnerability of the homosexual community or communities (Weeks 1977). There is no particular association of homosexuality with ballet prior to the time of the Ballets Russes. It is only with Diaghilev that ballet became an area in which homosexual men became involved as artists and as audiences, and that a homosexual approach developed to the appreciation and interpretation of ballet. Diaghilev's artistic affiliations (prior to his adoption of a more avant-garde approach on the eve of the First World War) were with the *fin de siècle* aesthetic and decadent movements in the arts, and with an ideology of art for art's sake. He seems to have gone out of his way to meet Oscar Wilde and Beardsley (Buckle 1975: 65) and was clearly aware of homosexual contributions to these movements. No one writing about the development of homosexual identity in the early years of the twentieth century has yet considered the role played by ballet, but the promotion of the male ballet dancer by Diaghilev and the development of new heterodox images by Nijinsky must have had some impact on this development.

Nijinsky's homosexuality is sometimes played down or discounted. His sister Bronislava Nijinska, in her *Early Memoirs* (1981), mentions a few of Nijinsky's infatuations with young girls in St Petersburg while he was a student. In Nijinsky's diaries as published by Romola, his wife, there are accounts of his tailing female prostitutes in Paris, and of his initial reluctance to give himself sexually to Diaghilev. There has been a general reluctance among those writing about ballet and modern dance to discuss male dance and male homosexuality. Some writers discount the significance of Nijinsky's sexuality in considering his work. This raises the question what exactly constitutes being homosexual. The widespread idea that homosexual men are men who have sex only with men (and are therefore entirely different from straight men) is neither true nor useful. The American researcher Alfred Kinsey suggested in the late 1940s that there was a range between entirely heterosexual and entirely homosexual sexual behaviour. More recently Jeffrey Weeks has suggested that homosexual identity is something that is assumed by the individual, and that there are men who have sex with other men who don't think of themselves as homosexual, while other men who aren't active at all sexually identify themselves as homosexual (Weeks 1985: 196). During the period 1909–13 Nijinsky was undeniably involved in a homosexual relationship with Diaghilev, and it therefore seems reasonable to take this into consideration where it is relevant and useful in looking at his work.

The prevalence of especially strong homophobia following the Wilde trials would have made it extremely unlikely that a heterosexual impresario in western Europe would have even considered looking at a male dancer let alone taking the initiative to present one in the way Diaghilev did. But consider the point of view of individuals who were aware that their sexual preferences made them different in relation to heterosexual norms. Their lack of allegiance to such norms would have given them an outside view of masculine identity. It is from such a point of view that the possibility of criticizing or even rejecting the legacy of nineteenth-century gender representations and ideologies becomes possible. The idea of enjoying the presentation of the male dancing body was conceivable at that time only by homosexual men, and it is homosexual men (together with heterosexual women) who would have appreciated the spectacle of male sexuality.

One shouldn't necessarily assume that, because some of these ballets gave expression to a homosexual point of view, they necessarily broke away altogether from nineteenth-century norms. There are three ways in which some of Nijinsky's roles, despite their heterodoxy, could nevertheless have been interpreted from a conservative point of view: in terms of male prowess, male 'genius' and their archaic, exotic or 'oriental' distance. It is these which are now considered. Following this it is argued that, in the modernist ballets of Nijinsky and Nijinska, new types of representations were developed which, in contrast, were critical of, and unassimilable within, conservative norms.

MALE PROWESS IN NIJINSKY'S ROLES

A much-reproduced drawing by Jean Cocteau shows Nijinsky in the wings after *Le Spectre de la rose*. Like a boxer between bouts, he lies back exhausted on a chair holding a glass of water while Vassili, Diaghilev's valet, fans

Figure 4 Cocteau's drawing of Nijinsky, exhausted in the wings after dancing
Le Spectre de la rose.
(Jean Cocteau, *Dessins*. Paris: Stock, 1924)

him with a towel. In the background, looking concerned, are Diaghilev, Bakst and Misia Edwards (later Sert) and her husband. Part of the mythology about Nijinsky concerns his incredible leap out through the window at the end of this piece, and, in general, the extraordinary agility and elevation of his jumps. It would appear that Cocteau's drawing is not a total invention as Marie Rambert describes the scene in her auto-biography.[6] Fokine, however, talked down Nijinsky's leap (Fokine 1961: 180–1). Anton Dolin claims that he had danced most of Nijinsky's roles either with the Ballets Russes or subsequently and with many dancers from the original casts. In his opinion Nijinsky's roles were not that demanding technically. This is perhaps to miss a crucial point about the attitude towards technical feats shared by Nijinsky, Pavlova, Fokine and other dancers of their generation from the Imperial Theatres. They disliked the *tours de forces* performed by the older generation of ballerinas and male dancers, feeling that these looked mechanical and were unsympathetic to the creation of an artistic feeling in performance. (But the younger dancers had all been trained to perform and all did perform the virtuoso roles in the Petipa repertoire.) Nijinsky's sister Bronislava, in her *Early Memoirs*, gives us several very detailed accounts of her brother's performances and how he prepared for them. She tells how his daily practice was geared towards developing his strength and that he would practise much more difficult feats than were needed for his roles. She says also that he would practise to minimize the preparations for jumps, and that he worked at finding how to land softly afterwards, so that when he was on stage his performance would appear effortless and flowing. The description that Rebecca West gives us of the effect is echoed in many other accounts:

> The climax of his art was his jump. He leaped high into the air, and there stayed for what seemed several seconds. Face and body suggested that he was to mount still further, do the Indian rope trick with himself as rope, hurl himself up into space through an invisible ceiling and disappear. But then he came down – and here was the second miracle – more slowly than he had gone up, landing as softly as a deer clearing a hedge of snow.
>
> (quoted in Buckle 1975: 390)

It would seem that Nijinsky did possess extraordinary strength and agility but that this was accompanied by hard work at creating an illusion of effortlessness. As Nijinska remarked: 'Do you remember how many transitions, how many nuances there were during the course of his leap? These transitions and nuances created the illusion that he never touched the ground' (Nijinska 1986: 86). What all this amounts to is that, whatever Dolin may have believed, Nijinsky did produce a spectacle of famed and mythologized agility on stage. While it was Diaghilev who commissioned these roles, it was Fokine who came up with the steps. As Garafola (1989) points out, Fokine is a transitional figure between the nineteenth-century ballet tradition and twentieth-century modernism. Judging by survivals like *Le Spectre de la rose* (1911), or from descriptions of ballets like *Narcisse* (1911), as far as the steps of Nijinsky's solos are concerned, these were fairly traditional. Compared with Nijinsky's subsequent innovations, Fokine's choreography is conventional, in phrasing and use of space: aided by Fokine and Nijinsky's musicality, jumps and effects coincide with appropriate musical climaxes, while spatially there are circles that boldly encompass the stage, and strong diagonals to give Nijinsky the appearance of mastering the space. These are devices for displaying traditional male virtuosity. Steve Neale, in Chapter 3, proposed that whereas women are a mystery to be investigated and exposed, men are tested. The evidence suggests that, in these virtuosic roles, Nijinsky passed the test. Fokine was keen to dance Nijinsky's roles himself in 1914 after the latter's break with Diaghilev and the company. Fokine's male solos clearly conformed to conventional expectations of male strength and prowess, and supported the notion that the Russian male dancers were less tainted by civilization and more in touch with 'natural' masculinity than their western contemporaries.

NIJINSKY AS GENIUS

Nijinsky was not famous just for his strength, agility and his exceptional skill in partnering a ballerina. He was also hailed for his extraordinary expressiveness and the uncanny way he 'got into' his roles. His performance as Petrouchka is the prime example of this.

The action of the ballet *Petrouchka* (1911) is set during a Lenten carnival fair in St Petersburg during the 1840s. The opening section is a big crowd scene full of incidental events leading up to the performance of three magic puppets – Petrouchka, the Doll and the Moor – all controlled by the menacing Magician. The second scene shows Petrouchka thrown by the Magician into his cell-like box, miming his hatred for the Magician, and getting over-excited when the latter brings his love, the Doll into the room. Frightened by Petrouchka's antics, she hastily retreats. The next scene shows the Moor, who hardly knows what to do with the Doll when she comes into his cell, but chases after Petrouchka when he comes in after her. The final scene shows the fairground, this time in full swing at night. Eventually the carousing of the crowd is interrupted by Petrouchka emerging from the Magician's booth chased by the Moor who in turn is followed by the Doll. Before a stunned crowd, the Moor kills Petrouchka. When a merchant calls a Guardian of the Peace, the Magician shows that Petrouchka is just an inanimate puppet and all disperse except for the Magician. As the music ends Petrouchka's ghost appears on top of the booth to frighten the Magician by frantically waving his arms.

Nijinsky's role contained both dynamic dancing and demanding mime. His sister records:

> When Petrouchka dances, his body remains the body of a doll; only the tragic eyes reflect his emotions, burning with passion or dimming with pain. . . . Petrouchka dances as if he is using only the heavy wooden parts of his body. Only the swinging, mechanical, soul-less motions jerk the sawdust-filled arms or legs upwards in extravagant movements to indicate transports of joy or despair.
>
> . . .Vaslav is astonishing in the unusual technique of his dance, and in the expressiveness of his body. In *Petrouchka*, Vaslav jumps as high as ever and executes as many *pirouettes* and *tours en l'air* as he usually does, even though his petrouchkian wooden feet do not have the flexibility of a dancer's feet.
>
> (Nijinska, 1981: 373–4)

It was for his dramatic expressiveness in roles like Petrouchka and the sensuality of his performance of roles like the Golden Slave in *Schéhérazade* (1910), as well as for his technical abilities, that Nijinsky was acclaimed as a genius. As Christine Battersby has argued (see Chapter 1), the idea of genius has sometimes been invoked to allow male artists to give expression to emotions that, over the last two centuries, have been characterized as feminine. In Nijinsky's case, the description is, in the hands of some writers, a back-handed compliment. Prince Peter Lieven for example suggested:

> I think the neatest and at the same time the truest estimate of Nijinsky's intellect was given me by Misia Sert, one of Diaghilev's best friends. She called him an 'idiot of genius'. This is no paradox. In our enthusiasm over the 'entity of genius' our admiration goes to the dancer's creative instincts and not to the conception of his brain, as for example, his role in *Petrouchka*.
>
> (Lieven 1980: 89)

Alexandre Benois is even more dismissive of Nijinsky's intelligence. For him Nijinsky was someone who came alive only for the stage. 'Having put on his costume, he gradually began to change into another being, the one he saw in the mirror. . . . The fact that Nijinsky's metamorphosis was predominantly subconscious is in my opinion, the very proof of his genius' (1941: 289). They are surely both putting Nijinsky down retrospectively. Both disapproved of the radicalism of his choreography, and are writing with benefit of hindsight, knowing of his subsequent mental illness. But the idea that Nijinsky was a genius in his dancing and in his on-stage creation of roles such as Petrouchka is a comparatively safe and unthreatening one. It can easily be recuperated within conservative definitions of masculinity.

NIJINSKY'S HETERODOX ROLES IN FOKINE'S BALLETS

But Nijinsky's roles were nevertheless transgressive. Most of them presented a spectacle of male sexuality. This raises the question of whom this spectacle was intended for, as, to recapitulate the argument earlier in the book, gender ideologies enforce that the dominant point of view is male, presuming that men are attracted to the spectacle of female sexuality but repelled by the male body. Heterosexual male norms are generally maintained through keeping male sexuality invisible. Any explicit expression of male sexuality was against the conventions of nineteenth-century middle-class gender ideologies. How far therefore did Nijinsky's roles in ballets like *Narcisse*, *Schéhérazade*, *Le Spectre de la rose* and in his own *L'Après-midi d'un faune* (1912) break with the nineteenth-century tradition, and to what extent were they still open to acceptable interpretation as essays on classical or 'oriental' themes?

Many contemporary descriptions of Nijinsky ascribe androgynous qualities to his dancing, stressing its male power and strength but female sensuousness. Richard Buckle quotes several descriptions of Nijinsky's performance of the Golden Slave in *Schéhérazade* (1910) including Fokine's comment that 'The lack of masculinity which was peculiar to this remarkable dancer . . . suited very well the role of the negro slave' (Fokine 1961: 155). (The ambiguity of Nijinsky's masculinity and sexuality in *Schéhérazade* would also be read in relation to a similar ambiguity about the role played by Ida Rubinstein as Zobeida, the Sultan's favourite (Wollen 1987: 5–33).) Fokine then likens Nijinsky to a 'half-feline animal' but also to a stallion 'overflowing with an abundant power, his feet impatiently pawing the floor' (1961: 155). Alexandre Benois, who wrote the libretto for this ballet, described Nijinsky's performance as 'half-cat, half-snake, fiendishly agile, feminine and yet wholly terrifying' (Buckle 1975: 160). It has already been pointed out that, within the technical range of male ballet dancing of his day, Nijinsky was considered to perform considerable technical feats. His roles often therefore allowed him to express sensuality and sensitivity (conventionally feminine) with extraordinary strength and dynamism (conventionally masculine).

None of the descriptions of Nijinsky suggest that he was actually effeminate. Moreover, according to Anton Dolin, Diaghilev disliked obvious homosexuality and hated any signs of effeminacy (Dolin 1985: 50). Garafola suggests that the androgynous quality of Nijinsky's dancing may have related to the image of the androgyne in the work of many homosexual visual artists of the aesthetic movement at the end of the nineteenth century (1989: 56). The androgyne presented the image of a graceful, innocent, often languid youth, unspoilt by the world. Emmanuel Cooper (1986) has suggested that many homosexual artists of the aesthetic movement saw in the androgynous male a positive image of the homosexual as a third sex. According to the 'scientific' explanation of homo-sexuality initially proposed by Karl Ulrichs, homosexual men were women born in men's bodies, and constituted a third sex. Those homo-sexuals who subscribed to the notion of a third sex saw this as a slightly effeminate 'in-between' man or woman.[7]

The role of Narcisse which Nijinsky created in Fokine's *Narcisse* (1911) can be interpreted as a straight piece of classical mythology, but is also open to interpretation as an image of the third sex. The figure of Narcissus is an image that has a history of use by homosexual artists that goes back to Caravaggio. Nijinska's description of *Narcisse* exemplifies all the qual-ities associated with the aesthetic androgyne – grace, innocence and unspoiltness:

> His body of the youth in love with his own image emanated health and the athletic prowess of the ancient Greek Games. It could have been dangerous to portray in a dance the sensual and erotic Narcisse, driven to ecstasy by his own reflection in the water. Vaslav had so interpreted this scene that all such implications disappeared, dis-solved in the beauty of his dance. Each pose on the ground, each movement in the air was a masterpiece.
>
> (Nijinska 1981: 366–7)

Alternatively the vigorous, classicism of Nijinsky's presentation of the role might be interpreted from another, different homosexual perspective that looked back to classical Greece as an example of a robust, manly culture in which male homosexuality was normal (see Dyer 1990: 22–5).

What made *Narcisse* acceptable to straight audiences, apart from its classical origins, was the fact that it is a moral fable that warns against the dangers of self-obsession.[8] For transgressing social norms, Narcissus is punished. On another level (following the argument in Chapter 3) he has to be punished also for being the erotic subject of the (male) spectator's gaze, as must the Golden Slave in *Schéhérazade*. In the Slave's case the discourse through which Nijinsky's highly ambiguous and exotic roles might nevertheless have appeared acceptable was that of orientalism. As Edward Said (1978) has pointed out, for the nineteenth-century European (and by implication for the Ballets Russes' audiences) the orient was associated with the freedom of licentious sex (see also Aldrich 1994). In the Romantic imagination, Mario Praz (1967) identifies a literary and artistic tradition which combined the imagery of exotic places, the cultiva-tion of sado-masochistic tastes, and a fascination with the macabre (see also Nochlin 1991: 41–3). *Schéhérazade*, with its orgy and subsequent execution, is clearly an example of this. All of this is within the discourse of orientalist art, with the qualification that Nijinsky, the Golden Slave in *Schéhérazade*, could, as a Russian dancer (though actually Polish by birth), claim to be part 'oriental'.

85

Those involved in the Ballets Russes, as Russians, were ambiguously both of the East and West. Peter Wollen points to the ambiguous nature of the identity of the Russian ballet: it was a fusion of French ballet traditions and indigenous Russian orientalist traditions – Pushkin, Rimsky-Korsakov. Drawing on dancers and visual artists from St Petersburg, it was part of European Russia in contrast to more 'eastern' Moscow. 'Yet by a strange reversal the trend was turned around and, in the form of the Ballets Russes, Paris (cultural capital of Europe, the "west") began to import Russia, the "east", in a deluge of exaggerated Orientalism' (Wollen 1987: 21).

The Ballets Russes never performed in Russia and both Diaghilev and Nijinsky were dismissed from the service of the Imperial Theatres.[9] Bakst, Benois and Roerich (who designed set and costumes for *Polovtsian Dances* and *Le Sacre du printemps* and worked with Stravinsky on the libretto for the latter) never worked for the Imperial Theatres after 1909, Fokine leaving in 1918. After 1911, Nijinsky was unable (or Diaghilev may have encouraged him to believe he was unable) to return to Russia because he had defaulted from his military service. Yet these artists claimed, as Benois put it, to be presenting Russian ballet to Europe, making new works that would embody 'all the beloved old with a fresh and stimulating manner of presentation' (Benois 1936: 194). One can therefore conclude that the project of the artists and intellectuals in Diaghilev's circle was to define through the ballet their identity as Russians, in ways that were impossible within and oppositional to the hegemonic Russian establishment.

For Diaghilev and Nijinsky as homosexual men, this marginal position also enabled a limited but contained expression of homosexual experience. Nijinsky's homosexuality was signified primarily through ambiguities within the stories, and through qualities of costume and decor. It was not signified by the virtuosic solos for which he became famous. In the case of the Golden Slave, Fokine's innovatory methods of combining mime and dance into expressive movement (Garafola 1989) was a vehicle for expressing a transgressively sensual and eroticized male image, but in a context within which transgression was seen to be punished. Punishment in the form of the violent ending of *Schéhérazade* might be appreciated as an erotic spectacle, but was made acceptable by being displaced from 'normal' Europeans on to 'oriental' 'Others'. Richard Dyer's comments on the Rudolph Valentino film *The Son of the Sheik* (1926) could equally be applied to *Schéhérazade*:

> The audience could take it two ways. Shocked by the sexual explicitness, it could dismiss the depicted events 'anthropologically' as foreign behaviour. Drawn to the characters, however, it could welcome the film as a sunlit dream of sexuality. In a period not yet saturated in Freudian ideas, such dreams were still possible.
>
> (Dyer 1992: 101)

The status quo of norms of traditional masculinity thus remained intact. It is only through the modernism of his own choreography that Nijinsky actually challenged and disrupted conservative gender ideologies.

THE RADICALISM OF EARLY MODERNISM

In every other context in which modernism occurs in this book, it is seen either as a means through which a universalizing distortion is applied to cultural representations or as a way of claiming that dance as art is not a representational practice. Most accounts of modernism, however, acknowledge that it possessed a more radical nature during the period up until the outbreak of the First World War, and that this was in some contexts maintained in the years immediately following.[10] What is argued here is that Nijinsky's ballets of 1913–14 and Nijinska's ballets of the early 1920s were able, through their modernism, to distance themselves from conservative gender ideologies and make representations of contemporary experiences of gender and sexuality.

One of the more contentious issues about modernism is, to what extent and in what contexts did modernist works of art have the power to attack and disrupt dominant ideologies? The question here is therefore whether Nijinsky and Nijinska's modernist point of view challenged the spectators of their pieces and created for them a detached and critical distance from which to perceive conservative gender norms, not as 'natural' and common-sense artefacts but as strange and threatening, and to challenge assumptions about 'natural' masculinity. The answer to this lies not just in analysing the evidence to be gleaned about gender representation in their surviving works from the period but in establishing the nature of their revolt.

A useful starting point for defining Nijinsky's and Stravinsky's modernism is another of Cocteau's drawings, showing Stravinsky playing *Le Sacre du printemps*. Growing out of the composer's shoulders, as he sits hunched over the piano, are closely packed rows of geometrically distorted figures. The word 'angular' has been used to describe both Stravinsky's music and the movements in Nijinsky's choreography. It conjures up both their modern feeling and their primitivism, as does Cocteau's drawing through its light-hearted evocation of the new vocabularies of cubist and futurist painting as well as its reference to 'primitive' African sculptures. Here is a seeming paradox that Nijinsky and Stravinsky, when producing their most 'advanced' works, were both involved in manipulating material gleaned from Russian academic research into archaic and defunct folkloric artefacts and traditions.

Simon Karlinsky has given us a useful account of the way Stravinsky used such material in his early ballets for Diaghilev. *The Firebird*, Karlinsky argues, is still a product of the nineteenth-century aesthetic. It mingles themes from Russian folklore with melodies from a reputable folk song collection, and couches them in 'the most advanced and elegant musical idiom of the time, French Impressionism' (Karlinsky 1983: 234). In *Petrouchka* Stravinsky turned his back on both 'the ethnographic approach and the western-style sugar-coating of folklore implicit in the Russian nineteenth century aesthetic' (*ibid.*), and went even further along this road in *Sacre* in which 'Lithuanian and Slavic materials were deformed . . . with a sovereign freedom that may be termed cubistic' (*ibid.*).

When one examines contemporary accounts of Nijinsky's work, a similar pattern emerges. First, these suggest that Nijinsky was reacting against the nineteenth-century tradition, and against the impressionistic vagueness of Fokine. When working secretly with her brother on *L'Après-midi d'un faune*, Nijinska wrote in her diary in 1911:

> Not long ago Fokine freed himself from the old classical school and the captivity of Petipa's choreography, and now Vaslav is freeing himself from the captivity of Fokine's choreography so that, again, we enter a new phase in our art.
>
> (1981: 328)

Stravinsky in 1912 also felt Fokine only went half way:

> At the beginnings of his career he appeared to be extraordinarily progressive. But the more I knew of his work, the more I saw that in essence he was not new at all. . . . New forms must be created, and the evil, the gifted, the greedy Fokine has not even dreamed of them.
>
> (quoted in Buckle 1975: 269–70)

In 1913 the composer told Henry Postel du Mas: 'Nijinsky is capable of giving life to the whole art of ballet. Not for a moment have we ceased to think along the same lines. Later you will see what he can do . . . he is capable of innovation and creation' (quoted in Craft 1976: 37).[11] Jacques Rivière also saw the general move towards modernism in dance as a reaction against the nineteenth century, characterized by the artificiality of Debussy. He detected in Fokine's work 'a certain artfulness, a certain vacillation, some sort of inner vagueness' (1983: 117) and felt that the innovation of Nijinsky's choreography for *Sacre* lay 'in doing away with dynamic artificiality, in the return to the body, in the effort to adhere more closely to its natural movements, in lending an ear only to its most immediate, most radical, most etymological expressions'.

Second, just as Stravinsky exercised a sovereign freedom in deforming folk idioms, Nijinsky took a high-handed approach towards his source material. Fokine had been highly critical of the inauthentic nature of the 'dances de caractère' (folk-derived dances that occur as divertissements) and period dances of the Maryinsky repertoire of the early 1900s.

When he himself choreographed such dances, he was proud of their imaginative realism. In his memoirs he speaks of learning folk dances on his travels in Russia and later in western Europe, and of his efforts to research the dances of classical Greece from sculptures and artefacts in museums and libraries (Fokine 1961). Nijinsky, however, wasn't interested in authenticity for its own sake. There is a story of how Bakst took him to the Louvre to look at Greek sculptural reliefs when Nijinsky was working on *Faune*; Nijinsky became far more interested in the galleries of Egyptian reliefs (Buckle 1975: 188). When Nijinsky was making *Sacre* he used the geometric patterns that Roerich had devised for the costumes as inspiration for choreographing circle dances (traditional Russian *khovorods*) and groups (Hodson 1986: 71). Nijinsky's interest in Gauguin's paintings (Buckle 1975: 107 and 331) is surely significant here. Linda Nochlin has argued that Gauguin:

> [rejected] what he conceived of as the lies of illusionism and the ideology of progress – in resorting to flatness, decorative simplification, and references to 'primitive' art – that is to say, by rejecting the signifiers of western rationalism, progress, and objectivity in toto.
>
> (1991: 51)

What was important for Nijinsky and Stravinsky was not the authenticity of the source material but the meanings it evoked in a dislocated modern context, and the expressive impact they could achieve through its use.

To some Russian audiences at the time, Stravinsky's progressive use of folk sources would have been interpreted as an expression of the Russian soul, achieved through rejection and purification of extraneous western European cultural influences. But Stravinsky was an immigrant, having more or less left Russia after 1909. The ballet scores that he wrote for Diaghilev were written in western Europe, are often best known by their French titles, and were premièred in Paris, the most advanced cultural metropolis of the day. Nijinsky also was in exile. Raymond Williams has suggested that the experience of exile, and of migrating to a foreign metropolis, was central to the creation of the formal innovations made by the early modernists. At the level of theme, Williams argues, the experience of being an immigrant:

> underlies in an obvious way, the elements of strangeness and distance, indeed of alienation, which so regularly form part of the repertory. But the decisive aesthetic effect is at a deeper level. Liberated or breaking from their national or provincial cultures, placed in quite new relations to those other native languages or visual traditions, encountering meanwhile a novel and dynamic common environment from which many of the older forms were obviously distant, the artists and writers and thinkers of this phase

found the only community available to them: a community of the medium; of their own practices.

(Williams 1989: 45)

It is this concentration on the medium itself that is of course the hallmark of modernist work, but it is also the key to understanding the revolution in representational practices.

What Nijinsky was doing was purging the ballet vocabulary of out-moded representational forms and conventions. For example, it took him numerous rehearsals to prepare *L'Après-midi d'un faune* (some accounts say 90, some 120), although the piece takes only eleven minutes to perform. As Nijinska commented:

the number of rehearsals was not excessive if one takes into account the ballet's completely new technique of presentation, and if one also remembers the marvellous level of execution finally achieved by the artists.

. . . Up to then the ballet artist had been free to project his own individuality as he felt. . . . Nijinsky was the first to demand that his whole choreographic material should be executed not only as he saw it but also according to his artistic interpretation.

(1981: 427)

The key to his new approach is that expression came through the movement material itself and not through mime or acting. Marie Rambert tells a story about Nijinsky rehearsing a new dancer in the role of one of the nymphs. He told her off for acting out a moment when the Faune frightens her. He wasn't interested in facial mannerisms. All she had to do was get the movements right (Rambert 1972: 62). It is the movement material on its own that is expressive. Jacques Rivière makes the same point while discussing *Sacre*:

In Nijinsky's dance . . . the face no longer plays a part of importance; it is merely an extension of the body – its flower. It is above all the body that speaks. . . .

By breaking up movement and bringing it back to the simple gesture, Nijinsky causes expression to return to the dance. All the angles, all the breaks in his choreography, are aimed only at pre-venting the escape of emotion.

(1983: 120)

These then are the new means at Nijinsky's and subsequently at Nijinska's disposal. What difference did they make where gender representations are concerned?

NIJINSKY'S BALLETS AND GENDER REPRESENTATION

Nijinsky's *Jeux* has not survived, and can only be glimpsed through descriptions, from the evidence of photographs and from drawings by Valentine Gross. It was the first 'modern' ballet to take a modern theme (tennis and a triangular relationship) and use a modern set and costume. Nijinsky was interested in Gauguin's paintings while working on *Jeux*.[12] Buckle points to ways in which the surviving drawings and photographs of *Jeux* resemble the monumental, sculptural qualities of Gauguin's compositions (1975: 339). But Nijinsky's attraction must also surely have been thematic. Gauguin rejected the sophisticated social mores of nineteenth-century Europe in preference for what he saw as the innocent freedom of social and sexual relations in Tahiti. In doing so Gauguin contributed to the European myth of the 'primitive'. To the western 'orientalist' imagination 'primitive' people were less inhibited about sexuality. *Jeux* was set in the present, and its theme was surely modern, uninhibited social and sexual relationships. His other ballets at the time, *Faune* and *Sacre*, deal with similar themes and are both set in the 'primitive' and mythic or mythological past.

Nijinsky's *L'Après-midi d'un faune* is set to Debussy's *Prelude à l'après-midi d'un faune* of 1894 that was itself inspired by Mallarmé's poem of 1876. The poem presents the reveries of a young faun. These include an encounter with two beautiful nymphs which may be recollected from a dream, a fantasy or a real event. Mallarmé was one of the poets whom Verlaine dubbed 'les poètes maudits', pure of heart but despised and rejected by both mother and society, and accursed (*maudits*) by God. Nijinsky's amoral interpretation of the poem is surely within this tradition.[13] The ballet's first performance provoked heated debate in the French press, and charges of indecency (Buckle 1975: 284–9). These largely concern the ballet's ending. The Faune, having surprised a group of nymphs, carries back to his rock a veil that one of them has dropped. As it is usually performed now, the Faune stretches out on top of the veil while making a couple of pelvic thrusts, jerks his head back in pleasure and then lies still. The first performance may have been more sexually explicit than this, or, as Richard Buckle suggests, Nijinsky may have been lying on his right arm, thus appearing to be masturbating (Buckle 1975: 284). According to *Figaro* the ending was changed after the first performance, thus eliminating the 'indecency'.

As a classical male role, the Faune superficially resembles the title role of Fokine's *Narcisse*. The difference, however, is in its attitude towards morality. Underlying the myth of Narcissus is a warning about unnatural behaviour – being unmoved by the love of Echo, being obsessed with personal appearance. The Faune however is 'pure', 'natural' and innocent. The movement style of the ballet is simple walking steps and jumps, dance stripped of every vestige of balletic style.[14] This exquisite surface thus, by being outside of balletic convention, created an ideological space for the ballet that was outside of social convention. The Faune, as Nijinsky shows him, is amoral, and the piece a deliberate provocation to society to condemn such spontaneous sexual behaviour, as if he were saying that only a depraved mind could see anything depraved in this. It was surely Nijinsky's homosexual point of view that allowed him to produce a representation of 'natural' masculinity that ran so strongly against convention. As Sokolova, who danced in the ballet with Nijinsky, recalls:

> Nijinsky as the Faune was thrilling. Although his movements were absolutely restrained, they were virile and powerful, and the manner in which he caressed and carried the nymph's veil was so animal that one expected to see him run up the side of the hill with it in his mouth.
>
> (1960: 41)

Nijinska's description of his other ballet for Diaghilev, *Sacre*, also stresses the animality of the male dancers.

> The men in *Sacre* are primitive. There is something almost bestial in their appearance. Their legs and feet are turned inwards, their fists clenched, their heads held down between hunched shoulders; their walk, on slightly bent knees, is heavy as they laboriously straggle up a winding trail, stamping in the rough, hilly terrain.
>
> (1981: 459)

In the reconstruction of *Sacre* that Millicent Hodson produced for the Joffrey Ballet the men look bestial. They characteristically make their entrances leaning forward as Nijinska describes above. Their postures are like those of the figures in the famous nineteenth-century Russian painting of *The Volga Boatmen* by I. Repin (1844–1930). The angle at which the men in *Sacre* lean, and the slightly pointed hats they wear, make them look as if they are about to jump forwards and upwards, and penetrate into one of the massed groups of women. In the first act men fight each other in the Games of the rival clans. The Ancients, in the second act, wear bear skins (Roerich: 'to show that the bear was man's ancestor' (MacDonald 1975: 89)) with the animals' heads fitting on their own like hoods. Grouped with other men round the circle in which the Chosen One is trapped and will dance herself to death, they perform a dance sequence which includes a movement where they drag their left feet across the floor like an animal pawing the ground. Throughout the Chosen One's sacrificial solo, they wait for her death spasm, the signal for them to rush in and grab her, hoisting her high in the air. All these are instances of the bestial quality in the male roles in *Sacre*.

Sokolova recalled the heat on stage every time *Sacre* was performed (Sokolova 1960: 44). Millicent Hodson suggests this may have been partly due to the ritualistic nature of the movement – circle dances that generated altered mental states (Hodson 1985: 41). It must also have come from the effort expended by both sexes in jumping, throwing themselves on the ground and straight away springing back up again, running, stamping. Within this, the male dancers have more dynamic leaps and jumps than the female ones. These are the sorts of movements for which Nijinsky himself was famous in his roles in other men's ballets. In *Sacre*, rather than hiding effort and exhaustion, these are if anything exaggerated. There is no way that the male dancers in *Sacre* could have been thought of as effeminate. If *Faune* presented a pure, 'natural' masculinity, in *Sacre* Nijinsky has stripped this of its acceptable classical setting, to produce a representation of masculinity at its nastiest and most abject. The first performance of *Sacre* on 29 May 1913 at the Théâtre des Champs-Elysées has gone down in history for the disturbance that split the audience; that what split them was the revolutionary character of the choreography and not the music is proved by the fact that the latter was ecstatically received when performed on its own in a concert in Paris early in 1914. It was Nijinsky's choreography, including the ways in which masculinity was represented in the ballet, that surely caused the most offence.

NIJINSKA AND GENDER REPRESENTATION

Nijinska saw her work as the further development of the choreographic advances initiated by her brother. At the end of her life she wrote:

> When the critics indicated the influence of *Faune* in my choreography of *Les Noces*, they were wrong. I was formed as a choreographer more by *Jeux* and *Le Sacre du printemps*. The unconscious art of those ballets inspired my initial work. From them, I sought to realize the potential of my brother's creativity in terms of neo-classical ballet and modern dance.
>
> (1981: 469)

The roles she made for herself in the ballets she made while working for Diaghilev in 1921–5 seem almost purposely to reflect Nijinsky's role in *Jeux*: like him she danced as a tennis player with a racket in *Le Train bleu* (1924), while as the Hostess in *Les Biches* (1924) she danced the Rag Mazurka in which she flirted with two young men, just as he had flirted with two young women in *Jeux*. *Les Noces* (1923) is a clear descendant of *Sacre*: in the sequence of Stravinsky's output it immediately follows *Sacre* (though it took him years to finish) and shares with it a similar rhythmic complexity and melodic harshness. Thematically both refer to Russian folk melodies and practices. In her choreography for *Les Noces*, Nijinska filled the stage with geometric groupings, and made the male dancers leap and stride in ways that recall *Sacre*.

Nijinska's point of view was very different from her brother's. Nijinsky was 24 in 1913 when he made *Jeux* and *Sacre*. For four crucial years he had led a protected life within the Diaghilev organization, within which he was isolated, ill at ease and probably lonely. Nijinska was 33 in 1924 when she had her triumph with *Les Noces*. She had always been more worldly than her brother, and was married, divorced and about to marry again, and supporting her mother and children (though she still led a circumscribed life). She could conjure up his intensity when the work demanded it, but elsewhere she had the ability to infuse her choreography with humour.

Crucially she was a woman in a man's job – one of the very few woman choreographers to have had the artistic and financial resources of a major ballet company at her disposal. Ninette de Valois is reported to have said that all choreographers are men 'except Nijinska, and she was a man really' (Early 1977: 17). Lydia Sokolova gave this description of Nijinska:

> in appearance she was a most unfeminine woman, though there was nothing particularly masculine about her character. Thin but immensely strong, she had iron muscles in her arms and legs, and her highly developed calf muscles resembled Vaslav's; she had the same way of jumping and pausing in the air.
>
> (1960: 203)

Her similarity with her brother would certainly have been most noticeable when she danced the role of the Faune in a revival of that ballet in 1922 (see Buckle 1979: 406). She danced a male role again in 1924 when Stanislas Idzikovsky refused at the last minute to dance the role of Lysandre the Dancing Master, which Nijinska had created for him, in *Les Fâcheux* (1924). Nijinska put on his costume and danced the role herself (*ibid.*: 424). For a woman to dance a male role had its precedents in the nineteenth century *travestie* dancers, and there is no evidence to suggest that Nijinska herself objected. It all goes to show what a versatile and adaptable dancer Nijinska was, but it also suggests that Nijinska had, at this time, an interestingly detached attitude towards signifiers of gender. There are other examples in which she can be seen to play consciously with these. For Anton Dolin as L'Elégant in *Les Fâcheux* Nijinska created a solo *en pointe*. This was to show the fussy, foppish manner of the seventeenth-century courtier. In *Les Biches*, as well as her own domineering Rag Mazurka, she created the androgynous role known as the Girl in Blue who dances a duet with one of the men, during which she never once makes eye contact with him. Sokolova says of this 'It was never quite clear whether or not she was meant to be a page-boy' (1960: 215). Arnold Haskell points out that the Girl in Blue wore a tight-fitting costume of the type usually worn by the male dancer (1928: 151).

Nijinska's distanced manipulation of these signifiers of gender is surely a consequence of her modernist aesthetic. This is certainly true of her modernist use of *pointe* work in *Les Noces*. *Pointe* has been, since its development in the early 1800s, the prime signifier of femininity in ballet. But rather than using it to create the atmosphere of delicate ethereality that one finds in the all-white acts of so many nineteenth-century ballets, Nijinska used *pointe* to emphasize the brittle nervousness of the Bride and her companions at what is for them the dreadful prospect of marriage.

One shouldn't overestimate the extent to which Nijinska had artistic control over her ballets and hence the sorts of representations of gender found in them. Although, like Fokine, she would have enjoyed relative autonomy over the actual process of choreography, decisions about music, design and libretto were Diaghilev's prerogative, and he and his circle also made contributions during rehearsals. For example he suggested that she should play with an extravagantly long cigarette holder as she danced the Rag Mazurka in *Les Biches*, having seen her constantly smoking on stage while running rehearsals; he, the ballet's designer, Marie Laurencin, and Misia Sert were all apparently involved in making changes to the Girl in Blue's costume for the same ballet (Baer 1987: 40; and Buckle 1979: 420). Both of these decisions contributed to the way gender is represented in these roles. It was Diaghilev who decided to make a ballet to showcase the talents of Anton Dolin, his current lover, and asked Cocteau to devise a libretto for what became *Le Train bleu*. Cocteau came up with the idea for Dolin's role Le Beau Gosse. This is often translated as the 'matinée idol', or the 'good-looking boy' – *gosse* is slang for kid, youngster or nipper. It was Cocteau who picked up on Dolin's prowess at acrobatics and suggested that this be incorporated into the role. Although the ballet is lost,[15] accounts suggest that Nijinska devised some brilliant sequences for Dolin that combined ballet with acrobatics. Nijinska's relationship with Cocteau while working on this ballet was famously fraught,[16] but collaborative relationships in the performing arts can often become strained, and the sort of enterprise which the Ballets Russes was at that time made many working relationships complex.

An insight into the way Diaghilev viewed Nijinska's abilities comes in a letter written in 1923 to his friend and secretary Boris Kochno while *Les Biches* was being made:

> Here everything is going along better than I expected. Poulenc [the composer] is enthusiastic about Bronia's choreography, and they get along excellently together. The choreography has delighted and astonished me. But then, this good woman, intemperate and anti-social as she is, does belong to the Nijinsky family. Here and there her choreography is a bit too ordinary, a bit too *feminine*, but on the whole it is very good.
>
> (Buckle 1979: 418)

Having said that he felt Nijinska's work was sometimes feminine,

Diaghilev goes on to talk about the entrance of the three young men (who have been described as sportsmen, bicyclists or Olympian athletes):

> The dance for the three young men has come out extremely well, and they perform it with bravura – weightily, like a cannon. It doesn't at all resemble *Les Noces*, any more than Tchaikovsky's *Eugene Onegin* resembles his *Queen of Spades*.
>
> (Buckle 1979: 418)

One gets the impression that it is the male dancers Diaghilev is most interested in, and likening them to a cannon is a most revealing simile. The men's entrance is a showy one. They are out to show off before the women, as Haskell puts it, 'like bucks before a groups of does (biches)' (Haskell 1928: 148). Despite this dazzling entrance, the women, however, behave as if unimpressed – two women ignoring the men altogether. This has the effect of making the audience see the men, and this sort of macho display, from a more complex point of view, and thus with a detachment which is surely a consequence of Nijinska's modernism. This detached view of the display of masculine energy is at its most extreme in *Les Noces*.

The music for *Les Noces* is sometimes said to be the piece of Stravinsky's which Europeans find most inaccessible. It takes as its starting point texts that record rituals and superstitions surrounding Russian peasant wedding celebrations. The Russian peasant world-view remained a mixture of Christian and pagan superstitions much longer than it did in most western countries. From the founding of Christianity in Russia in 988 through until the communist revolution, there was never a period of religious reform like the Reformation and Counter-Reformation in Europe. Simon Karlinsky suggests that in *Les Noces* some of the invocations sung by the wedding guests are thinly disguised pagan survivals (Karlinsky 1983: 236). Boris Asaf'yev, writing in Russia in 1929, proposed that two conflicting themes are bound together in Stravinsky's music for *Les Noces*: the women's grim, downtrodden threnody (lament) and the men's grotesque, drunken buffoonery. The first and third sections – blessing the Bride, departure of the Bride – are strident laments, while the second and last sections – blessing the Groom, the wedding feast – are bawdy and grotesque.

The traditional Russian wedding, Asaf'yev says, is virtually a funeral rite. He does not imply that *Les Noces* divides simply into feminine and masculine sections, but argues that these themes are inexorably but conflictually connected: 'The authority of tradition speaks to women: life is a burden, bear it come what may, bury your maidenhead, and with it your will. The buffoon says: life is mime, the rite of the family is theatrical farce' and 'The laughter of buffoonery . . . serves to assuage the bitterness of female grief and blunt the wild impulsiveness of the male procreative energy' (Asaf'yev 1982: 130). The ballet, like the music, is the battle between these two powerful old themes. Asaf'yev, cut off from the West

96

in post-revolutionary Russia, would not have seen the ballet performed. In Nijinska's choreography the themes of the piece divide clearly along gendered lines, and there is never any compromise or let-up in the bitterness of female grief. The Bride remains totally frigid and slightly turned away from her husband all through the final wedding feast (this is more obvious in the British Royal Ballet's version (1966) than in the Paris Opera version (1976)). In the feast, the two families are seated on a platform, back stage, while the guests dance in front of them side by side in segregated blocks and wedges. The music here is at its rowdiest, with sometimes two or three different things being sung at once. The male and female dancers never completely come together; sometimes the men are jumping up at the moment that the women are landing from their own jump which is following a different rhythm in the music.

It is in the earlier scenes that the differences between the material given to the male and female dancers is most apparent. The groups formed by the women are generally in lines, strung out on either side of the Bride as they weave patterns holding the yards of rope-like hair that are being ceremonially braided. This linearity matches the accompanying thin, strident lament of the soprano who sings the part of the Bride. The men's groups have more depth, just as the male voices that accompany them are more resonant. The men form a semicircle behind the Groom at the beginning of the second scene, form up in groups two or three lines deep, and at the end of the scene perform a vigorous circle dance that could almost be straight out of *Sacre* (see Garafola 1992: 66–7).

One of the most striking aspects of Nijinska's choreography is the extraordinary pyramidal tableaux in the first two scenes. At the end of the blessing of the Bride, the women guests, one after the other on alternate sides, lay their heads one on top of the other in a vertical line. The last two each lay a rope-like hair braid on their side which emphasizes the triangular shape of the group. Finally the Bride takes her place, putting her elbows on top of the pile and propping her head on her hands, while her mother and father stand symmetrically at either side blessing her with raised arms. There is a similar group in Blessing the Groom, but here four men kneel forward at the front, three men then lie back to back on top of them with their arms spread wide, two more men do the same on top of them, and then the Groom walks easily into position behind so that his head is at the apex.

The energy in the women's pyramid is downwards with the weight of all those heads precariously held in line. In the men's group the energy is upwards: it is like a football scrum, and the way they support one another is much easier, recalling the ease with which men sometimes touch one another in all-male situations. In another similar motif, each man in a group lays his head on his forearm and walks sideways in an awkward crouch. This unnatural pose, moving sideways across the stage while facing front, recalls typical Nijinsky poses in *Sacre* and *Faune*. A block of men form up in this position and move sideways across the stage like a screen behind the Groom. Here and elsewhere, this motif is surely a reference to lying in bed, and thus to the bedding of the couple at the end of the feast. Both this and the pyramid speak of these men's almost insolent male ease in their bodies and happiness at their status in patriarchal society: this contrasts with the female lack of ease about the power men have over theirs. What Nijinska does is to make the audience uncomfortably aware of the men's ease by stressing the women's lack of it.

MODERNISM AND THE MALE BODY

Rivière argued that the difference between Nijinsky's work and that of Fokine was a new focus on the body: Fokine was too artful, vacillating and vague, but Nijinsky did away with artificiality in 'a return to the body'. Fokine had nevertheless, in his roles for Nijinsky, expanded the range of male dance to include both sensitive and sensual movement, and strong and dynamic expression. Fokine's ballets might hint at aspects of male sexuality whose expression had not previously been acceptable, but these occurred within exotic, 'oriental' or classical settings that were far enough removed from contemporary, modern European ones to defuse any potential threat. In addition Nijinsky as a dancer was so dynamic and skillful that he was hailed as a (male) genius. This in itself was a convenient excuse for any eccentricities. Thus although Fokine may have been introducing types of representation that were new to dance, they could nevertheless be fitted into existing conservative gender ideologies.

It is these two aspects of Nijinsky's star persona – the dynamic solo and the homoerotic spectacle – that have left an active legacy for much of the twentieth century. First, the myth of Nijinsky's leap has fascinated many male ballet dancers and set a standard to which they have aspired. (This fascination with Nijinsky becomes apparent for example in an incident Dolin recalls in his late autobiography (1985). He describes how he forced an unwilling Diaghilev to take him to meet the mentally ill Nijinsky living with Romola in Paris.) Second, photographs and drawings of Nijinsky in revealing costumes were a prototype for a genre of homoerotic images of male ballet dancers – to give two random examples, Pedro Pruna's 1925 portrait of Serge Lifar dressed only in trunks and wearing the sailor's hat from *Les Matelots* (1925) and Baron's photographs of Jean Babilée in Cocteau and Petit's *Le Jeune Homme et la mort* (Baron 1950: 41–50).

It is only in the last few years that Nijinsky and Nijinska's contribution to radical dance practice has been rediscovered by dance historians. *Sacre* can now be seen to have revealed the division in the audience for early modernism – between liberals and radicals who were sympathetic to changing social mores and those conservatives who responded to the anti-

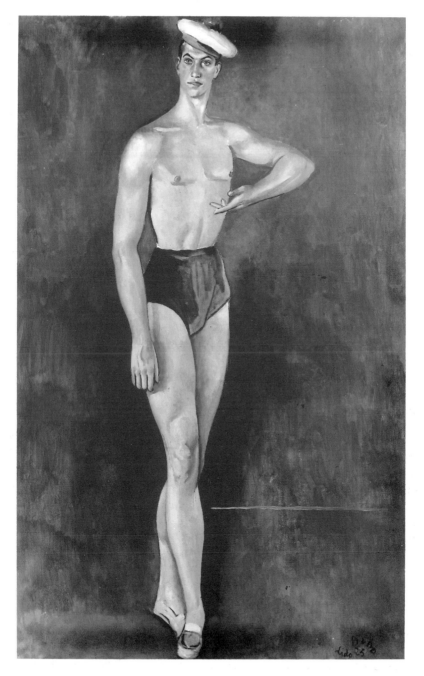

Figure 5 Since Nijinsky, paintings, drawings and photographs of male dancers in teasing costumes have developed into a homoerotic genre.
Serge Lifar in *Les Matelots*, painting by Pedro Pruna, 1925. (Private collection)

bourgeois sentiments of modernism. Nijinska is only now being seen as the real founder of neoclassicism in ballet – the use of the traditional ballet vocabulary in new expressive ways. If the re-emergence of the male body in dance and ballet at the beginning of the twentieth century can be seen as a disruptive force, it was not through the renewal of bravura male dancing nor the founding of a homoerotic tradition but through the radicalism of early modernism. By denaturalizing and destabilizing the representation of gender in theatre dance, Nijinsky and Nijinska were using the kinds of deconstructive strategies that are more familiarly associated with the work of the postmodern choreographers discussed in Chapter 7.

5

MEN, MODERNISM AND MODERN AMERICAN DANCE

'Men don't dance.' This, according to Walter Terry, was the message that one of Ted Shawn's fellow divinity students had for Shawn, after the latter's first public dance performance in Denver in 1911. When Shawn cited as examples the men of the Russian ballet, and the dances of men in almost every culture, the reply came 'that's all right for Russians and pagans but not for Americans' (Terry 1976: 41). This is a witty anecdote but also a telling one, in that it brings together key issues facing white men in the United States who go into serious theatre dance.

First, 'Men don't dance' is not far from '"real" men don't dance', i.e. there must be something wrong with those who do. With this go all the homophobic pressures on white men to conform to prevalent and culturally specific heterosexual norms of masculine behaviour. Second, what is or is not all right for Americans is a question of American cultural identity. By the end of the twentieth century, while Russian men have continued to have a high profile on the international ballet scene, American men are now dancing on stage and have played a large part in the development of American modern dance. It must to some extent be as a result of Cold War rhetoric (Gilbaut 1990b) that there has been and still is among some critics and commentators a deep-rooted belief that the United States leads the world in the modern arts. To adapt a good line from the television series *Star Trek*, modern dance is seen as a new frontier where American men have been able to boldly go where no man has gone before.

Third, there is the comment about pagans. One should beware of underestimating the impact of Christian ideas on dance during the first half of the twentieth century, particularly when looking back from 1990s points of view. Shawn and his fellow student were studying for the Methodist ministry. Christian beliefs were sufficiently important for him and for the other three main choreographers whose work is discussed in this chapter – Martha Graham, José Limón and Alvin Ailey – to create a number of dance pieces on biblical themes (see Manor 1980 and 1992). What is argued in this chapter is that representations of masculinity in modern dance in the United States have been informed largely by White

Anglo-Saxon Protestant (WASP) values. Shawn and Graham, each in their own way, developed in dance the image of a heroic masculinity which is valorized with reference to nature, heterosexuality and religion, and presented in a style and vocabulary that looks muscular and hard. The masculine ideal, which their work evokes, is entirely a product of white, western social forces and depends upon an ideologically distorted view of non-western masculinity. Ailey was black and Limón was, in his words, 'of Mexican origin reared in the United States' (Limón 1967: 23). One aim of this chapter is to explore the ways in which the dominance of hegemonic, white gender ideologies in modern dance affected or limited the way Limón and Ailey were able to express through their work their identity as black or immigrant American men.

This chapter does not therefore set out to recount the history of American modern dance, nor the development of roles for men in modern dance in the United States. Instead the main body of the chapter presents readings of a few well-known pieces by these choreographers. What emerges from these readings is a recurring image of 'natural', essential masculinity as expressed through dance.

It is argued that this image, and the masculine ideal to which it corresponds, is a conservative and defensive response to challenges to male hegemony. The image has persisted on the dance stage for a large part of this century, and has developed an autonomy of its own. Choreographers have not been able to ignore it: they have had to take it on board, adapt it, reject it or react against it. It is an image with which choreographers have tried to map out different positions in relation to the problems surrounding masculine identities as they have experienced them themselves. What therefore are these problems and what are the threads that bind modern dance in the United States to essentialist ideals of American manhood?

AMERICAN MEN

The American association of masculinity with toughness renders male dance problematic, dancing still being, in many people's minds, a feminine realm. Marcia Siegel sums this up thus:

> Dancing is an equivocal activity in any society that places a low value on the arts in general, but it becomes even more dubious where men have been celebrated as kings of the frontier, masters of the gun, the ax, and the plow.
>
> (Siegel 1981: 305)

This may be how American men have been celebrated, but the reality has of course been somewhat different. Throughout the period which this chapter covers, there have been continual conflicts and sources of insecurity about the nature of masculine identity as various sometimes contradictory factors have seemed to threaten to weaken or undermine it. A heavy-handed return to ideals of 'natural', essential, instinctive and 'traditional' masculinity is of course only one of many differing responses to such insecurities: but it is these sorts of ideals that underpin the representations of masculinity one finds in the choreography of Shawn and Graham. Why then has this idea of American man as a gun-slinging, axe- and plough-wielding frontiersman developed?

By the beginning of the twentieth century, the prairie was increasingly being ploughed up and the expansion westwards into unsettled land was ended. While American men might still dream of the frontier life as a viable avenue through which to establish their identity as men, the frontier had effectively ceased to exist. In general, modern civilized lifestyles and values were widely perceived to be having a softening and degenerating influence on the effete, educated, Eastern male elite. There was widespread concern about the feminization of American culture (see Douglas 1977) which had a softening and degenerating influence on traditional male lifestyles and ideals. When Shawn first became interested in dancing around 1910, dance in the United States was almost exclusively a female preserve. Other factors also were affecting men, and white-collar male workers in particular. The rise of women's suffrage and changes in the world of work, with women increasingly entering the job market, meant that jobs which until then had been the preserve of white-collar male workers were now being done by women.

One response to these pressures and sources of insecurity about the changing nature of masculine identity was the development of an essentialist reassertion of 'natural' male energy that could be read as a reassuring rebuttal of the charge that men are growing soft. Michael S. Kimmel (1987) has called this sort of conservative reaction to changing masculine norms of identity a 'pro-male' response.

In the last chapter, Lord Baden-Powell's ideas on the need to stay in touch with 'essential' masculinity were considered. His career and jingoistic outlook begs comparison with that of Theodore Roosevelt (1858–1919), President of the United States (1901–9). Both shared what might be called a pro-male attitude towards masculinity. The writer Edgar Rice Burroughs (1875–1950) was closer in age to Shawn (1891–1975), and the image of 'natural' masculinity embodied in Burroughs's great fictional character Tarzan is a useful reference point for Shawn's early male solos. Shawn's first performance as a dancer was the year before the publication of the first Tarzan novel. In the latter, masculinity is conceived of as 'natural' and innate, while civilized behaviour is a thin veneer which is learned because of women. This is in line with the pro-male, misogynistic view that, while it is women's function to uphold and maintain the values of civilization, the consequent feminization of culture leads to the weakening of manhood.

This is the opposite of the view (considered in Chapter 1) that women are closer to nature and their emotions, while men are more rational and more cultured. In the first novel *Tarzan and the Apes* (1912) it is only through contact with Jane Porter that the eponymous ape man decides to enter into civilized society. As Joseph Bristow points out,

> Tarzan obviously bears the traces of earlier varieties of man – the gentleman of Victorian fiction; the imperial soldier on the battle-front; the Scout making himself at home out of doors – but he is, for all to see [when he first kisses Jane], a belatedly Darwinian being whose sexual passion knows no reason. The political imperative to survive has here been transformed into a sexual imperative to be a man.
>
> (Bristow 1991: 217)

This political and sexual imperative is a homophobic one. The idea of a 'natural' and instinctive masculinity evoked by Tarzan, and asserted by figures like Roosevelt and Baden-Powell, was a reassuring myth to hold on to during a period in which traditional gender norms were perceived to be under threat. This myth is, of course, largely a product of white, Anglo-Saxon social forces, but one which draws on an ideologically distorted view of non-western masculinity. Tarzan is not unlike the later film heroes that Martin Pumphrey has commented on. Like Stallone's Rambo and Schwarzenegger's Terminator, Tarzan can be seen as a hero who directs his violence against an externalization of contemporary crises rather than acknowledging the internal contradictions his identity encompasses (see Chapter 1).

By the 1940s and 1950s there were similar pressures on traditional tough norms of masculine identity and behaviour. The Second World War had a decisive impact on the development of gay and lesbian communities in the United States. It brought large numbers of people together and thus created situations in which individuals came to recognize their sexual orientations, and in which homosexual behaviour became far more commonplace for large numbers of people. The plus side of this was that, by the 1950s, there was increasing tolerance of gays and gay communities, but there was also substantial harassment which was in part stimulated by McCarthy's witch-hunts (D'Emilio 1983: 41–53). There were other factors, in the 1950s, that undermined 'traditional' notions of masculinity in the world of managerial work and suburban family life in the United States. Barbara Ehrenreich has discussed the pressures on these sorts of office-working, family men. The rise, in the 1950s, of the affluent consumer economy in the United States, she suggests, gradually eroded the opportunities for men to live up to the traditional American male values to which Siegel refers above. David Riesman proposed that the requirements of business dictated that the male role should move away from the goal-oriented, entrepreneurial man (who might have dreamed about frontier-breaking) to the easy-going, likeable male colleague. In this new industrial society, it is not things that matter or are a problem, but other people. 'Today it is the "softness" of men,' he wrote, 'rather than the "hardness" of material that calls on talent and opens channels of social mobility' (Riesman 1950: 127). If there were pressures in new styles of management for men to move away from traditional masculine norms of behaviour, it was also necessary for the US economy for these men to abandon the Protestant work ethic and spend, consumerism being the motor for post-war industrial growth. Motivational researcher Dr Ernest Dichter told American businessmen:

> We are confronted with the problem of permitting the average American to feel moral . . . even when he is spending, even when he is not saving, even when he is taking two vacations a year and buying a second or third car. One of the basic problems of prosperity, then, is to demonstrate that the hedonistic approach to life is a moral, not an immoral one.
>
> (quoted in Ehrenreich 1983: 45)

It is these issues and concerns which affected thinking about masculine identity (or identities) during the period covered by this chapter. Many of the ideas which Ted Shawn developed about dance and masculinity can be seen as a product of the debates about the nature of masculine identity around the turn of the century. It is largely through Ted Shawn that the sort of masculine identity that can be described as western, Christian, Darwinian, pro-male and mythical became a norm of American modern dance. It is this image of the male dancer which was inherited by Graham, Ailey and to a lesser extent Limón, and mediated the ways in which they responded to the gender ideologies of the 1940s and 1950s.

Ideologies of American modernism

For Americans until the 1940s, modernism in the arts was associated largely with Europe in general and Paris in particular. Modernism was international – the modern movement in architecture was called the International Style – while the United States was, in terms of political outlook, isolationist for most of the twentieth century up until 1943. American entry into the Second World War was accompanied by a change of political direction – the idea that the American people should take on the mantle of world leadership and make the twentieth century the American century (see Gilbaut 1985; Wilkie 1943). Eva Cockcroft (1985) and Serge Gilbaut (1985 and 1990b) have described the transitional process through which American abstract expressionist painting was taken up and promoted abroad through State-Department-sponsored exhibitions as part of the internationalization of American culture. American modern dance companies were also sent on foreign tours by the State Department as part of this process. Gilbaut argues that the anti-capitalist criticism of some of the foremost American painters became hidden and silenced as they were cast in the role of the 'free', progressive and above all modern artists of the 'free world', in contrast to socialist realism, the politically restrained and old-fashioned representational art advocated by the Communist Party in Europe. What was stressed in new liberal American politics was these artists' individualism. As Gilbaut puts it, 'In the modern world which brutally stifles the individual, the artist [became] a rampart, an example of will against the uniformity of totalitarian society' (1985: 162). The spectre of bland uniformity also, as Ehrenreich suggests, faced American businessmen in the United States. At any rate the 1940s and 1950s were a time when American modern dancers were highly individualistic. As Marcia Siegel puts it: 'In this period before eclectic, ballet-based training reduced most modern dancing to stylelessness, great dancing personalities could be accepted as interpreters of particular points of view' (1987: 237). In painting, this American individualism had a specifically masculine quality: 'Only the virility of an art like [Jackson] Pollock's, its brutality, ruggedness, and individualism, could revitalize modern culture, traditionally represented by Paris, and effeminized by too much praise' (Gilbaut 1985: 161). As we shall see, representations of masculinity in American modern dance have also been characterized as ruggedly virile in comparison with the supposed effeteness of the European ballet tradition. This is the modernist, artistic context within which Graham, Limón and Ailey created the male roles discussed below.

TED SHAWN, AMERICAN-NESS AND NATURAL MASCULINITY

Marcia Siegel sees Ted Shawn's choreography for the male dancer as an expression of American cultural values which could not be represented within the European dance tradition. She argues that Shawn's principal contribution to choreographic development was his focusing of attention on heroic male body images.

> He must have decided early on that there was no reason the arms and upper body had to be round, light, and delicate, as dictated by the decorative European ballet. They could be strong and ready for work just as well. As a corrective, his thinking was quite logical. The things men do when dancing are strong and do demand great physical endurance, precision, and daring. The whole ballet convention consisted in more or less hiding these attributes, with elaborate costuming, passive role-play, and that soft, aggression-denying upper body.... Shawn wanted to restore or complete the energy

106

system that has been emasculated by tradition. The clumsiness of his efforts at choreography doesn't invalidate his vision.

(Siegel 1979: 307)

Whereas Siegel suggests he completed an energy system that had been emasculated by tradition, her description suggests that his choreography expressed only the 'positive' male attributes of strength and expansiveness, narrowing the range of the male dancer's expressiveness to the more macho side of male behaviour. She argues this by equating on the one hand America with the modern and on the other hand Europe with ballet. When Shawn argued with his fellow divinity student in 1911 he cited the men of the Russian ballet as positive examples of male dancers. He may well have been thinking of Mikhail Mordkin, who toured the USA with Pavlova in 1909 and then with his own company in 1911–12. No one surely would have said of Mordkin that he indulged in passive role-play, or presented a soft, aggression-denying upper body. It was the American exponents of ballet that were problematic. Writing in 1946, Shawn recalled:

> At the beginning of my own career, the dance parts performed by men had become less and less creditable – men ballet dancers were being largely used as props for a danseuse during an arabesque – while the training of men was such that men and women were trained together and there was little differentiation of the movement, with the result that dancing for men was under a cloud; but in these later years, my group of men dancers, focusing on masculine problems of the dance, have also enriched the field until today no one who has seen my men dance can tolerate effeminacy in the male dance.
>
> (1946: 98–9)

Shawn developed his own style through gradually rejecting the conventions of European ballet movement, and replacing balletic mime with vocabularies of gesture derived from the work of Francois Delsarte (1811–71), as did many early American modern dancers.[1] The aggressive masculine stance of his work should not therefore be seen solely as a consequence of rejecting ballet. It needs also to be located within specifically modern American social and religious ideologies.

Shawn's earliest solos such as *Savage Dance* and *Dagger Dance*, both of 1912, and *Dance Slav* (1913) were concerned with primitive or non-western warrior cultures, as were subsequent pieces like *Invocation to the Thunderbird* (1918), *Spear Dance Japonaise* (1919) and *Pyrrhic Warriors* (1918). In these Shawn seems, like Edgar Rice Burroughs, to have been borrowing the outer appearances of primitive and non-western cultures in order to evoke a 'natural' masculinity with which these 'Others' were believed to be in touch. This notion of masculinity bore little relation to the realities of non-western social structure, and only really meant anything in the context of contemporary western society.

The assertion of 'positive' male attributes of strength and expansiveness can be related to what has been called Muscular Christianity (see Kimmel 1987). Shawn initially trained to become a Methodist minister, and started going to dance classes for exercise after recovering from diphtheria. Notions of manliness in the late nineteenth century were associated with the practice of sports and athletics within the spheres of education and the church. One American preacher at that time pronounced that Jesus was no dough-faced lick-spittle proposition, but the biggest scrapper that ever lived (Kimmel 1987: 140). Shawn choreographed a church service, and many pieces based on biblical and religious themes. For his company Ted Shawn and his Male Dancers in the 1930s he choreographed many evocations of the male world of work such as *Cutting the Sugar Cane* (1933), *Dance of the Threshing Floor* (1934), *Labour Symphony* (1934) and *Workers' Songs from Middle Europe* (1931). It is probably coincidental that Shawn settled on this theme at around the same time that the Workers Dance League were beginning to explore it (Prickett 1989 and 1990). But male work as a subject offered a safe, unequivocally masculine range of movements. In 1946 he wrote about this in an essay on the male dancer:

> in watching movements of men in manual labour all over the world, continuously and carefully, I have come to the conclusion that most of them are big movements of the whole body and the arm movement is a continuation of the body movement, as for example the movement of a man using a scythe.

> (Shawn 1946: 104)

Shawn thus argues that men's work is totally different from women's work and that it is neither right nor natural for women to do male work. 'We felt that it was best when woman was working in the home, taking care of the needs of her husband and children, and so most religious and moral education has come from mother to children' (Shawn 1946: 105). Thus his assertion of the supposedly essential difference between male and female movement as a basis for dance is in line with the conventions of conservative Christian propriety.

If it is all right in the late twentieth century for American men to dance, this is largely due to Shawn;[2] but, in bringing this about, he and his dancers portrayed men in almost every culture but that of modern America. (Even his worker pieces referred to Eastern Europe, sugar cane plantations or to modern machines rather than to modern American men.) What is significant is the position of power that Shawn as a member of the dominant Anglo-Saxon American social group enjoyed in relation to the subject societies whose cultural forms he and St Denis chose to borrow. The cultural and racial stereotypes which their work retailed are part of the period's nativist and racialist ideologies (see Kendall 1979: 105–6). That there were no black dancers in the Denishawn company (Shawn and Denis's dance company) is hardly surprising in a period when a colour bar forbade black performers appearing on stage with white ones. But Shawn saw the influence of black dance on American social dance as a degenerate one, saying so in his 1926 book *The American Ballet*. Looking back at this period in 1946, Shawn again deplored the way white people had adopted black social dances:

> I was sick at heart that we, this whole vast country of millions of white people, still kept on dancing dances of negro derivation. Have we lost completely the qualities that made us a great nation? We were capable in the past of creating our own dances. Why is it in this last period that we have let this negroid influence so completely ob-literate everything else?

> (1946: 84)

Doris Humphrey suggests in her unfinished autobiography that Shawn and Denis might have been anti-semitic (Cohen 1972: 62). In relation to the native American and non-western dance traditions from which his work borrowed, Shawn's ethnocentric point of view ensured that he found only what he wanted to see – a confirmation of conservative, western gender ideologies. If the only way western male norms could be represented in dance was by referring to non-western men, this is a curious example of the discontinuities and double-binds inherent in the construction of western masculinity at that time.

While Shawn succeeded in raising the status of male dance in the United States, he achieved this by remaining within hegemonic norms rather than confronting them. The strong, positive qualities of his choreography for men are in line with the continuum between conservative Muscular Christian ideologies and the contemporary appeal of 'natural' masculinity identified above; but they are also open to appreciation from a manly, classical homosexual point of view. There was a chapter on nudity in Shawn's *The American Ballet* that extolled the Greek ideal of nudity, 'of youths at the ancient Olympics, entering races and wrestling matches with gleaming, oiled, nude bodies' (Terry 1976: 39). In his solo *Death of Adonis: Plastique* (1923), made up as a classical marble statue and wearing only a fig leaf, Shawn moved through a series of thirty-two choreographed poses on a sculptural plinth. In the context of a larger dance spectacle of the ancient world for which the solo was devised, the piece seem to have been acceptable.[3] It clearly evokes an acceptable, classical male image; but it can also be related to homosexual thematics. As was stated in Chapter 4, some nineteenth- and twentieth-century homosexuals have looked to Ancient Greek society as an ideal manly culture within which homosexuality was considered normal (see Dyer 1990: 22–5).

Shawn became engaged to his first dance teacher and dancing partner Hazel Wallack, and in 1914 married Ruth St Denis (later separating), but his subsequent relationships were all with men. Terry says that Shawn's homosexual side was latent 'during all but the last days of Denishawn, and his acceptance of his homosexuality was known only to a few' (1976: 140; see also Sherman and Mumaw 1986). In his society at that time Shawn would have had many reasons for keeping his sexual orientation a secret, not least the fear that any suspicions about his sexuality and that of his male dancers would, at the least, have seriously affected the financial viability of his company, let alone the possibilities of blackmail, persecution or even prosecution (D'Emilio 1983: 40 and *passim*). Nude and semi-nude photographs of Shawn and his male dancers clearly relate to an American genre of male erotica (see Cooper 1986: 233 and *passim*), but could also double as acceptable images of athletic, classical males. It was these sorts of acceptable values that Shawn stressed in his polemical writings in support of male dance (Shawn 1916, 1933, 1936, 1946 and 1966) and in the 1930s with his all-male company. A review, in the *Berkshire Evening Eagle*, of a 1937 performance by the company is typical of notices the company received.

> Men, brought the first time by their wives, returned of their own accord, and found that the dance, as an exhibition of art, muscular poise and coordination, was as exciting as a track meet and a wrestling match. They agreed with Shawn, that 'dancing is not a sissy art'.
>
> (Schlundt 1967: 47)

This last quote appears in variations in many of the reviews quoted by Schlundt (1967), and must have been said often by Shawn. By arguing that dance was not 'pansy' or 'sissy', Shawn seems to have attempted to fit in with dominant heterosexual male norms, rather than challenging them. Shawn's work thus tried, within the social restrictions of the period, to occupy common ground, albeit of a problematic kind, between a gay and straight point of view. But such value-free common ground never exists. The restrictions may allow a limited expression but at the same time they block and deform it. Shawn undoubtedly did a lot for male dance, but, by keeping carefully within the bounds of propriety, he unfortunately limited the range of male dancing to tough, aggressive expression.

MARTHA GRAHAM AND SHAWN'S LEGACY

Though Terry may have claimed for Shawn the accolade of father of modern dance, the field in the United States was, of course, until the 1950s, dominated by women dancers and choreographers. If one is concerned with questions of genealogy or status then Martha Graham was one of the most important figures in this development. Where images of the male

Figure 6 Ted Shawn's group of male dancers proved that 'dancing is not a sissy art' by narrowing the range of the dancer's expressiveness to the more macho side of male behaviour. Photo of Ted Shawn and his male dancers in 1936 dancing *Kinetic Molpai*.

(Photo: Sherman; New York Public Library, Shapiro Dance Collection) dancer are concerned, Graham can be seen to have continued and extended the way of presenting the male dancer which Shawn initiated. When, in 1922, Shawn temporarily split from Ruth St Denis and toured with his own company, it was Martha Graham who was his principal partner. Graham started choreographing group pieces in 1926 but it was not until 1938 that she included male dancers in her company. When one examines the sorts of qualities Graham choreographed for her male dancers, these seem to owe more to her association with Ted Shawn than is sometimes acknowledged.

Erick Hawkins joined Graham's company to be its first male dancer in 1938 and was subsequently, for a while, her husband. Merce Cunningham joined her company in 1939. Hawkins came to her from Lincoln Kirstein's Ballet Caravan, and she suggested to Cunningham that he should take ballet classes at Balanchine's School of American Ballet. According to Bertram Ross (who joined Graham's company in 1954 after her split with Hawkins), when Graham choreographed parts for men she didn't like demonstrating movements 'because she did not have a man's body'; she would give movement directions verbally instead (Mazo 1991: 44). This is confirmed by Tim Wengerd, who danced with the Graham company in the 1970s: 'This being the case, Hawkins and Cunningham probably had major shares in the creation of their roles from the start, and Martha shaped the material to suit her purposes' (Wengerd 1991: 52). Between 1938 and 1944 Graham made a number of works that present a central female character (performed by herself) and two male roles initially danced by Cunningham and Hawkins. These pieces are generally acknowledged to present her most rounded and interesting male roles, but it could be argued that this was sometimes achieved at the cost of subordinating the roles she created for herself – for example the bride in *Appalachian Spring* (1944). In these two-man pieces, Deborah Jowitt suggests, Graham presented herself poised between two antithetical males.

Hawkins was called 'The Dark Beloved' in the sombre, seething *Deaths and Entrances*, and he played this role – sexually alluring, masterful, potentially dangerous – in more than one dance. Cunningham was 'The Poetic Beloved,' a slightly mystical, even androgynous figure: he was the blithe acrobat to Hawkins's whip-wielding ringmaster (*Every Soul Is a Circus*), the winged Pegasus to his swaggering husband (*Punch and the Judy*), the gentle Christ figure in *El Penitente*, the fanatic Revivalist in *Appalachian Spring*. After Merce Cunningham left the company, Graham made no more dances that expressed this double image of man. Perhaps the male roles also embodied a duality within herself: sensuality and idealism; or the taskmaster/perfectionist and the undisciplined, irrational visionary.

(Jowitt 1988: 228–9)

112

Appalachian Spring is a particularly interesting example of how she was dealing with the male image at that time. The piece shows an American wedding in a small frontier farmhouse in the first half of the nineteenth century. The cast consists of the Bride, Husbandman, Revivalist preacher, the older Pioneer Woman, and four young women who are followers of the Revivalist. They all come on stage in a formal procession, and throughout the piece, as well as a duet for Bride and Husbandman, the principal characters each have a solo during which everyone else is frozen still.

Following Jowitt's suggestions above, the two male roles can be seen as projections of different sides of Graham's own desires and aspirations, although it doesn't make much sense to see them as those of the Bride – the role Graham herself danced in the piece. As Marcia Siegel points out, *Appalachian Spring* reworks themes originally explored in her earlier solo *Frontier* (1935). In this earlier piece, a woman dancing by a fence on the prairie seems torn between repressive religious feelings and the spatial freedom symbolized by the new land of the (open) frontier of unsettled country. She was thus evoking imagery that, as we have seen, was clearly associated with American masculine values. In *Appalachian Spring*, the two men could be said to represent these two sets of opposing values: the Husbandman expresses a straightforward love of freedom, space and the natural cycle, while the Revivalist vents the tortured and convoluted feelings of his (and Graham's) puritanical fervour.

The movement material which the Husbandman performs is very straightforward in contrast to the mercuric distortions of the Revivalist's solos or the nervous temperamental quality of the Bride's role. Marcia Siegel conjures up the flavour of the Husbandman's role:

> The husband's movements are large and expansive. The actual steps he does when he first takes centre stage are a conglomeration of knee-slapping, rein-pulling mime motifs; balletic turns in the air; and leggy, travelling jumps, reachings, and stampings. You feel he's showing off, but not in a narcissistic way; rather, he's giving vent to his happy feelings and pride, his natural assertiveness and drive.
>
> (Siegel 1979: 147)

He also surveys the horizons and makes some gestures which suggest ploughing or working the land. Edwin Denby in 1945 wrote that the Husbandman's role 'suggests farmer vigour and clumsy farmer mirth' (Denby 1986: 314). The stamping gestures he makes are part of the traditional image of the farmer: in the folk song 'Oats and beans and barley grow'

> First the farmer sows his seed
> Then he stands and takes his ease
> Stamps his foot and claps his hand
> And turns around to view the land.

This recalls atavistic notions of fertility. The Husbandman is supposed to be virile and fertile. The quality and nature of his movements fit in remarkably with Shawn's description of the way male dance movements relate to the movements of male work activities referred to earlier.[4] Like Shawn's manly Christian male dancer, the Husbandman looks hard and muscular in a role that is expansive and tough, if not exactly aggressive, and he definitely does not have a soft, aggression-denying body.

For all that, the Husbandman is hardly a deeply observed character. Like most of the men in Graham's pieces he is flat and one-dimensional. The role of the Revivalist is the exception to this; as both Jowitt and Siegel suggest, he is more rounded. This is surely because this role articulates one of Graham's central themes, the contradictory pull of repressive, old-fashioned evangelical Protestantism. There is a quality of torture and inner contradiction at the heart of some of Graham's best work that comes from her Presbyterian upbringing and her consequent love–hate relationship with Christianity.

The Revivalist's main solo represents a sermon that is all hellfire and damnation. He starts it by stamping one foot repeatedly on the ground and then hitting himself with a clenched fist on the side of the trunk. There are stamping movements in the Husbandman's solos, that, it has been suggested, connote virility and fertility. By stamping and then hitting himself, the Revivalist is starting off his sermon by condemning everything the Bride and Husbandman are looking forward to enjoying, the pleasure both of being close to the land, and of being close to each other.

The solo continues with wild, angular movements and asymmetrical gestures, bewildering leaps and risky falls. Two films of *Appalachian Spring* show differing interpretations of the Revivalist's role. David Hatch Walker in the 1976 film[5] projects the hellfire straight at the bride and groom. Bertram Ross, however, in the 1959 film[6] is less fierce; his Revivalist is surely aware that he himself is not immune to the perils and weaknesses of the flesh. The Revivalist is surely meant to enjoy playing up to, and exerting his power over, the four excitable girls – at one moment rolling from the floor up into their laps. The virtuosity demanded by the Revivalist's role makes the straightforward manliness of the Husbandman's movement material look boring in comparison. It is noticeable that the expressive range of movement in the Revivalist's solo is far greater than that of the Husbandman or of Shawn's Muscular Christian dancers. Paradoxically then, Ross's (Christian) Revivalist seems less restricted than them by the need to maintain a decorous, Christian propriety.

Male roles in later Graham pieces also recall Shawn's work. Wengerd says that Jason's big solo in *Cave of the Heart* (1946) includes a large number of movements that are to be found in Shawn's *Spear Dance Japonaise.*

114

Whether she suggested them to Hawkins or whether he had seen them before and felt their appropriateness for this dance we cannot know, but this figure is often pointed out as being 'typical' Graham choreography for men. In reality, there is nothing like him up to this point, and while similar treatments of men are found in later 'Greek' pieces, this is the first and most extreme.

(1991: 52)

The way most of Graham's male dancers move may have much in common with Shawn's Muscular Christians, but Graham's view of woman is radically different. For Shawn, a woman's place is in the home. The Bride in *Appalachian Spring* (1944) is the nearest Graham gets to this. In other pieces from around this time, such as *Letter to the World* (1940) and *Deaths and Entrances* (1943), the home is the scene of tensions. Her later heroines are powerful and dangerous, and a threat to the family home. In the 'Greek' pieces in particular, women are incestuous – Jocasta in *Night Journey* (1947) – or murder their children – Medea in *Cave of the Heart* – or murder their husband – *Clytemnestra* (1958). This is the context within which Graham's heroines simultaneously fear and desire their leading men, and it is from their point of view that these male dancers are seen. Then, starting with *Diversion of Angels* (1948) in which she herself did not dance, Graham created pieces which are generally lighter and have much less narrative in them, but which present the dancers as idealized 'celestial acrobats'.

Wengerd suggests that the same basic male types recurred throughout her career: adored men, men feared, man the unattainable, even man dehumanized. 'Few men in dance are allowed to be as thoroughly tortured as Orestes, as adored as Oedipus, as loathsome as Jason, and as simply joyous as all the men in *Adoration of Angels*' (*ibid.*: 52). The fact that Graham was producing work from a woman's point of view for a predominantly female audience constitutes the context within which the male roles in her work were produced. Within Graham's female-centred stories, men are seen as desirable while they act out an erotic display. In doing this, Graham is subverting the norms of gender representation by reappropriating images of men for her own pleasure and that of other women, almost thirty years before feminist visual artists started controversially dealing with similar eroticized representations of the male body (see Walters 1979; Kent and Morreau (eds) 1985).

In retrospect, although one can infer that the male body was desirable for Shawn, this was never admitted either in the subjects and themes of his pieces or in his polemical writings in support of male dance. If within Graham's pieces male dancers are subversively seen as desirable, at least the framework within which female desire operates is clearly marked as heterosexual. As Lynn Garafola has suggested

Although Graham's works of these decades take the heroine's point of view, it is maleness that fuels the drama; it is what stokes the passion of her heroines and destroys it, what drives them again and again to seek what they cannot have, to desire what they should not want.

(Garafola 1993: 172)

Graham's men and women seem in Graham's own eyes to have represented differing but positive ideals – men and women in abstracted images of heterosexual relations, not fixed in any historical period.[7] Graham's readings from Jung no doubt led her to see the actors in her 'Greek' pieces as perennial, archetypal beings alive in the collective unconscious. Pieces like *Diversion of Angels* suggest, by their modernity, the type of ideal, mythical beings discussed in Chapter 3: their movement suggests beings who are more intense, more energetic and more physically aware, more masculine and more feminine than ordinary people. One could say of these modernist male roles that they represent 'belatedly Darwinian beings' for whom the imperative to survive has been 'transformed into a sexual imperative to be a man'. This, it will be recalled, is Joseph Bristow's description of Tarzan when first kissing Jane.

The most flat and caricatural male role Graham choreographed seems to have been Jason in *Cave of the Heart*. This is the role whose movements, Wengerd suggests, resemble Shawn's *Spear Dance Japonaise*. Wengerd describes Jason as 'a sort of cardboard-cutout Greek Hell's Angel' who is allowed only 'to show his humanness after he has been utterly undone, but prior to that he is one hundred percent male chauvinist pig' (1991: 52). There is nothing, however, to suggest that Graham here was criticizing men in roles like this. Medea may have hated Jason (who in the myth leaves her for another woman) but only because she still desired him. Nevertheless, compared with the roles in *Appalachian Spring*, male roles in the dark, brooding 'Greek' dances, and in pieces like *Diversion of Angels*, are reduced to caricatures of posturing machismo. Deborah Jowitt suggests that these men are all prick and no personality.

The movements [Graham] devised for them – stiff-legged walks and jumps, bows bending like a V at the hips, assertive gestures – imbued them with phallic significance. ('We're usually stiff foils, or something large and naked for women to climb on' is how Paul Taylor put it.)

(Jowitt 1988: 230 quoting Taylor 1975: 85)

What is it, then, that stops Graham's 'Greek' men from being so grotesque as to appear inhuman, and thus a challenge and critique of dominant masculine norms? Because they are seen by the central female character – through Graham's eyes – it becomes possible to discount what is disturbing

116

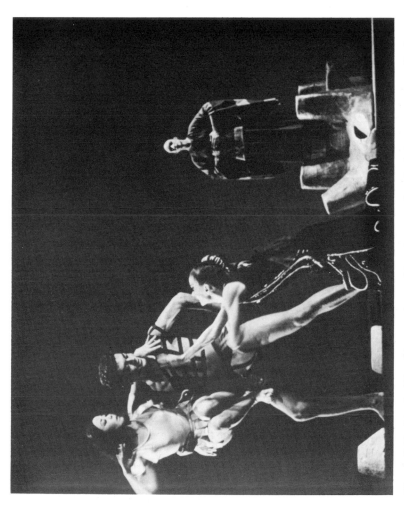

Figure 7 Graham's 'Greek' men: 'something large and naked for women to climb on'. Yuriko, Robert Cohan, Helen McGhee and Matt Turney in *Cave of the Heart*.

(Photo: Martha Swope)

about these representations of masculinity and see it as just an aberration, a personal quirk of Graham's. Of course 'we' don't see them the way she does. As Martha Siegel puts it, 'Graham had been making display dances for men since she had first had men in her company' and she 'didn't gloss over the idea that the woman was physically turned on by what [the male dancer] was doing. All through the 1940s and 1950s men were Graham's villains, and though to us they may look pompous and grotesque, to her heroines they were fatally erotic' (Siegel 1979: 316).

Like Shawn's male dancers, Graham's 'Greek' men's movement range is 'limited' to represent only the more macho side of male behaviour. They are tough – so much so as to be tight and insecure about their boundaries (Theweleit), defending themselves against repressed developmental conflicts (Chodorow). The tight qualities of the movements should not be attributed entirely to Graham. She didn't demonstrate them but gave verbal instructions: the male dancers she was working with found these tensions within their own bodies. In compensating for the embarrassment of being the object of Graham's erotic gaze (when Bertram Ross first started learning male solos he rehearsed in private with Graham without telling anyone (Mazo 1991: 44)), they turned themselves into the one-dimensional macho 'Greek' Hell's Angels of modern dance.

This was a male image which had particular social resonance in the United States in the late 1940s and early 1950s. This was, as Ehrenreich points out, a time when social and economic forces were eroding traditional male values. This was also the cold war and McCarthy period, and a time of repression of homosexuals (discussed in the next chapter). Graham's male dancers, in their excessively physical, excessively masculine form were surely an example of a pro-male reassertion of traditional masculine qualities – strength, hardness, aggressiveness, expansiveness. The male dancer in her work may be subject to a female erotic gaze, but it is a heterosexual one in which the power of the male body is acknowledged as an unproblematic norm.

Graham jotted in a notebook:

> The aching muscles
> the remembered glories
> the agonies of the future
> (Graham 1973: 304)

But, as Robert Cohan put it, 'She loved you to want to kill her'.[8]

DANCE, MODERNISM AND THE 'OTHER'

What Cohan and Graham are talking about here has far-reaching implications for the way masculinity is represented in modern dance. It means that a particularly strong tradition that comes from Shawn and is developed by Graham has become associated with a heroic masculinity which is valorized with reference to nature, heterosexuality and religion, and presented in a style and vocabulary that looks muscular and hard. It has been argued that this tradition is determined by the need to repress the internal contradictions of dominant, white, masculine identities.

One difference between Denishawn (in which Graham and Humphrey both started to perform) and the subsequent work of Graham and Doris Humphrey is the modernism of the latter. In contrast to the blue-eyed, blond whiteness of Denishawn, Humphrey's and Graham's companies in the 1930s and 1940s were ethnically diverse, reflecting the social make-up of urban America. Metropolitan experience was among the factors which Raymond Williams associated with the development of the formal innovations of early modernism (discussed in Chapter 4). The abstracted works that Graham and Humphrey created in the late 1920s and early 1930s – such as Humphrey's *Colour Harmony* (1928) or Graham's *Lamentations* (1930) – must in part be seen as a reaction against the exotic and period costume dances that they had performed in while members of the Denishawn company. Writing about her teaching with Charles Weidman in New York in 1928, Doris Humphrey stated:

> The students were stimulated by our enthusiasm for some discoveries about movement, which had to do with ourselves as Americans – not Europeans or American Indians or East Indians, which most of the Denishawn work consisted of, but as young people of the twentieth century living in the United States.
>
> (Cohen 1972: 61)

Unhindered by the need to create an identifiable setting or social reference, Graham and Humphrey were able to look at the expressive potential of movement itself. This kind of concern with the medium of dance itself is an attribute of modernism. It is this concern with expressive movement, together with emergent ideologies of American rugged individualism, which, from the 1940s onwards, informed the work of José Limón and Alvin Ailey. In turning now to look at them there is a shift to two modern dance choreographers who were definitely not white Anglo-Saxon Americans.

A major problem facing black and immigrant or 'hyphenated' American dancers is how to deal with or avoid the effects of stereotypes. Stereotypes are not natural or inevitable but socially constructed and reproduced in cultural forms including dance. Black male dancers may in some cases be able to appear less soft and effete, less contaminated by civilization and thus more 'essentially' and 'naturally' masculine than white dancers of European origin; but black dancers can often be

119

stereotyped. J. Aschenbrenner has pointed out that reviews by American dance critics of black dance performances have tended to reinforce general stereotypes of black people. Aschenbrenner notes that reviewers often comment on the supposedly innate ability of black dancers rather than acknowledging the work that goes into preparing for performance or in attaining a degree of technical proficiency. Reviewers also attribute mysterious qualities to black performers, and Aschenbrenner notes that there is an overemphasis on the physicality of dancers (Aschenbrenner 1980a, b). Black dancers, as Christy Adair observes, have to fight these stereotypes in order to establish themselves as serious creative artists using their rich African American heritage (Adair 1992: 180).

Stereotypes do not work just by putting down groups deemed inferior, but also carry with them a degree of ambivalence. As the photographer David A. Bailey has pointed out,

> The process of stereotyping is not as simple as one group dis-criminating against another. There is a complex *ambivalence* in operation. This is a concept in psychoanalysis based on *otherness* and *difference*. Here the stereotype derives from an underlying fear of the subject which is combined with desire and fascination. For instance, blacks pose a threat to white society, yet within this fear there is a desire and fascination with the physical, textual and sexual physique of the black subject's body.
>
> (Bailey 1988: 36, emphasis in the original)

Some of the pleasures derived by white spectators from the spectacle of black dancing bodies must surely be determined by the conjunction of fear, desire and fascination which Bailey describes. This may also be a factor for black spectators, to the extent that black people internalize negative images of themselves developed within white societies.[9] Limón and Ailey's ethnic or racial backgrounds are relevant to a consideration of representations of masculinity in their choreography. Where postmodern choreographers, including some considered in Chapter 7, have chosen to deal with issues of race and ethnicity, their work constitutes a political intervention within the dominant modes of representations. Such an intervention was inconceivable for choreographers such as Limón and Ailey because of the underlying ideology of modernism within which their work was situated.

It has been argued that, where representations of masculinity are concerned, non-white masculinities appear from a dominant, white point of view to be in touch with 'essential', 'natural' masculinity. These are of a kind with which modern whites of European origin believe them-selves to be out of touch. Representations of non-white masculinity therefore pose a threat to white masculine identity in so far as they highlight the inadequacies of the latter; but, as Bailey points out, they are also a source of desire and fascination. In the following discussion of Ailey's work it is argued that modernism in dance had the effect of limiting the threat while maximizing the desirable and fascinating spectacle of the non-white body.

LIMÓN, MODERNISM AND ETHNICITY

Limón recalls in his autobiography that when he first showed Doris Humphrey his piece *Chaconne* (1942) she commented: 'This is one of the most magnificent dances I have ever seen. It is that for a number of reasons, but chiefly because it is a man dancing' (quoted in Siegel 1987: 210). As one of the principal dancers of the Humphrey–Weidman company during the 1930s and then with his own company from 1947 onwards, Limón was a powerful and handsome dancer. One of his greatest assets as a dancer was his ability to look manly and virile on stage.[10] For this, Limón's Mexican origin must have worked to his advantage: a personal sense of pride derived from his cultural inheritance as a Mexican and as someone of Spanish origin (Pollack 1993: 2).

It is difficult, in the absence of more biographical information, to judge exactly what being American meant to Limón.[11] Barbara Pollack has described the way that Limón's father (who was of Spanish and French origin, his mother being part Spanish and part Indian) brought him up speaking pure Castilian Spanish which accorded the family some status in Mexico (*ibid.*: 4). The family moved to the United States in 1915 when Limón was 7 years old. As a Mexican immigrant living in poorer districts of Arizona and California (*ibid.*: 4–7), he must personally have experienced some racism, and have subsequently been aware of racist attitudes towards others of Mexican origin. He grew up in California and returned there for a few years after he left the Humphrey–Weidman company in 1940. While on the West Coast, he danced with May O'Donnell before returning to New York in the summer of 1942. Limón was thus in San Francisco during the period immediately preceding the so-called Zoot Suit riots of 1943 in Los Angeles between street gangs of Mexican immigrants and white American servicemen. Stuart Cosgrove points out that the zoot-suited *pachuco* youths were second-generation working-class immigrants who were 'stripped of their customs, beliefs and language' (Cosgrove 1989: 7); they thus constituted a disinherited generation within disadvantaged sectors of North American society, and were alienated both from the aspirations of their parents and from the dominant assumptions of the society in which they lived. Drawing on Joan Moore's study of Los Angeles street gangs, Cosgrove distinguishes between machismo and pachuquismo:

The concept of pachuquismo is too readily and unproblematically equated with the better known concept of machismo. Undoubtedly, they share certain ideological traits, not least a swaggering and at times aggressive sense of power and bravado; but the two concepts derive from different sets of social definitions. Whereas machismo can be defined in terms of male power and sexuality, pachuquismo predominantly derives from ethnic, generational and class-based aspirations, and is less evidently a question of gender.

(*ibid.*: 13–14)

It would be ridiculous to try to make some direct connection between Limón and the pachuco gangs. He was not disadvantaged, nor was he ever particularly out of touch with his Mexican roots.[12] By all accounts, far from being swaggering, Limón's dancing was highly lyrical – Humphrey, as we shall see, attributed to Limón's performance of his *Chaconne* (1942) an appearance of authority without boastfulness, of power tempered with intelligence. The roles he created for himself, such as Othello in *The Moor's Pavane* (1949) or Emperor Jones in the dance of that name which he made in 1956, conveyed a sense of tragic nobility. In fact, compared with the *pachuco* gangs, Limón was an example of a successful Mexican American who had kept in touch with his roots. This was doubtless a factor behind tours of the José Limón Dance Company sponsored by the American State Department to Mexico, South America and Europe.[13] According to Pollack,- Limón told South American audiences (speaking in Spanish):

In North America, with all our crudities, we are Americans. We are not afraid to declare ourselves, and have done so in our dance. The academic dance from Europe is not adequate to express what we have to say. Hemingway and Faulkner write in English, but they write as Americans. In the same way, we are trying to find a new language for American dance.

(Pollack 1993: 37)

The difference between Spanish- and English-speaking Americans seems therefore, for Limón, to have been less than the difference between Americans (Northern and Southern) and Europeans. Where there are signs of a certain male superiority and aggressiveness in Limón's roles, these should nevertheless be seen as deriving from Latino cultural traditions, and would have been recognized as such by audiences in the United States and abroad. The 'new language for American dance' which Limón used to create these roles was a modernist one.

One aspect of the modernism of American modern dance was a move away from imagery informed by a particular reference or content that might carry specific social and political meanings, towards the generalized, the universal and the humanistic. A movement towards the exploration of more individualistic, non-specific material would also have been a response to the rise of McCarthyism in the 1940s. We have already seen how Graham moved from her 'American' pieces of the late 1930s and early 1940s to her abstracted 'Greek' pieces and even more abstracted 'celestial acrobat' pieces like *Diversion of Angels*. Limón choreographed abstracted musical visualizations (which recall Humphrey's work) like his *Chaconne* and *Fantasy and Fugue in C minor* (1952) as well as narrative works throughout his career. The latter exhibit a progression that is similar to Graham's. Limón seems to have had left-wing sympathies in the 1930s, for example dancing as a revolutionary in his *Danzas Mexicanas* (1939). From Mexican and American themes in this and works like *Danza de la Muerte* (1938), *Western Folk Suite* (1943) and *La Malinche* (1947), Limón moves gradually towards more universal and humanistic themes,[14] and subsequently to abstracted ones in late works such as *The Winged* (1966) and *The Unsung* (1970/1).

A number of Limón's pieces centre on a conflict between two men. One of Limón's early pieces for the José Limón Dance Company was *La Malinche* (1947) in which he danced the role of a Mexican Indian in a conflict with a European conquistador played by Lucas Hoving. In *The Moor's Pavane*, made later the same year, Hoving played Iago, another European courtier, while Limón danced the role of Othello, the Moor. In both roles Limón was non-European, but whereas he was cast to type as a Mexican in *La Malinche*, he was more universally 'Other' while playing Othello in *The Moor's Pavane*. Later in *The Traitor* (1954), where Limón as Judas comes into conflict with Hoving as Jesus, Limón is not even noticeably black, but even more despised and 'Other'. The move from the specifically Mexican towards a more generalized and universal role is a modernist one. Beatrice Gottlieb, writing in 1951, criticized Limón for his 'limited sense of tragic action [which] reduces drama to a struggle between two people' and which ran the risk of sentimentality (Siegel 1987: 262). The narrative situations that his works explored were not over-complex, with the consequent danger of stereotyping. The danger for Limón of being looked down upon as a Mexican could to some extent be averted through the ideology of modernism: an abstracted, highly expressive modernist dance vocabulary which evoked generalized, universal values.

One aspect, at least, of what Humphrey admired in Limón's dancing was that she felt it expressed universal, modern male values. This is one implication that can be drawn from a passage she wrote about Limón's performance in his *Chaconne*. It comes in her reply to a review by John Martin in the *New York Times*:

I see in the Chaconne implications of what one of the Greek philosophers meant when he said, 'every good citizen should dance

123

in order to understand the State and be a good citizen.' Here are courage, balance in every sense, authority without boastfulness, power tempered with intelligence, the possibilities of the whole mature man brought to a high degree of perfection.[15]

Humphrey's own work often stressed shared, communitarian values, and, where it had any narrative content, the characters or roles were of a generalized, humanistic view of somewhat impersonal 'man' and 'woman' in society. Her vision was not a particularly optimistic one. One motto she adopted from the American Shaker sect (whose rituals she used as a source for her piece *The Shakers* (1931)) was 'Ye shall be saved when ye are shaken free from sin'. One might surmise that, for her, dance was the expression of the individual's best contribution to human society, and modern dance a modern expression of this.

Limón later quoted Humphrey when searching for a definition of the unique power of dance:[16]

The human body is the most powerful expressive medium there is. It is quite possible to hide behind words, or to mask facial expression. It is conceivable that one can dissimulate and deceive with paints, clay, stone, prints, sounds. But the body reveals. Movement and gesture are the oldest language known to man. They are still the most revealing. When you move you stand revealed for what you are.

(Limón 1979: 100)

Limón himself argues in his essay 'The virile dance' (written in 1948)[17] that a man dancing reveals himself for what he is, and thus expresses the 'truth' about masculinity: 'Since dance and gesture were his long before the spoken word, he still has the power to reveal himself more truly in this atavistic language [dance] not only as an individual but also "en masse"' (Limón 1966: 82). What Limón is arguing is not Graham's view that the body cannot lie but the idea that man as a dancer can choose between the good of revealing himself truly and the evil of dissembling through dance. These are the alternatives facing the three Kings that Limón writes about in 'The virile dance'. The biblical King David danced 'a ritual of surpassing purity and power and showed the man as dancer at his most sublime' (*ibid.*: 83). Louis XIV of France danced too, but for Limón this was an arrogant, mincing expression of the cynical, licentiousness of his regime. An (unidentified) twentieth-century European king,[18] who has been deposed and lives out a seedy exile dancing in night clubs in Paris, represents 'the fearful spectacle of a sick world *in extremis*' (*ibid.*: 85). Limón expressed the hope that 'it will be a saner world when the President of the United States, as chief magistrate, will lead the nation in solemn dance on great occasions before the Dome of the Capitol' (*ibid.*: 86). All of this is clearly in line with Humphrey's idea that, as man dances, he expresses his status and maturity as a member of society. Since man, for Limón, has the power to reveal himself truly through dancing, Limón feels affronted by what he perceives as dancing that lies, dissembles and betrays other signs of degeneracy. His conclusion is therefore that there is hope for saneness and propriety only in a modern American setting – before the Capitol, in a dance that presumably expresses the 'truth' about masculinity. Limón himself expressed this 'virile dance' in his most famous role, Othello[19] in *The Moor's Pavane*.

The Moor's Pavane

The Moor's Pavane (1949) is based on the play *Othello*, Shakespeare's plot being reduced to a simple narrative involving the handkerchief which Othello gives to Desdemona. In one duet Iago makes his wife Emilia aware that he wants her to get it for him, and Emilia achieves this when Desdemona drops it during a group sequence. Emilia then teases Iago with it, playing hard to get, and then in turn Iago taunts Othello with it provoking him into killing Desdemona. This last takes place on stage hidden behind Iago's and Emilia's backs, and is followed by a denouement.

The piece starts with a 'pavane'[20] – a formal, centrally focused, symmetrical group section for the four dancers – which evokes an image of flowing, balanced, stately, ideal social relations. The dancers return to this in variations and developments throughout the piece, which, as the narrative tensions increase, gradually degenerates into a tense, anguished ritual. The tempo varies and the initial square floor patterns become increasingly unbalanced, finally veering into a skewed diamond on a steep diagonal out of which Othello and Desdemona break to run wildly around the stage. Thus the unfolding narrative of increasing tension between the community of characters is expressed as much within this group dance as within the duets and mimed sections. Only Othello himself remains stately, ideal and noble throughout the piece, expressing the 'truth' about masculinity, although it leads him to a tragic end.

Shakespeare's Iago is European and, in contrast with Othello's blackness, is probably a blond, blue-eyed white. Limón gives his role a gracefulness of carriage and gesture that hints at the European ballet tradition. Hoving, who created the role, was born and brought up in the Netherlands and had worked with Jooss and Laban before coming to the United States. From Limón's point of view, the role of Iago must have represented the sort of European courtier about whom Limón had expressed such dislike in his essay 'The virile dance'. Iago is light on his feet, and uses his hands and arms precisely extended to make obsequious gestures. He taunts Othello, then steps back, smiling, to watch the result.

By contrast, Othello is much more grounded and weighty in his movements, and his increasing emotional turmoil is conveyed through a repertoire of expressive mannerisms. He grasps a taut fist, then pushes it away from him, turning his fingers outwards into a tortuously twisted shape; he bends over forwards or arches backwards, almost as if he has a terrible pain in the stomach. Othello confronts people eye to eye, pulling their heads towards his own to search their souls. It is through this repertoire of mannerisms that Limón surely believed he was evoking the 'truth' about masculinity. The contrast between Iago's and Othello's gaze thus conveys both gender (active male looking) and notions of honesty and guile.

Lucas Hoving, commenting on the role of Iago, mentioned the possibility that there is a homoerotic motivation behind Iago's hatred of Othello.[21] This suggests the possibility of reading the violence and aggression between this pair of men (and other similar pairs in Limón's *oeuvre*) as an expression of the tensions in male–male relations that result from homophobic conditioning. It was argued in Chapter 1 that homophobia is a mechanism for regulating the behaviour of all men rather than just self-identified homosexuals. Men are in a double bind in that, while they are encouraged to work closely together in the interests of men, there is no clear dividing line between approved forms of male homosocial bonding and expressions of male homosexuality. Iago's relationship with Othello could be seen as an example of this double-bind. As Othello's second-in-command on Cyprus he is in a position in which he has to work as closely as possible with Othello in the interests of maintaining Venetian (patriarchal, Christian) hegemony. But as a white spectator, following David A. Bailey, Iago simultaneously fears and is fascinated by Othello's (black) body. This conclusion can be derived not only from the relationships as mapped out in Shakespeare's play but from key elements within the choreographed encounters Limón devised between Othello and Iago. These can be interpreted as sexual and homoerotic.

Several times Iago comes up behind Othello to whisper in his ear, elegantly placing his hands on Othello's shoulders, and crooking his right leg forwards to partially encircle Othello's body. It is as if he is about to press his body up tightly against Othello from behind. In his combative duets with Othello, Iago is more than once dragged across the stage, lying on Othello's back. On one level Othello's expressed disgust and his rejection of Iago is because of what the latter is telling him (that Desdemona is unfaithful to Othello), but it also surely has to do with the manner in which Iago makes his approach. In the sequence where Iago taunts Othello with Desdemona's handkerchief, Iago gets down on his knees and arches his back as he twice rubs the handkerchief against his own body from his crotch up to his face. Iago is implying that he has had sex with Desdemona and thus that Othello is a cuckold (in Shakespeare's play, he suggests Desdemona has slept with Cassio); but the manner in which Iago conveys this draws Othello's attention to the sexual attractions of Iago's own body. He is thus revealing himself as a (male) erotic object to Othello's (male) gaze, thus evoking the forbidden realm of homosexual sexuality.

What is argued here is not that the suppressed homoeroticism in Limón's *The Moor's Pavane* is an expression of Limón's sexual orientation but that it is conditioned by the problems underlying male–male bonding in a homophobic society. Othello represents an attractive, ideal masculine type, a man's man. But because he is so attractive, this brings up the problem of homophobic constraints on male bonding. What Bristow calls Tarzan's imperative to be a man is an imperative to be heterosexual. Men must violently reject any approach that might be interpreted as homosexual. Thus the two men's relationship in Limón's choreography turns from dignified, ideal bonding into an aggressive, combative and ultimately destructive tie. Othello's problems are further complicated and exacerbated through the sexual connotations of a male dancer's body when he is identified as 'Other'. These sorts of issues would undoubtedly have been unacceptable ones for explicit exploration in cultural products such as dance during the cold war period. It was the universal, humanistic ideologies of modernism that restrained Limón's work from recognizing and dealing with these issues directly, while the aggression in pieces like *The Moor's Pavane* unite Limón's and Graham's male dancers.

ALVIN AILEY AND BLACK MASCULINITY

Alvin Ailey is recognized as a key choreographer in the development of black dance in the United States. At the time of writing, although it is a few years now since Ailey's death, the Alvin Ailey American Dance Theatre is still one of the largest and most successful American dance companies, attracting both black and white audiences.[22] It is generally recognized that Ailey, along with Talley Beatty and Donald McKayle, was responsible for making black modern dance respectable. As Lynne Fauley Emery observed, 'It is [Ailey's] blending of the black heritage with modern dance that results in his greatness' (Emery 1972: 275). White modern dance artists had used black music (for example both Helen Tamiris and, surprisingly, Ted Shawn used negro spirituals), but Ailey integrated modern dance forms with a black thematic.

Joseph Mazo likened Ailey's popular manner of presentation to that of Ted Shawn:

> In some ways Ailey is a throwback to Denishawn with its direct chor-
> eographic style, its emphasis on theatrical presentation, and its amal-
> gam of dances drawn from the various traditions of the world. The

naive muscularity of the dances Shawn made for his all male company is sometimes echoed in the exuberant athleticism of Ailey's work.

(Mazo 1978: 8)

Mazo's use of the word 'various' is, however, a pointer to some key differences between Shawn and Ailey. Shawn, as we have seen, drew on a variety of dance styles and traditions, mostly from Eastern Asia and from Europe, none of which had any direct connection with his identity as a white, Anglo-Saxon American. Ailey, however, drew on a range of traditions all of which related to his black identity – styles ranging from Africa and the Caribbean to the black American vernacular. It is these, as Emery observed, that he combined with modern American dance.

Ailey, like Graham and Limón, can be seen to have moved from the culturally specific towards a more generalized, modernist stance. His first piece, *Blues Suite* (1958), for his newly founded Alvin Ailey American Dance Company, took as its starting point his memories of black people in the Brazos Valley in California where Ailey had lived until the age of 11. Two years later with *Revelations* (1960) Ailey explored the more generalized subject of religious faith and communal spirit found in black Baptist rituals. Ailey's later pieces to music by Duke Ellington – such as *Night Creature* (1974) – are more generalized again, evoking celestial jazzy acrobats. Underlying the direction Ailey's work took was a belief in an integrationist politics. In the 1970s he told Joseph Mazo:

> I wanted my dancers to feel that they were not just 'black dancers', that they were part of society. There was one white girl with us on the tour in 1962 [of south-east Asia], but I discovered as we travelled through Asia that there were blues in all cultures, and that there were spirituals in all cultures, and that the people of any culture can express them. I got a lot of flack about it during the 1960s, but I think that an integrated company enlarges the statement I've been trying to make.
>
> (1978: 13)

Whether or not he actually held this position throughout his career, what concerns us here is not Ailey's politics but the ideologies of modernism within which his work was situated. The modernist emphasis on the generalized and universal ('there are blues in all cultures') precluded any exploration of the critical potential of oppositional black cultural experiences. It has already been argued that where representations of masculinity are concerned, non-white masculinities appear from a dominant, white point of view to be in touch with 'essential', 'natural' masculinity. These are of a kind with which modern whites of European origin generally believe themselves to be out of touch. Representations of black masculinity, therefore, pose a threat to white male identity, in so far as they highlight the inadequacies of the latter; but, as Bailey points out, they are also a source of desire and fascination.

Most of the choreography Ailey created for male dancers fits into the sorts of representations of masculinity that have already been discussed in this chapter. The male dancers' bodies are shown off in the trio 'Sinner man' in *Revelation* in a similar way to the male display dances which Graham made in her Greek pieces. Some of the more celebratory sections in Ailey's works contain passages for dancers that could be compared to Graham's passages for what she called 'celestial acrobats', though Ailey's choreography is more balletic (with high extensions and pirouettes) and jazzy (with fluid and rhythmic movements of the pelvis). Ailey worked on his early *Blues Suite* (1958) after working with Anna Sokolow, from whom he said he had learned 'how to go inside one's self for themes' (quoted in Mazo 1978: 11). In key roles in this piece, it could be said that Ailey, like Limón, seems to be trying to express the 'truth' about masculinity in dance. But the main difference between Ailey's choreography for male dancers and that of these other choreographers is the meanings his work derives from the fact that his dancers are (predominantly) black.

Where Ailey's work deals with themes or imagery that are specifically to do with black experience (and least reducible to a notional universal experience) it is potentially at its most threatening to the dominant white point of view. The function of stereotype is to defuse the threat posed by the threatening 'Other'. Because of Ailey's adherence to popular modes of theatrical and choreographic discourse, the representations of black people that he made are in danger of tending towards the stereotypical. The popular is a source of pleasure because it is familiar. Stereotypes are also familiar and may be pleasurable for some spectators. They may not even necessarily be recognized as stereotypes by members of the oppressed group in question. In what areas, then, are representations of masculinity in Ailey's work in danger of being read in relation to stereotypes?

Most of Ailey's choreography falls into two broad categories: either his dancers present a jazzy spectacle of their joy in dancing, or they make a sincere expression of emotions that often refer to religious experiences. Representations of masculinity in the former type of dance piece are in particular danger of being read as stereotypes. As Aschenbrenner points out, white reviewers (and by implication the dominant white male point of view) have come to expect black male dancers to be highly energetic in performance and display a supposedly innate sense of rhythm. The high kicks and balletic pirouettes of Ailey's jazzy celestial acrobats can thus be seen to conform to popular, conservative notions of a high-quality dance product, without the dancers gaining recognition for their achievement in attaining desired qualities. This sort of dancing can, however, be appreciated in a different way from a black point of view. First, the jazzy spectacle is a popular, positive and to a certain extent exemplary black image. Second, modern dance, like athletics and boxing, has been one of the acknowledged avenues through which young black men of working-class origin can gain recognition and develop a career.[23] And even if they don't, dancing in black venues to the latest in black music has, for most of this century, been an outlet for the expression of black identity, equally for Malcolm X and his contemporaries in Harlem during the early 1940s as for young black men 'vogue' dancing in Britain in the 1990s.[24] This is the *mise en scène* for several of Ailey's pieces including *Blues Suite*, *The Mooch* (1974), and *For 'Bird' – With Love* (1984).

Where work is rooted in specifically black experience, its consequent authenticity might give it a power and directness that overrides or dispels the stereotype. But even where Ailey can be seen to be trying to express black experience and create representations of masculinity that are meaningful to black audiences, white definitions of dance aesthetic, of gender and of 'Otherness' intervene. The stereotype condemns the black male dancer to be seen as a body and as the objectification of black male sexuality and virility – the source of thrills and fears to which David A. Bailey refers. Two of the male roles in *Blues Suite* offer a useful example of the way the dominant white point of view affects the way representations in this dance can be read.

Blues Suite

In his first piece, *Blues Suite*, Alvin Ailey drew on his childhood memories of night life in the Honky Tonk saloons of Brazos Valley in California. Joseph Mazo describes the suite's central theme as 'the dragging routine of a small town, with no work and no place to go' (1978: 39). 'Backwater blues', the central duet[25] of *Blues Suite*, explores a tense, teasing relationship between a stud, whose bare torso gleams behind his open black leather waistcoat,[26] and his lady in high heels and wearing a feather boa, who, as the piece opens, is posed half way up a ladder. When she comes down, the spectator might expect an imperceptible transition into partnered dancing; but instead the song comes to an end, and in the ensuing awkward silence the woman glares at the man and gives him the cold shoulder. 'Backwater blues' plays with the expectation that the couple will execute a culminating sequence of ever higher and more technically demanding lifts. This is what the stud clearly wants to happen. Because his desire coincides with that of the spectator, the structure of the piece invites, if not compels, the audience to gaze from a male point of view. One might almost say they become accomplices in rape, when he more or less forces her to dance with him in a duet full of showy and precarious lifts.

Steve Neale's observation (in Chapter 3) that women are a problem and a mystery certainly applies to 'Backwater blues'. The stud, as bearer of the audience's gaze, clearly cannot understand what she wants, or at least why she doesn't want him. As a man there is no mystery about him, though. His movements and the gestures through which he expresses his self-confident manner – his swaggering walk and the dismissive shrugs with which he responds to each rejection – are open, large, unambiguous. But when the audience look at him, testing him and challenging him to prove himself, they are also objectifying the 'Otherness' of his race and colour.

This is a key to understanding the stud's macho behaviour. All he has of value is his body and his sexuality. Robert Staples (1982) describes black macho behaviour as the destructive passing on by a poor black of the negative image of himself which society succeeds in making him internal-ize. The only way he has of establishing his value is through projecting his negative image of himself onto others more abject than himself, in this case the black woman on the ladder, and by behaving in an oppressive way towards her. By 'putting her down', he further reinforces the abject, oppressed status they both share as blacks.

'Backwater blues' contains wonderful roles that are a gift for the right performers. But however well or badly these are performed, the roles themselves are trapped within stereotypical conventions which reinforce the terms of their own oppression. The stud is responding, as Bristow puts it, to the sexual imperative to be a man, by asserting that he is a belatedly Darwinian being whose sexual passion knows no reason. Where a white dancer asserts that his sexual passion knows no reason, he is implying that white men have not entirely lost touch with their essential, 'primitive' biological nature. But where a black dancer evokes the same imagery, there is a danger that he will merely reinforce the racist stereotype of blacks as an archaic link in the evolutionary chain, and over-sexed to boot.

Another aspect of this negative image is represented in the misfit or loser in the final section of *Blues Suite*. When he is first introduced, this character is a clown-like figure. While everyone else is 'getting down' with a partner in a dance that seems to be degenerating into a sexual romp, the misfit is on his own, and his attempts to join in are repulsed with increasing finality. By the end, sitting cut off from the rest of the dancers, he is an abject wreck: his shoulders twitch up and down like someone who is suffering a nervous breakdown. When one of the women notices this and lays a friendly arm on his shoulder, he reacts as if she has given him an electric shock, recoiling away from her in a paranoid manner. The misfit and the stud are opposite faces of the same coin. Both characters are driven, in their different ways, by the same sexual imperative to prove themselves as men. Ailey, however, shows us that, largely because of their blackness, the imperative is so absolute and extreme that they cannot possibly achieve anything through responding to it.

Although Ailey's work does not avoid or question stereotypes, it is in moments like these that the terms of the underlying racist oppression are revealed. But such moments are rare. More often Ailey presented dancing roles that were celebratory, presenting the spectacle of dance for dance's sake. In the later *For 'Bird' – With Love*, Ailey depicted another misfit in the role of Charlie Parker. The movement style of the dancer playing Parker at times verges on the twitchy, abject quality of the misfit in *Blues Suite*. But the overall impression of the piece is one of celebration, as Ailey dazzles us with sequined show girls and smooth male dancers who execute high stepping, jazzy routines. To celebrate and to harrow don't go well together.

Ailey, like Shawn, attempted to find common ground between his own minority position as a black and those of dominant, white interests. Such value-free common ground never exists, although the ideologies of modernism must have seemed to Ailey to offer that possibility. Ailey tried to work within the conventions and traditions of modernist dance, substituting his own point of view for the dominant one. Because he trusted in the supposed universality of these conventions, he didn't block the possibility that his representations of black experience could be viewed in a negative, stereotypical way.

MODERNISM AND THE UNIVERSAL MALE

The simple conclusion to be drawn from this discussion is that Ailey, Graham, Limón and Shawn all produced representations of masculinity that conformed to prevalent, conservative notions of masculinity. In Shawn's case it has been suggested that this may to some extent have been intentional. The others, however, might well have denied the existence of any grounds for such an accusation. They subscribed to modernist views about the nature of art which posited the universality of modernist expression.

To reiterate what has been argued in Chapter 2, the widely held view of modernist dance as a purist move towards increasing abstraction – dance about nothing other than dance movement itself – is an inadequate one. All the works by Ailey, Graham and Limón discussed in this chapter are modernist in their concern with exploring the expressive potential of movement as a medium. Yet all involve a degree of characterization and narrative. All three choreographers, in their different ways, were involved in a modernist rejection of the narrative and mimetic conventions of earlier ballet and theatre dance. Their work constituted a search for new forms through which to express modernity, through which to express the experience of modern life and particularly a supposedly universal metropolitan experience. Thus representations of masculinity in modern American dance came to stand for the universal in American men. The male modern dancer as a belatedly Darwinian being expressed a political imperative to be a man, an imperative that was socially and politically specific but nevertheless unvaryingly heterosexual. This male, humanist modernism had particular meanings in relation to American expansionism commercially and politically on the international scene.

The ways in which this modern masculinity was expressed are different in Graham's and Limón's work. In the Humphrey/Limón tradition, the overall pattern of the choreography was used to express the communal and the social. The pavane movement material in *The Moor's Pavane* is shared by both male and female dancers and gender differences are not specifically signified through particular steps and patterns at this level. Gender is signified instead through the way the individual interpreted the material in the dance as a whole, through use of weight and expansiveness and in details of the choreography like Iago and Othello's masculine, active gaze and the gestures that signify their masculine aggression. In Graham's work, these levels and vocabularies are more integrated into the movement material itself. Her male and female roles differ radically at the level of steps and movement patterns, as well as looks and gestures. What unites male roles in the work of Ailey, Graham and Limón is the use of highly expressive movement and gesture and their aggression through which these choreographers each, in their different ways, believed 'truths' could be communicated. In the 1950s all three produced highly individualistic performances so that their male roles were in line with contemporary notions of ruggedly virile American culture.

This 'modern dance' of course now looks outmoded. Some of the highly expressive movement material, through which it is suggested Limón tried to express the 'truth' about masculinity, probably now looks rather overdone. Jill Johnston's verdict in 1960 on Limón's *The Traitor* (1954) is apposite here. She complains that some of the more tortured passages are 'like bagsful of hot air': 'This is modern dance at its rhetorical worst. A few well-known movements from a personal style are contrived to "express" a profound emotion' (Johnston 1992: 34). As Marcia Siegel suggests, Graham's male dancers of the late 1940s and 1950s may now look pompous and grotesque. If these dancers' *oeuvres* now look to some people rather clichéd, it is not just because of changes in style and taste, but because both 'truth' and masculinity now seem problematic concepts. The idea of being able to define absolute truths appears inconceivable when we now, as Janet Wolff points out, see all knowledge as socially and historically situated and therefore partial (Wolff 1990: 89). As has already been discussed in Chapter 1, a crucial consequence of seeing identity as socially constructed is that we have become aware of the partial and problematic nature of concepts such as gender and race. The monolithic masculinity, which the male American modern dancer signified, was in effect a denial of the possibility of a plethora of possible masculine identities, differing in relation to class, race, sexuality and so on. To be fair, Ailey, Graham and Limón did not altogether set out to speak the truth about this universal masculinity but to give expression to the truth of their individual experiences of gender and gendered relationships. It was the ideology of modernism that encouraged them to set this in universal terms. It was then the differences between this putative universality and the reality of their individual experiences that gave rise to some of the more intriguing passages in their work.

6

AVANT-GARDE
STRATEGIES

Merce Cunningham, and in the next generation Steve Paxton, Trisha Brown, Yvonne Rainer and other dancers in the Judson Group, between them brought about influential cross-overs between the practices of American choreographers and avant-garde traditions and strategies current in the New York art world community during the 1950s and 1960s. The avant-garde ways in which these choreographers have attacked and subverted conventional expectations of dance structure and aesthetics can be described as 'practices of negation'. This is a term which Tim Clark has coined to describe such avant-garde strategies in the visual arts. In avant-garde painting, Clark argues, these are forms of decisive innovation, in method or material or imagery,

> whereby a previously established set of skills or frame of reference – skills and references which up until then had been taken as essential to art-making of any seriousness – are deliberately avoided or travestied, in such a way as to imply that only *by* such incompetence or obscurity will genuine picturing be done.
>
> (Clark in Frascina 1985: 55 note, emphasis in the original)

By using such strategies to disrupt or destabilize the conventions and traditions of mainstream modern dance and ballet, Brown, Cunningham and Paxton opened up the idea of what constitutes choreography in ways that have made possible the development of the eclectic, pluralist and postmodern work of the 1980s and 1990s.

The example of the work of Cunningham and the development of contact improvisation by Paxton were two of the most significant influences on the way masculinity has been represented by postmodern American choreographers in the late 1970s and 1980s. To look at Brown's, Cunningham's and Paxton's work in terms of the use of avant-garde strategies is a useful way of considering representations of gender in their work.[1]

Cunningham was closely associated with the composer John Cage, and the painters Jasper Johns and Robert Rauschenberg. Cage first met the veteran French avant-garde artist Marcel Duchamp in 1942 and by the 1960s Cage, Cunningham and Johns were close friends with Duchamp. This connection was primarily responsible for continuities in a number of different areas between the New York avant-garde and earlier European developments. As Yvonne Rainer put it in 1981, Cunningham and Cage

> succeeded in opening a veritable Pandora's Box, an act that launched in due course a thousand dancers', composers', writers', and performance artists' ships, to say nothing of the swarms of salubriously nasty ideas it loosed upon an increasingly general populace, ideas which are even apparent today in fluxus-like punk performances.
>
> (Rainer 1981: 66)

Paxton was a member of Cunningham's company in the early 1960s and, along with Brown and Rainer, attended Robert Dunn's composition classes in Cunningham's studios; these were based largely on Cage's ideas. Most of the dancers involved in these classes went on to organize performances at the Judson Church where dancers and visual artists involved in happenings put on performances. During the 1960s Paxton was involved not only in dance work but also in cross-over types of events with Rauschenberg and Alex Hay. In the 1970s and 1980s Brown has worked with Rauschenberg and other leading avant-garde or minimalist artists.

This then is the context of the work discussed below which is being seen as avant-garde. Where questions of gender representation are concerned, what advantage is there in seeing the work of these dancers as avant-garde rather than modernist? The French Utopian Socialist thinker Saint-Simon's first connection of the term avant-garde with the arts in 1825 is a useful starting point: 'It is we artists who will serve you as avant-garde . . . the power of the arts is in fact most immediate and most rapid; when we wish to spread new ideas among men, we inscribe them on marble or on canvas' (quoted in Nochlin 1991: 2). Peter Bürger, in his *Theory of the Avant-garde* (1984), has distinguished between the authentic historical avant-garde, which questions art's institutional status, and modernist art, which asserts its own autonomy and formal, aesthetic concerns. One aspect of institutionalized art is surely the way it reinforces dominant norms of sexual difference. Since the advent of the women's movement there has been a groundswell of opinion in favour of greater equality between the sexes, so that, given Saint-Simon's view of the connection between 'advanced' art and political ideas, one would expect these opinions to be supported by the artistic avant-garde. To what extent, therefore, are there differences between the ways in which gender has been represented in, on the one hand, the works of Brown, Cunningham and Paxton and dancers performing contact improvisation, and on the other hand in mainstream theatre dance during the same period? Can these differences be attributed to avant-garde strategies, and with what consequences in terms of their influence on subsequent dance?

Brown has mostly worked with an all-female company, so that the way she created material in the early 1980s for male dancers can only have had any influence from that time. Her piece *Set and Reset* (1983) is discussed at the end of this chapter as a counter-example to the way masculinity has been represented in contact improvisation. Where Cunningham's and Paxton's work is concerned, the usual argument is that, in different ways, there is a certain blurring of the conventional differences between what male and female dancers can do on stage, arising from each choreographer's own, very different commitments to the discovery of new possibilities of movement. The claim made for contact improvisation is that it is an egalitarian form that allows women to lift women or men with comparative ease, and that in contact dance men often dance without embarrassment with other men (Novack 1990: 168). How true this has proved in practice is examined below.

In Cunningham's case, it could be said that he, more or less, pioneered the presentation of what might be termed unisex choreography – theatre dance in which, superficially at least, differences between male and female dancers are not especially important to the sorts of formal, aesthetic qualities presented in dance material. On the evidence of the many public or printed interviews that Cunningham has given about his work, one can assume that he would not consider questions relating to his dancers' gender to be relevant to an appreciation of his work. He has tended, over the years, not to give a direct answer to questions about meaning in his work, preferring to talk about the formal properties in his choreography instead. This shouldn't necessarily be taken to mean that the issue of gender is irrelevant to him as an artist. The assumption which this chapter makes is that the issue is a relevant one. What Cunningham's work means to Cunningham himself and a handful of his close friends who are artistic associates – the late John Cage, Robert Rauschenberg and Jasper Johns – is private, and is not revealed to audiences of his work. The stated view is that there are no right or wrong ways of looking at his work: it is up to spectators to devise their own. 'There are no symbols, relax and enjoy', Cunningham says at the end of a short talk about his work during the 1976 film *Event for Television*.[2] It is nevertheless a legitimate line of inquiry to consider what sorts of representations of masculinity are created in Cunningham's work and, in particular, how his presence as a performer can be seen to contradict and subvert the mythology associated with the male artist's body. It is this revisionist view of Cunningham's work which is considered in the first part of this chapter. The next section of the chapter looks at representations of gender in the choreography of Steve Paxton and in contact improvisation. The argument put forward here is that Paxton's own work develops the contradictory and subversive manner of representing masculinity that is latent in Cunningham's work. When contact improvisation is looked at, however, much more conservative and Romantic representations of masculinity are often found which can sometimes be the antithesis of the example of Paxton's own practice. The chapter concludes by looking briefly at Trisha Brown's *Set and Reset* (1983). Through avant-garde compositional practices and through the use of experimental approaches to movement that are parallel to Paxton's interests, Brown choreographed material for male dancers in this piece that create the sorts of dynamic and expansive qualities generally associated with bravura male dancing ways. But, it is argued, the male body is revealed in *Set and Reset* in such a way as to subvert, denaturalize and destabilize the meanings such movement qualities generally signify.

MERCE CUNNINGHAM

Jill Johnston, reviewing Cunningham's *Roaratorio* (1983), challenged the opinion that Cunningham has questioned and reacted against, or subverted, most aspects of the nineteenth-century ballet tradition. Within the deep, or a priori, structure of his pieces, she argues, Cunningham has not questioned traditional ways in which gender is represented, while younger choreographers (Johnston mentions David Gordon, Mark Morris, Steve Paxton, Lucinda Childs) have done so. The way she states her case deserves to be quoted at length.

> Most apparent, and most boring, in the range of male/female breaching in his work is the traditional lift. *Roaratorio*, with its extensive social partnering, has more than the full complement of lifts to be expected in a Cunningham dance. Again, he inherits this convention from the ballet, yet generally the way his men lift or carry or place or drag his women is much more like a vestigial echo of ballet than anything resembling the no-nonsense support of the ballerina for the purpose of exposing her line and 'sex' and sweeping her through pedestals in the air. Although Cunningham's manipulations of women are comparatively matter-of-fact, frequently like an afterthought, *en passant* really, they still appear to affirm, if only perfunctorily, the assumed dependency, weakness, helplessness, etc., of women. Certainly his women remain armless this way, except in the conventional decorative sense. But Cunningham would no doubt say that lifting is, simply, along with leaps, jumps, turns, etc., part of the raw material of his medium, something that bodies can do on stage, and to which he can apply his chance operations, obtaining the most interesting variations in rhythm and sequence.
>
> (1987: 105)

Johnston here is arguing along the lines discussed in Chapter 3 concerning the male gaze. A little context about Cunningham's practice is necessary here. Where Johnston observes that *Roaratorio* presents rather more traditional ballet lifts than are usually found in Cunningham's work, one might add that this is partly a consequence of the fact that, increasingly in the late 1970s and 1980s, Cunningham has used ballet-trained dancers, which had not been the case earlier. In the 1950s and 1960s, he was approximately the same age as the dancers in his company, and danced as much, and in more or less the same way, as them; at that time, there was in each dancer's movement style more individuality, quirkiness and often a somewhat ironic or disrespectful attitude in relation to the polished presentation of academic dance steps; and the way lifts were used in partnering was more unconventional than later. This quirky, unacademic style is clearly no longer there in his later company.

In an earlier work like *Septet* (1953) there are definitely fewer lifts, and women are not as conventionally partnered as Johnston says they are in *Roaratorio*. If one applies to *Septet* the sort of rough test that Sarah Rubidge suggested concerning signs of dominance and equality (see Chapter 3) it doesn't come off too badly: men don't always initiate lifts and, for example, women sometimes purposely hang from their male partner; there is an appearance of co-operation in lifts that to some extent detracts from the way women who are being lifted appear passive, dependent and objectified.[3] As far as the relationship between the spectator's gaze and that of the dancers is concerned, again *Septet* varies considerably from traditional conventions: throughout the piece, dancers' gaze, like dancers' use of space, is highly erratic and unpredictable. In a way now recognized as typical of a Cunningham dancer (Novack 1990: 132–7) they almost appear to be purposely ignoring the audience. The penultimate section of *Septet* (originally titled 'In the distance') is for one man – initially Cunningham – and three women dancers: together they slowly present a series of extremely beautiful shapes with linked or touching arms, while all direct their eyes laterally, either towards the floor or up into the wings. In a few instances in *Septet* dancers look directly at the audience. The duet in the third section starts with the 'ballerina' – initially Carolyn Brown – facing the audience with her arms out sideways, and her partner lifts her by placing a hand under each armpit. She is carried towards the audience and stares directly at them with a gaze that is reminiscent of that of some of the painter Manet's models – in *Olympia* (1863) or *The Bar at the Folies-Bergères* (1881–2). As in Manet's paintings the 'ballerina's' open gaze disrupts and challenges the audience's gaze. When Johnston argues that Cunningham has done nothing to question traditional ways in which gender is represented, the evidence of *Septet* suggests that, in the 1950s, this was not altogether the case. It is nevertheless true that he has not consciously chosen to break up the conventions of partnering in the sorts of ways that the younger choreographers Johnston mentions have done (see below and Chapter 7).

An important part of what Johnston is saying is that she is disappointed by Cunningham, as if he has broken faith with the avant-garde through not questioning the gender-given aspects of his practice. Can work truly be avant-garde if it leaves such an important area untouched? In the light of the discussion of the avant-garde above, one could argue about whether or not Cunningham's avant-gardism has turned into high modernism, or whether he has become institutionalized.[4] But this isn't particularly productive in advancing our understanding of the very influential ways of representing gender in dance which Cunningham has developed. It is difficult not to accept the justice of Johnston's criticism of the way women are lifted in works like *Roaratorio*. Johnston is surely also correct in her suggestion that Cunningham would answer a question about the way he uses lifts without mentioning sexual politics. But, rather than attempting to defend Cunningham against Johnston's charges, what is suggested below is that there is a sexual politics implicit in the way he has developed his role as a (male) artist both off and on stage.

Modernism and mastery

In the last chapter a particular kind of heroic image of the male dancer has been identified within modern dance in the United States. Underlying this image was a rhetoric of male creativity, not only in the work of the modern dancers but also, as Christine Battersby (see Chapter 1) has argued, the work of the writers and painters who were in fashion in the 1950s (1989: 40–44). This was the time when Merce Cunningham and his close artistic associates John Cage, Jasper Johns and Robert Rauschenberg (the four of them are referred to in the following as Cage and friends) were developing their own artistic identities. When one considers the neutral stance which Cage and friends adopted in relation to content and expressiveness, the possibility emerges that this was a reaction against the fashionable, virile creativity of the time. Cage and friends, in rejecting the expressionism of modern artists such as Jackson Pollock, Willem De Kooning and modern dance artists such as Martha Graham, Erick Hawkins or José Limón, can be seen to reject the idea of interpreting strong, powerful and energetic gestures as an expression of personal and psychological concerns.

At that time, it was generally thought that the (male) artist's body was an important expressed content in the work of modern painters. Harold Rosenberg proposed, in an influential article in 1952, that a work by an abstract expressionist painter was not a picture of something but the record of an event in which the painter engaged in an encounter or skirmish with the canvas, which retained an impression of the artist's body. 'He went up to it with material in his hand to do something to that other piece of material in front of him' (Rosenberg 1968: 569). This is surely a description of 'a man having to do what a man's gotta do'. The paint marks showed the male energy with which the artist engaged in the encounter.

Certain works by Cage and friends can be seen as a subversive comment on these tendencies in the work of their predecessors; for example Rauschenberg's *Erased De Kooning Drawing* (1953), Jasper Johns's *Scent* (1973–4) (referring to an earlier painting by Pollock of the same name) or Cunningham's parody of the style of Martha Graham in the 'Bacchus and cohorts' section of *Antic Meet* (1958).

In erasing the drawing by De Kooning, Rauschenberg was erasing the expressionistic marks which, in Rosenberg's view, could be interpreted as signs of the (male) artist's physical engagement with his medium. The surface of the paper, after Rauschenberg had worked at it, still showed signs of De Kooning's gestures and of Rauschenberg's actions in rubbing them out; the piece, however, is no longer read as a direct expression of a heroic struggle but can only be understood in the context of Rauschenberg's conceptual project. It is still a work by a male artist (or two male artists) but stripped of those signs which are conventionally read as signifying manly physical struggle.[5]

Tim Clark has argued that Jackson Pollock's drip paintings are

clearly implicated in a whole informing metaphorics of masculinity: the very concepts that seem immediately to apply to them – space, scale, action, trace, energy, 'organic intensity', being 'IN the painting', being 'One' – are all, among other things, operators of sexual difference.

(Clark 1990: 229)

He goes on to suggest that Pollock wanted his viewers to see the encounter involved in making the drip paintings, and appreciate the physical powers he had at his command, seeing them as part of being a man. The concepts which Clark picks out recall Battersby's description of the Romantic (male) genius battling against nature (see Chapter 1), and it fits in with Rosenberg's definition of modernist practice advanced earlier. Thus the male modernist artist engages in an organic struggle to create a whole, a oneness, through his mastery of a sublime and terrifying (male) nature. Relevant here are Martin Pumphrey's observations about the violence associated with masculinity in some cultural forms (see Chapter 1). Men, he suggests, do not recognize that what is wrong with modernity might have anything to do with the internal contradictions of contemporary masculine identities. Instead the ills of modernity are projected on to something outside, against which men contend. Signs of struggle and violence in the work of an artist like Limón or Pollock could be seen as an example of this sort of psychological projection. Their violence is directed against an externalization of contemporary ills and represents an attempt to master them. As artists they violently master and control their material.

It is precisely a rejection of this sort of mastery which characterizes one of the most commented-upon aspects of Cunningham's choreographic process – his use of chance procedures. Cunningham's refusal to master his material in this way but to accept uncontrolled occurrences is an implicit rejection of a Romantic view of the male artist's role.

Cunningham's use of chance is a key instance of the problematic relationship between avant-garde strategies and the masculine authority inherent in the role of the artist. Cunningham may say 'relax and enjoy' but this is somewhat disingenuous. The decentred ways in which dancers in his choreography are distributed across the stage, and the abrupt discontinuities or overlaps between different dancers' material generally put individual spectators in the position of consciously deciding what and how to watch, rather than leaning back and passively letting it wash over them. This is an avant-garde approach to aesthetic appreciation and one which goes against the grain of a traditional Kantian view of aesthetics. The spectator of a ballet by Balanchine or Petipa may indeed relax and enjoy, confident that the choreography has been consciously fashioned by the artist, and that it contains a formal arrangement that is aesthetically pleasing. Cunningham and Cage's use of chance challenges and disrupts this view of art. This is precisely what Marcel Duchamp was doing when he exhibited his first 'ready made' *Bottle Rack*, in 1914. The *Bottle Rack* had not been fashioned by the artist and was not intended to be an aesthetically pleasing arrangement. It only became art if and when a spectator consciously looked at it. Duchamp proposed this view of appreciation in a lecture in 1957, *The Creative Act* (Duchamp 1973). It is in this way that, as Bürger suggested, avant-garde art questions the status of art, using what Clark calls practices of negation.

However, Cunningham's use of chance procedures in his choreography cannot altogether match up with Duchamp's 'ready mades'. The 'ready mades' were everyday objects which in themselves challenged conventional expectations of what art should be. Cunningham's use of a ballet-derived movement vocabulary did not challenge these expectations in the same way, unlike a piece that included 'everyday' movement – such as the walking in Steve Paxton's *Satisfyin' Lover* (1967) considered below. Furthermore, although he uses chance, Cunningham has always kept control of his material. Yvonne Rainer (1981) has criticized John Cage for retaining on a conceptual level a god-like position as creator in control of his material. The same observation might be made about Cunningham.

Having made these qualifications, the argument still stands that the sorts of power involved in Cunningham's position as choreographer are qualitatively different from those exercised by the artists of what Battersby has called the Virility School of creativity. Cunningham's role as author and creator conditions the spectator's response to Cunningham's appearance on stage within his own work. The ways in which Cunningham has, over the years, exploited this to disrupt conventional expectations is considered shortly.

Modernism and the Cold War

While it is usually presumed that the work of Cage and friends doesn't deal in private meanings, Fred Orton (1988) has suggested that these artists have developed a range of concerns and themes which remain private. Cage and friends, he argues, outwardly cultivate a carefully managed indifference towards personal and psychologically charged material with which the earlier 'modern' artists dealt, developing instead an artistic style of ironic detachment. Orton argues that Jasper Johns uses a variety of clever, formalistic devices in his work which:

> attract the attention, and distract the enquiring mind. They seem to hide the subject, give the explainer something to find, and keep explanations cutaneous. Johns's surfaces play hide and seek, impose and simultaneously resist interpretation in terms of subject.
>
> (1988: 9)

This could be applied equally to the way Cunningham offers his interviewers detailed explanations of the systems and random processes which he uses within the choreographic process. As Carolyn Brown, who was a leading member of the Merce Cunningham Dance Company from 1953 to 1972, has observed:

> Perhaps Merce feels that his dances need have no meaning for anyone but him; certainly he has taken precautions to see that little of it is intelligible to an outsider, or even for that matter to an insider. But he does leave clues.
>
> (Brown 1975: 25)

Orton argues that Cage and friends' evasion of questions about meaning can in part be seen as a response to the social and political climate in the United States during the early 1950s, the period when these artists established their artistic philosophy. As was noted in the last chapter, it was at this time that abstract expressionism was taken up as an important element in the way the United States presented itself internationally. It was cast in the role of the 'free', progressive and above all modern art of the 'free world' in contrast to socialist realism, the politically restrained and old-fashioned representational art advocated by the Communist Party. As Serge Gilbaut has observed,

> In the process though, modern art, in order to be acceptable to the U.S. for strategic reasons, had to lose its negative, traditionally oppositional edge and be somewhat toned down, so as to be able to

enter into the international arena as a positive alternative to Communist Culture.

(Gilbaut 1990b: 36)

Domestically, this was accompanied by a pervasive climate of oppression – this was the so-called McCarthy period. As well as investigating communism, the House Un-American Activities Committee persecuted homosexuals. Cage himself, the artists Rauschenberg, Johns, Warhol and Duchamp – all of whom were involved in designing sets for Cunningham's work – as well as the poet and museum curator Frank O'Hara who was also a close friend and associate, were all gay. Various writers have connected the repressive atmosphere during the Cold War period to the development of individual artistic practices (Roth 1977; Craven 1985; Orton 1988). Roth points out that Johns painted his first American flag in 1954 in the year following the trial and execution of the Rosenbergs, and she questions Johns's claim that the flag was merely inspired by a dream (1977: 51). The flag was, according to critical orthodoxy, an unimpeachably modernist work – flat, avant-garde, self-referential – and it would have been hard to accuse Johns of being un-American for painting an American flag.[6] Orton argues that Johns, in opting for the flag, and the artistic direction it suggested, withdrew for the rest of the 1950s 'from the dangers – real or imagined – of self exposure' (1988: 13).

Johns had destroyed all his paintings prior to 1954. According to Carolyn Brown, Cunningham stopped, around this time, giving information about any personal meanings his work might have had; he asked that information about meanings in his earlier work be taken out of an article being written by Remy Charlip (a member of his company) for *Dance* magazine in January 1954 (Vaughan *et al*. 1987: 28). In both cases the artists are hiding things about what their works mean to them. Their personal reasons for doing this were surely influenced by the the climate of domestic repression, and the manner in which abstract expressionism was appropriated as the 'modern American' art form. Johns's and Cunningham's resulting public stances, their aesthetic of indifference as Roth has called it, might therefore be seen as part of a strategy by these artists to survive the McCarthy period with their personal integrity intact.

Imagery in the work of Johns and Cunningham

Johns himself has more recently been willing to discuss this indifferent stance, and it is noticeable that during the 1980s the personal meanings and concerns in his work have been more openly discussed. Interviewed in 1978 by Peter Fuller, Johns said:

> In my early work I tried to hide my personality, my psychological state, my emotions. This was partly due to my feelings about myself

144

and partly due to my feelings about painting at the time. I sort of stuck to my guns for a while but eventually it seemed like a losing battle. Finally one must simply drop the reserve. I think some of the changes in my work relate to that.

(Fuller 1978: 7)

Cunningham too has dropped his reserve a little:

I have many references, many images, so in that sense I have no images. Because I could just as well substitute one image for another, in the Joycean sense of there being not *a* symbol but multiple [symbols] – one thing can build on another, or you can suddenly have something – the same thing – being something else. . . . That seems to me the way life is anyway.

(quoted in Dalva 1992: 181, emphasis in original)

One of the few cases where there are clues to the meanings of images in Cunningham's work is *Septet* (1953). This is performed to the seven piano pieces of Satie's *Trois morceau en forme de poire* (1903). When *Septet* was initially performed each of the seven sections had a title: these were (in order) 'In the garden', 'In the music hall', 'In the tea house', 'In the playground', 'In the morgue', 'In the distance', 'In the end'.[7] These suggest some sort of narrative, and Carolyn Brown suggests that this was indeed the case (Vaughan *et al.* 1990: 28). A programme note for 1950s perform- ances reads: 'The poetic ambiguity of the music and dance titles express the character of this ballet, the subject of which is Eros, and the occurrence of which is at the intersection of joy and sorrow' (quoted in Siegel 1979: 325). When one looks at the piece itself, the way signs of sorrow relate to signs of joy is surely an instance of Cunningham's stated interest in the Joycean way one image can change into another. In his book *Changes* (1968), Cunningham wrote of *Septet*: 'What makes a movement at one moment grave, and the same at the next, humorous?'[8] One obvious moment in *Septet* where this idea is explored is in Cunningham's solo in the second section, 'In the music hall'. At more than one moment in this, he brings his hands up in front of him to hide his face, then suddenly whisks them up and away to reveal a clown-like facial expression, his mouth pursed in a big 'O'.

Cunningham is presenting emotions as arbitrary and conventional signs. As such he is contradicting the idea that emotional expression in dance is an eruption of underlying psychological pressures. This is, of course, the idea of theatre underlying not only the modern dance of Graham and Limón but also the direction in which some choreographers like MacMillan have developed ballet. In *Septet*, Cunningham danced a role that slips between joy and sorrow, Eros (love) and Thanatos (death). Two moments in the piece which surely refer to death are the endings of

145

the last two sections. At the end of the penultimate section 'In the distance', Cunningham, having danced with three women, leads them off diagonally, backwards towards the wings. Cunningham is at the head of the procession. Two of the women, side by side, each hold one of his hands and with their other hand hold the hand of the third woman who brings up the rear. With slow, unison steps which he initiates, they are pulled away.[9] As the curtain comes down on the final section 'In the end', Cunningham is again leading someone away: this time it is one woman (Viola Farber in the original production) who walks backwards with her back arched and her head leaning right back. Her arms are stretched out and Cunningham seems to be pushing her. In both cases he is surely Death leading them out of life.

There are two other cases where imagery in Cunningham's choreography tangentially signifies death. The first example is in *Antic Meet*. During this there is a section which parodies Graham's style and contains a reference to the death of Jocasta in Graham's *Night Journey*.[10] It comes at the end of the sequence where Cunningham is struggling to put on a four-armed, but neckless, jumper. He eventually knots two sleeves together and pulls them tight, letting his head lean sideways. Given the context of other references to Graham in this section, this image is clearly intended to be recognized as Graham's image of Jocasta hanging herself with a rope. The other case is *Second Hand* (1970). According to Carolyn Brown, this piece, which was performed to Cage's piano version of Erik Satie's *Socrate*,[11] actually acts out parts of the story of the death of Socrates. One would never guess this, of course, from what Cunningham told Jacqueline Lesschaeve about *Second Hand*:

> In the final movement, 'Mort de Socrate', in an attempt to keep the space from being static, I decided to choreograph it in such a way that the dancers would have made a complete circle by the end of the piece. I began the movement standing alone at the back of the stage, and the dancers gradually entered and throughout the dance we make this spiralling circle before the final exit of the dancers leaving me on the stage alone.
>
> (Lesschaeve 1985: 89)

Brown, however, reveals: 'It was about Socrates's death, and it was very clear. It was very moving and very touching – the gestures that we all make towards Socrates at the end, dying in the back – it's all there' (Vaughan *et al.* 1990: 28). Cunningham described for Lesschaeve a complex system through which dancers determine when to perform a sequence of hand and finger movements during this section (Lesschaeve 1985: 87). On one level these must signify Socrates' friends waving farewell.

Brown tells the following story. During the final rehearsal of the middle section of *Second Hand*, which was a duet for Cunningham and herself, she was startled by Cunningham's anguished facial expression. Concerned that he might have strained himself or be ill, she mentioned it afterwards to John Cage. Next day Cage told her Cunningham had said that at that moment in the duet, Socrates is preparing to meet death (Brown 1975: 25). Note that Cunningham didn't tell her directly. The middle section of Satie's *Socrate* is a Platonic dialogue between Socrates and Phaedrus. So, Brown concludes, 'the duet is not actually a duet of male and female; it should be a duet with two males' (Vaughan *et al.* 1990: 28)

The first section of *Second Hand* is a solo which Cunningham revived from his 1944 piece *Idyllic Song* which was set to the first section of Satie's *Socrate*. In *Socrate* the first section is a dialogue between Socrates and Alcibiades from Plato's *Symposium* and is thus about sexual love. So, like *Septet*, *Second Hand* deals with imagery or material associated with both love and death. This is not expressed in a mawkish or sentimental way. Carolyn Brown and Stephen Smoliar both described *Second Hand* as Cunningham's most programmatic work (Smoliar 1992: 87–8; Brown 1975: 25). Cunningham's choreographic procedures ensure the removal of sentiment.

One can point to the presence of these sorts of images in some of Cunningham's work, but what they really mean to Cunningham and his closest associates remains a matter of speculation. What can be stated, however, is the method through which these images signify. Fred Orton has argued that the images in Johns's paintings do not signify through the use of metaphors but through metonymy. Similarly in Cunningham's case, the references to love and death are not metaphoric but metonymic. In Nelson Goodman's account (see Chapter 2), a metaphor links qualities of the thing itself to other qualities in the thing with which it is being associated. In 'a frosty reception' the quality of an individual's manner is linked to sub-zero temperatures. In *The Moor's Pavane* (see Chapter 5) the material where the group dance together in the pavane functions as a metaphor for the social relations of the group. Orton applies the idea of metonymy to the chains of association that he uncovers in Johns's images. A metonymic image is one that refers to something else by way of a code. Thus 'Downing Street refused to comment' can be understood if one knows that the British Prime Minister and her or his officials are based in Downing Street, London. The spiralling circle that Cunningham created in the last section of *Second Hand* and the sequence of hand and finger movements the dancers perform do not metaphorically express the grief of Socrates' friends saying farewell. The dance material only signifies 'farewell' if you know Satie's *Socrate* and thus realize what is happening at this moment.[12] Images co-exist together with other levels of material. The dance is the dance movement itself and is not a metaphor or symbol for something else; but there is a level on which chains of associations allow private, metonymic meanings to be detected.

It has been argued that the expressionist struggle of many modern

147

American artists in the 1950s metaphorically signified masculinity and that Cunningham has always refused such signs of mastery. It is proposed instead that masculinity is signified metonymically in his work. More or less throughout his career, Cunningham has been a dominating presence on stage with his company. Both the critics and his dancers have described instances when he has completely upstaged the latter.[13] Invariably he does not in fact do this by being more energetic or dynamic or stronger than them, or by dancing material which covers space in a more commanding way – the ways in which, it has been argued, masculinity is conventionally signified in western theatre dance; instead he commands attention through his quality of attention and the clarity with which he executes his material. To command attention on stage signifies leadership and is a masculine characteristic, but the qualities through which Cunningham achieves this are not ones which can be metaphorically connected with masculinity. In fact Cunningham's stage presence, particularly in his idiosyncratic solos, can be comic, disconcerting or even disturbing.[14] As he has commented in a much-quoted remark, 'I think dance only comes alive when it gets awkward again' (Brown 1975: 26; Johnston 1971: 151). One source of awkwardness is his refusal to use the conventional metaphoric signs of masculinity to mediate his presence as a man on the dance stage.

STEVE PAXTON

Steve Paxton has taken Cunningham's use of avant-garde strategies much further in terms of researching new possibilities of dance movement. Paxton's own dancing invariably presents unconventional uses of the body which challenge the spectator to reassess aspects of masculine identity and experience that are generally denied or rendered invisible in mainstream cultural forms. Contact improvisation is a separate and distinct movement form initially developed by Paxton which developed logically from Paxton's earlier performance work. Contact dance has, in some ways, expanded the ways in which the male dancer can appear on stage, but the male contact dancer can sometimes appear strong, dynamic, powerful and controlling – qualities that support, and conform to, conservative notions of masculine identity. The case of contact improvisation is a useful example of the uneasy relationship between radical social and aesthetic ideas.

Contact improvisation, which developed in the 1970s, is, as Cynthia Novack (1990) has shown, imbued with and informed by non-hierarchical structures. Paxton's interest in such structures can be traced back to earlier stages in his artistic development. Egalitarian concerns can be clearly recognized in two features of Paxton's pieces during the 1960s: non-hierarchical ways of structuring group works, and the use of everyday or pedestrian movements – walking, standing still, sitting down, smiling, etc.

– which any able person can do. For example, Paxton's *Satisfyin' Lover* (1967) is a piece for a large number of performers (anything from thirty to eighty-four) who just walk one by one or in groups from one side of the performance space then off the other in a prearranged sequence (for score see Banes 1980: 71–4). Jill Johnston, in a 1968 review of a performance of Paxton's work, pointed to his interest in using an 'incredible assortment of bodies, the any old bodies of our any old lives'. She goes on:

> And here they all were in this concert in the last dance, thirty-two any old wonderful people in *Satisfyin' Lover* walking one after the other across the gymnasium in their any old clothes. The fat, the skinny, the medium, the slouched and the slumped, the straight and tall, the bowlegged and knock-kneed, the awkward, the elegant, the coarse, the delicate, the pregnant, the virginal, the you name it, by implication every postural possibility in the postural spectrum, that's you and me in all our ordinary everyday who cares postural splendour.
>
> (1971: 137)

It may be stating the obvious but the sorts of movement skills demanded by this sort of piece do not, in themselves, depend upon, or draw any particular attention to, the differences between the male and female performers. One might call it an example of unisex anti-choreography. Paxton therefore, like Cunningham, could be said to be aiming at making choreography in which sexual difference is not important or significant.

Paxton's own performance of his work, like Cunningham's own personal solos, can be seen to use avant-garde devices that, in effect, avoid or reject the ways in which masculinity is conventionally represented. An early example that illustrates this is *Flat* (1964). In this Paxton walked in a rectangular path around the performance space, occasionally stopping or sitting down (mimed – without a chair). After doing this for a while he took off an item of clothing, hanging it on one of three hooks attached to his chest with surgical tape. The walking then continued for a while before another item was removed, and the piece proceeded in this way until Paxton was dressed only in his underpants (see Banes 1987). *Flat*, by revealing the male body as something to hang clothes on, dismantled, more radically than Cunningham, the metaphysical meanings associated with the male dancer's solo. The slow pace, the lack of any development, climactic or otherwise, the lack of any physical tension or excitement in his everyday movements, Paxton's dead-pan facial expressions – all of these can be seen as the antithesis of the bravura male solo. In *Flat*, as in many of his later solos, such as the series of improvisations he called *Dancing* (1973 on) and *Goldberg Variations* (1986), Paxton has continued to produce work which consistently dodges or defuses expectations of masculine display. Paxton's refusal to acknowledge the challenge of the spectators' gaze to prove himself as a man (see Chapter 3), opens up the

Figure 8 Steve Paxton's solos have consistently dodged or defused expectations
of masculine display.
(Photo: Ray Abbott)

possibility of male dancers exploring a greater range of movement qualities; this expanded range is precisely what contact improvisation has offered.

Contact improvisation is a duet form where two partners improvise and explore movement that arises from contact with each other. It often involves doing things like leaning and giving weight, lifting and carrying or maybe wrestling, giving in to the floor and gravity. A frequently used starting point for contact is standing.[15] Paxton points out that, when standing 'still', relaxing all the voluntary muscles which can be used to assume and maintain a particular posture, one finds that one's skeletal muscles, which are not voluntary, continue to hold one upright. Even in this state one can sense tiny adjustments in one's posture that come with the flow of breath and in order to allow blood to circulate. One is not strictly speaking standing still, and Paxton calls this the 'Small dance' (1977: 3). A common way of starting to do contact in classes is to lean over and rest the top of your head against the top of your partner's head while standing still. By placing yourself in contact with a partner in this way you can feel a small dance develop between the two of you, as you let these tiny movements develop into an improvised duet.

There are some ways in which the movement skills and qualities involved in contact derive from forms and practices that are generally associated with masculine rather than feminine behaviour. Paxton has been interested in the martial art Aikido, and suggests that what he learned in Aikido had unconsciously been used in developing contact. He commented that:

> Contact improvisation resembles Aikido quite a lot, in that they are both partnering forms and are both concerned with a very light and appropriate use of energy in fairly dangerous situations, one an act of aggression and the other an act of dance. They both rely on training or manipulating the instinctual reactions in some ways.
>
> (1982: 13)

As well as physical dangers and risks, there are also aesthetic ones involved in improvisation. As Paxton has observed, Cage and Cunningham's use of chance procedures avoids aesthetic risks: 'chance and indeterminacy allow the aesthetic pratfall wide berth' (Paxton 1972: 133). The contacter however risks pratfalls. But both physical and aesthetic risks, when taken by a male dancer, can be read as part of what Tim Clark calls an informing metaphorics of masculinity. What is at issue here is not aesthetics but representation, and how the sorts of movement involved in contact dance create social meanings.

In an interview in 1977, Paxton says he found, in his 1960s pedestrian pieces, that standing still was not really, in its pure state, an everyday activity like walking or sitting, because 'it's rarely done in its pure state

... walking and sitting are more common' (1977: 6); so common that, Paxton goes on to say, the body's potential is under-used by people living western urban or suburban lifestyles.

> Watching the body for a long time, mainly in New York where I lived, and seeing the city life, seeing the many, many people sit, and watch television, and go to bed. They have two positions: they get up and walk a little bit, then they sit on their transportation to the office, where they sit all day.
>
> (1982: 13)

Paxton suggests that this way of living uses one per cent of our potential, whereas, the more the body is employed, and trained, and becomes strong, 'the better adjusted you are to what is occurring on all levels' (*ibid.*).

Contact therefore develops from a critique of the stale inertia of urban lifestyles and, by implication, the industrial capitalist system that those who live like this service. Members of the emergent political counter-culture of the 1970s would doubtless have agreed with this. This counter-culture can be broadly characterized as a series of loose alliances, or shared concerns and responses to ecological issues, passivism and non-violent protest, gay politics, feminism and new age mysticism, along with beliefs in the efficacy of consciousness-raising, therapy, and meditation. Common to most of the counter-cultural groupings was a commitment to personal change summed up in the slogan 'the personal is political' and leading to exploration of consciousness-raising in groups. Contact dance and other related forms of movement research were sometimes explored as a means towards consciousness-raising. There are examples of such uses of contact improvisation by groups of men in Britain in the late 1970s.[16] One aspect of the counter-culture in Britain was the formation of men's groups and the men against sexism movement. For the men involved in these men's groups, part of the process of change, and of taking on board the sorts of criticisms being made of them by feminists, could include working on the body through the sorts of work being developed in new dance. Dance workshops did sometimes occur during men's anti-sexist events and meetings. A report in the British men's movement magazine *Achilles Heel* number 2 on the Men's Week at Laurieston Hall[17] lists activities that include discussion groups on sexuality, gayness, patriarchy, splitting up when you have children, anti-semitism, racism and sexism. There were also workshops in dance, Arica (*sic*) exercises, movement and contact dance, a massage workshop, a therapy group involving primal therapy, co-counselling and group bio-energetic work (Weld 1979: 30–1). The radical nature of contact improvisation matched the radical aspirations of such groups.

Cynthia Novack records that, in the United States, contact was used and practised during the 1970s in contexts where it mediated extremely diverse interests and concerns (1990: 78 and *passim*). The fact that Paxton, in a newsletter in 1975, spoke out against incorporating symbolism, mysticism, psychology and spiritualism in the teaching of contact (*ibid*.: 81–2) testifies to the fact that contact was being used by people involved in therapy and encounter groups and 'new age'-type mysticism. Paxton went on to comment that 'personally I think we underestimate the extent of the "real"' (*ibid*.: 82), a sentiment with which Cage and friends might not have disagreed.

Contact acquired its aesthetic radicalism from Paxton and the avant-garde dance and art tradition. This radicalism must be seen as simultaneously making possible the mediation of counter-cultural values while at the same time limiting and redefining them. As Novack shows, those involved in contact often argue that the form allows more egalitarian representations of gender compared with other styles of theatre dance. She argues that contact redefines women's strength capacities and possibilities, and offers men opportunities to be physically close to both men and women without being thought to be confrontational or sexual. Contact dance makes representations that are socially expressive: women performing contact dance together, or a woman lifting a man in a contact duet, might be seen as an image which subverts and dismantles traditional images of women dancers. A female dancer, by performing moves that demand a use of energy generally considered to be masculine – such as the sort of strength and energy needed to perform contact lifts – can get to be 'one of the boys'. Nancy Stark Smith seems to be acknowledging this when, reminiscing about the early days of contact improvisation, she comments on the difference between 'the jocks' and the softness of dancers with a background in Mary Fulkerson's releasing work: 'the jocks, and I guess I was one of them, . . . were out there rolling around and crashing about' (Novack 1990: 64). For women to do this may destabilize and denaturalize certain assumptions about images of women in dance. It is positive for women to have the opportunities to do activities traditionally thought of as male – for example to earn a living in 'male' jobs such as driving heavy goods vehicles or building work. Contact improvisation enables women to do some of the sorts of strong and risky movements generally associated with male dance. The same argument cannot be applied to men dancing contact. There is nothing subversive about men appearing strong and assertive (though the men and women in both cases might appear to be 'being themselves', which, in the context of consciousness-raising and therapy groups, was valued).

What then is positive about men dancing with other men? Through unconventional uses of the body, the spectacle of a man and a women or two men dancing in contact may in some cases challenge the spectator to reassess aspects of masculine identity and experience that are generally denied or rendered invisible in mainstream cultural forms – softness, non-

153

competitiveness, responsiveness, caring. This can in some contexts de-naturalize the dominance implicit in the male dancer's presence. There have been instances where male dancers have used movement related to or derived from contact to explore issues relating to gender and sexuality – for example Mangrove and Men Working.[18] The way contact impro-visation brings men into close proximity with each other goes against social convention. Chodorow and Theweleit (in Chapters 1 and 3) have both pointed to the significance of tight bodily boundaries in the psycho-logical construction of male identity. Contact is a way in which men can develop a more relaxed awareness of the boundaries of their bodies, through flowing in and out of contact with another male body. For two men to exhibit such a free attitude towards bodily intimacy in performance might make them look vulnerable. In terms of social convention, this kind of physical proximity between two men would ordinarily be interpreted as either sexual or confrontational – getting 'too' close may trigger off homophobic fears. The aesthetic radicalism of contact improvisation, however, allows such interpretations to be suspended. For example, Danny Lepkoff has said that, when doing contact improvisation, he enjoys 'being able to dance with men without being homosexual or even dealing with that issue at all' (Novack 1990: 171–2). This may be fine from a therapeutic point of view, but not 'dealing with that issue' implies not thinking about sexual politics in performance. 'Being oneself' regardless of gender, as some contacters have suggested the form allows, may mean having no sexual politics. The problem is that libertarian and egalitarian ideologies are not necessarily feminist ones. Without a sexual politics, there is no method of ensuring that brave new ways of dancing are necessarily any better, in a political sense, than the bad old ones.

Contact improvisation, through its emphasis on individualism and self-expression, can fall back on traditional notions of artistic genius, and very traditional representations of masculinity can sometimes be found in some risky or organic performances of contact improvisation. Organic and 'natural' qualities in the performance of contact improvisation have sometimes been informed by holistic or 'new age'-type counter-cultural values. Where a male contact dancer creates, through his improvisation, a sense of organic oneness within what would otherwise be disparate elements, he is being in control and mastering his material; in Clark's terms these attributes are implicated in an informing metaphorics of masculinity. It is noticeable that Paxton in his own performances has tended to avoid these sorts of organic and holistic qualities. The influence of contact in postmodern choreography of the 1980s and 1990s has been largely to reintroduce a risky and/or organic male style of dancing.[19] Some choreo-graphers have set contact movements for performance. Here the risks are, generally, of a spectacular kind rather than coming from the fact of their being improvised and risking, as Paxton put it, the aesthetic pratfall.

Contact, in these cases, is used not as a means of finding new and previously unknown ways of moving, but as another style with which a choreographer can create effects.

SET AND RESET

There was one moment in Trisha Brown's *Set and Reset*, beautifully caught in a photograph by Jack Mitchell, where Stephen Petronio and Randy Warshaw jump powerfully into the air and Petronio catches Warshaw. Both are barefoot and are bare from the waist: all they are wearing are semi-transparent, loose silk trousers printed with collaged imagery designed by Robert Rauschenberg. Warshaw has taken a running jump and Petronio catches him by curling his hand and arm around Warshaw's stomach and smoothly diverting the direction in which Warshaw's jump was taking him. It is a very dynamic and exciting image in which both dancers are moving with a level of energy that is comparable to that of a male bravura ballet solo. Their bare upper bodies reveal their strong, muscular male bodies in a way that recalls Shawn's male dancers, or even those of Graham and Ailey, although the basis for the movement in *Set and Reset* is rather different, being similar to contact improvisation. What stops this spectacular image from being an assertion of male dominance is the way this one brief moment fits into the piece as a whole.

Petronio and Warshaw had both studied contact improvisation and were members of the improvisational dance company Channel Z. Improvisation has played an important role in Brown's development. Although she has never actually studied contact improvisation, she had a close working relationship with Paxton, improvising with him as early as 1963 in *Lightfall* and was subsequently, along with Paxton, a founder member of the dance improvisation company Grand Union in the early 1970s around the time Paxton was developing contact. Paxton even danced in some performances of Brown's *Line-Up* (1977). *Set and Reset* was not, however, improvised but, as its name implies, carefully structured.

Brown and many of the dancers in her company in the early 1980s practised the Alexander Technique; this is not a dance technique but a method of improving bodily alignment through working to free inhibiting muscular tensions in order to gain a more stress-free, 'natural' posture. Brown herself described her approach to movement in the late 1970s and early 1980s as making 'animal dance' in comparison with the highly intellectual, conceptual structures she had employed in choreographing pieces during the 1970s.

Set and Reset presents a seemingly continuous flow of lyrical dance movements that have the sort of fresh, impulsive and spontaneous quality that is generally found only in improvised dance. There is a clear structure to the piece: dancers explore the periphery of the performance space and

Figure 9 When Stephen Petronio catches Randy Warshaw during Trisha Brown's
Set and Reset (1983), it seems quite unpremeditated.
(Photo: Jack Mitchell)

continually come into the middle to engage in duets and trios. There are many instances in the piece, as Henry Sayre points out, when dancers come 'in and out of sync with one another, forming duets and dissolving them, or of dancers following the gestures of another, "resetting" them, across the space of the stage' (1992: 144). Dancers also define, with their hands, arms and legs, an imaginary wall across the middle of the stage 're-establishing and dis-establishing the line'.[20] This line then reforms in the centre of the space and wheels around its middle so that everyone in the auditorium gets to see it end on. A generalized overall structure is thus created through the distribution of movements all over space: this is done in a way that is initially not centrally focused, but then, as the central line rotates, the central focus is projected to every possible viewing position in the auditorium. It is the antithesis of the balanced, symmetrical groupings found in, for example, the ballets of Petipa. Furthermore the piece avoids any sense of development or climax through its almost minimalist uni-formity of incident and through its continuous, fast, strong but free pace.

The dancers in *Set and Reset* seemingly ignore the audience and adopt a neutral gaze. They appear to be concentrating on the physical sensations involved in executing the choreography, as Cunningham's dancers can also appear to do, although they occasionally smile to one another in passing – it is a piece they evidently enjoy performing. Petronio and Warshaw are both facing away from each other at the moment they make contact. Neither is looking actively outwards or upwards (in what Dyer calls an elevated way). Petronio, in Mitchell's photograph, is looking down while Warshaw's gaze is horizontal. When Petronio catches Warshaw, the act seems quite unpremeditated. It is not a climactic moment; and indeed as has already been stated there are no climaxes in the piece. In this event, as elsewhere, in the piece Brown makes full use of the strength and dynamism these two male dancers possess. There are few lifts as such in *Set and Reset* but several instances where dancers catch others who jump or dive into their arms. The men do perhaps more than their fair share of this and are themselves caught a few times. But their powerful contribu-tions are redistributed into the texture of the piece as a whole, through the way dancers' gaze is contained, and through the other formal devices with which Brown creates an overall, decentralized structure. In effect, she destabilizes the power implicit in male display by absorbing it into a collective whole.

UNISEX LEGACIES

Despite their neutral stance towards gender, a real blurring of masculinity and femininity rarely if ever occurs either in the work of Cunningham or within contact improvisation. Male dancers rarely take on movement qualities and conventions that are in the range associated with feminine behaviour. Female dancers, however, get to dance material or movement qualities conventionally associated with masculinity. Carolyn Brown suggested that the duet in *Second Hand* was not actually a duet of a male and a female but a duet with two males. Nancy Stark Smith talked about being 'one of the jocks'. Despite claims about their radicalism, contact improvisation and Cunningham's work has done more to reinforce dominant norms of masculinity that it has to dismantle or undermine them. Nor do either offer much by way of a positive alternative for women.

What is found in both Cunningham's work and in contact dance is an attempt to ignore the differences between male and female dancers. Masculinity is not itself questioned but taken as axiomatic, an unproblematic norm. Women thus get to be 'normal' rather than the mysterious, problematic, feminine. As Johnston's review of *Roaratorio* shows, this attempt fails because the power implicit in a male presence on the dance stage is problematic and will not just go away when it is ignored. It will continually reassert itself, unless or until a conscious attempt is made to dismantle it or absorb and redirect it as in *Set and Reset*. Aesthetic radicalism on its own does not necessarily guarantee this. In his own work, Steve Paxton is far more radical in the way he deals with gender than Cunningham is; but when one looks narrowly at the ways in which masculinity is represented in other dancers' use of contact improvisation and compares it with the 'awkward' way masculinity is represented in Cunningham's personal solos, Cunningham denaturalizes the conventions through which masculinity is represented more successfully than do most contact dancers. The neutral aesthetic disposition, which is contact improvisation's legacy from Cunningham and Paxton, does not itself denaturalize and destabilize dominant notions of gender and masculinity, although some dancers have used it in ways which are subversive and deconstructive of the traditions and conventions through which masculinity is constructed. If in the 1990s women are also dancing with a new kind of energy and aggression, a cynic might say that all this does is reinforce ways in which masculinity constitutes a norm. The search for new possibilities of movement, in which Cunningham and Paxton are involved, has not in itself brought about a situation in which the normality of the movement qualities traditionally associated with masculinity are questioned. If Brown's search, in works like *Set and Reset*, has lead to a different conclusion, this is because, rather than trying to ignore the differences between male and female dancers, she has acknowledged and made use of these differences, thus allowing spectators the possibility of enjoying the spectacle of male dancing bodies.

7

POST MEN

This chapter looks at radical, new ways of representing masculinity in experimental, new, progressive – call it what you will – theatre dance of the 1980s and 1990s. What radically separates these new representations of masculinity from those discussed in the previous three chapters is the strategic stance the new works take up in relation to mainstream theatre dance. The debates about the nature of gender, ethnicity and sexuality that were started by feminists and black and gay activists in the 1960s and 1970s have informed the work of the younger generation of dance makers. Particularly influential have been new theories about the relationship between cultural forms and the construction of identities.

I have so far avoided calling all this new dance work postmodern. Yvonne Rainer has suggested that Cunningham and Cage put together an act that 'launched in due course a thousand dancers', composers', writers' and performance artists' ships' (Rainer 1981: 66). In retrospect this act pointed the performing arts in the direction of postmodernism (although, as was argued in the previous chapter, Cunningham and Cage's own work can also be usefully thought of as avant-garde). The label 'postmodern' is becoming less and less useful as a descriptive term as time passes. It is confusing to use the same word to cover the dance work produced by Paxton, Rainer and their colleagues in New York in the early 1960s and the progressive, experimental American and European dance of the 1970s, 1980s and 1990s. Then there is the question of how to relate post-modernism in dance to uses of the term in relation to other cultural forms and in critical theory. A plethora of competing and sometimes conflicting definitions of postmodernity, postmodernism and postmodern culture have been put forward, together with a riotous proliferation of books and articles on these subjects.

The social and political background to all this has been one of a shift to the right: Jean-François Lyotard in 1984 called it a period of slackening 'when a worried public opinion encourages authority to a politics of totalitarian surveillance' (1984: 72). Patrick Kelly and Otis Stuart, writing in *Dance Magazine* about new male American choreographers, commented that the 1980s had opened with the onset of the AIDS threat and concluded with the election of a former CIA Director to the White House (1989: 34–8). Old-fashioned Marxist academics like Fredric Jameson have seen in the new pluralist philosophies of postmodernism a danger of collusion with the interests of capitalism.

Noticeably absent from most of the literature on postmodernism, particularly that written in the late 1970s and early 1980s, is any discussion about gender representation.[1] Much of the writing about postmodernism in the visual arts has been concerned with the return of figurative expressionist painting, almost entirely by male artists, prompting Sarah Kent to write:

> Postmodern painting is often referred to as post-political. One might equally name it as post-moral, post-idealist or retrovisionary. It is a form of mourning for lost power, lost belief and lost confidence, in which actual significance is replaced by over-blown self-importance, inflated scale and hysterical bombast. It is a masculine artform – a witness to the crumbling of certainty.
>
> (1984: 61)

Some feminist writers have suggested that the areas of concern addressed within postmodern theory are a distraction from the important questions still unanswered about how women's experiences can be represented in cultural forms. Janet Wolff, for example, has argued that 'the radical relativism and skepticism of much postmodern thought is misplaced, unjustified, and incompatible with feminist (and indeed any radical) politics' (1990: 99). But she also cautiously suggests that the deconstructive strategies of postmodern cultural practice – re-appropriating and sub-verting imagery, self-reflexivity, decentring the subject, consciousness of, and attention to, the medium itself, use of new media and so on – are invaluable to feminists, 'and a realistic politics for artists is one that judges the availability and effectivity of particular strategies in the moment' (1990: 8).

Deconstruction is a way of reading or criticizing a text or a theoretical concept which reveals inconsistencies and discontinuities that normally remain invisible. As Christopher Norris has put it,

> Deconstruction is the vigilant seeking-out of those 'aporias', blind-spots or moments of self-contradiction where a text involuntarily betrays a tension between rhetoric and logic, between what it manifestly *means to say* and what it is nonetheless *constrained to mean*.
>
> (1982: 19, emphasis in original)

Masculinity as a socially constructed identity is, it has been argued, full of contradictions and discontinuities. A deconstructive reading of repres-entations of masculinity in a text is one that seeks out and makes evident the self-contradictions within it which are a sign of institutionalized defences: these, it has been argued, are the ways in which men repress strongly experienced developmental conflicts.[2] Wolff is suggesting, above, that radical artists can use deconstructive strategies within their work to destabilize and denaturalize the way gender is represented in mainstream cultural forms. Given that one development in the new dance of the 1980s was a return to representation (in reaction against the formalist abstraction of high modernism), how then have deconstructive strategies informed the making of representations of masculinity in recent progressive theatre dance?

Progress or change in theatre dance (as in all cultural forms) is not just a matter of a unilateral decision by the artist to change forms or conventions but a process of finding ways of making the spectator see differently. Sometimes this means making the spectator aware of the fact that what she or he has taken for granted – what has seemed normal or natural – is actually manufactured and contingent. Dance artists who are not white, male, heterosexual or privileged have to make representations differently in order to express their point of view, their sense of identity or their cultural values in theatre dance. In order to make the spectator see gender, race, sexuality or other components of identity differently, it is necessary to deconstruct those conventions and traditions which, in their effects, maintain these dance artists' marginal and oppressed status.

Norris suggests also that deconstructive strategies reveal a tension between the rhetoric of a work – what it means to say – and the logical meaning that is signified by the signs that make up the work. Some recent dance seems almost purposely to exaggerate these sorts of tensions through ambiguous uses of representation. In some works nothing has a straightforward meaning: it is as if meanings are disavowed or put in inverted commas. One example of this approach has been described by Fredric Jameson in his discussion of postmodern pastiche:

> Pastiche is, like parody, the imitation of a peculiar or unique style, the wearing of a stylistic mask, speech in a dead language: but it is a neutral practice of mimicry, without parody's ulterior motive, without the satirical impulse, without laughter, without that still latent feeling that there exists something *normal* compared to which what is being imitated is rather comic. Pastiche is blank parody, parody that has lost its sense of humour.
>
> (1985: 114)

Within the context of the essay, Jameson seems to have meant to criticize the use of pastiche in postmodern culture: consequently he doesn't consider the possibility that its use might constitute an implicit criticism of the subject or style being imitated. But to imply that the subject of the imitation was not *normal* in the first place is to destabilize and denaturalize it.

161

Judith Butler (1990) has suggested that the artificiality of the way masculinity or femininity is portrayed in the work of some female and gay male artists – the element of masquerade or pastiche – challenges the idea that gendered identities in western society are any more than a necessary fiction determined by the conventions and traditions of mainstream cultural forms. In Norris's terms, the masquerade or pastiche refers logically to masculine or feminine identity and is constrained to do so by mainstream conventions; but the spectator is aware of inconsistencies between this and what it manifestly *means to say* – that what should appear 'normal' nevertheless seems nothing of the kind. Think for example of the little-girl look of the female dancers in Anne Teresa de Keersmaeker's company Rosas or the besuited respectability of some of the men in Pina Bausch's work (both discussed later in this chapter). De Keersmaeker and Bausch surely do not intend these to be interpreted straightforwardly as positive role models. Some critics question whether the presentation of these depressing images actually provokes what they perceive to be the necessary critical response. Such a humanistic and moralistic approach misses the ways in which strategic uses of textual ambiguities and tensions constitute a radical, destabilizing intervention within mainstream norms and conventions. As Wolff argues, however, an endless process of decon-struction leads towards a radical relativism, and what use would any resulting dispersed and fragmented politics be? The only political use deconstructive strategies have is to create a space within which to make visible and representable what has remained invisible and unrepre-sentable within patriarchal culture.

What is being described here is a guerrilla warfare conducted by those who recognize the strategic value of being on the margins. Work which mobilizes such strategies 'bears witness' as Lyotard puts it 'to the un-presentable' (1984: 82), showing the spectator that which is rendered invisible by the institutionalized defences of the dominant male point of view. In previous chapters examples have been given of the ways in which women's images of men and gay men's images of men are generally deformed by mainstream conventions. The discussion of Ailey's work suggests that similar difficulties surround the creation of black men's images of blackness that are different from white stereotypes of blacks. What this chapter focuses on is the work of those choreographers who, since the late 1970s and 1980s, have sought to undermine the dominant ways in which gender has been and still goes on being represented in that massive and repressive order – the mainstream institutionalized dance and ballet companies.

It should be borne in mind that far more people go to performances of mainstream work than go to see new and experimental works, and that the resources available to the choreographers discussed in this chapter are, in nearly all cases, minute in comparison to the scale of those available to choreographers working within institutionalized companies. Artistic guerrilla warfare against the mainstream therefore not only entails opposition on a theoretical level but is also experienced materially. But working outside the constraining obligations of tradition allows the radical choreographer to respond to changing norms of gendered behaviour with a freedom that is manifestly missing within the mainstream.

In previous chapters, the exploration of different approaches to representing masculinity in dance has been focused on discussions of a restricted number of different choreographers' work. It has never been the intention to present a general survey in this book. However, in looking at developments in more recent work a slightly wider selection is called for, including examples of British, continental European and American pieces. While most of the examples considered were made between the mid-1980s and the early 1990s, the first and last pieces looked at are by two dancers from an older generation – Fergus Early and Pina Bausch – who it is argued, each in very different ways, caught on to aspects of how to break the rules about images of men a lot earlier than most other dance artists. This chapter considers first different ways of challenging, disrupting or dismantling the mainstream conventions by looking at the varying means through which masculinity is represented in the work of Fergus Early, Lea Anderson and Ralph Lemon, whose work in different ways seems to focus particularly on issues to do with masculinity and whose approach is clearly informed by feminism and critical theory. It then examines how the male dancer's body has been presented, contrary to convention, as the object of either female or male desire within recent uses of partnering and the duet form. Finally it considers what happens when images of masculinity are pushed to the limits, through Michael Clark's and Mark Morris's manipulations of style and parody, and finally in the abject and horrifying representations of masculinity in Pina Bausch's *Bluebeard* and DV8's *Dead Dreams of Monochrome Men*.

SEEING MASCULINITY DIFFERENTLY

Perhaps the key element of the 'alternative' or deconstructive practices of this new European and North American dance is a new politics of the body which radically challenges the traditional ways in which dance movement creates meanings. New representations of masculinity assert the physicality of the masculine body in ways that have the potential to make visible repressed aspects of the construction of masculine identity. On a private level, to uncover and become aware of repressed conflicts might be therapeutic, but to do so within a performance can have the effect of subverting norms and changing attitudes. Strategies for doing this can be identified both on the levels at which narrative, spoken texts, visual images, etc. challenge the spectators to reassess their idea of what constitutes theatre dance, and on the level at which the dancer's body presents a body politics through movement. An early example of a dance artist working along these lines and dealing with issues relating to masculinity is the veteran British new dance artist Fergus Early.

Early trained at the Royal Ballet School and then danced with the Royal Ballet from 1964 to 1969 and then with the Royal Ballet's Ballet For All Company from 1969 to 1971. In the 1970s he was one of the group of dancers, mostly like himself dissidents from ballet companies, who broke away and started to create the conditions for an alternative new dance. This included founding the X6 Dance Space in London's Docklands and starting the magazine *New Dance*. The question of how to apply sexual politics to dance is one that concerned many contributors to early issues of *New Dance* and is also evident in many of Early's works at the time including *Three Satie Dances* (1976), *Sunrise* (1979) based on Albrecht's role in the ballet *Giselle* (1841) and, with Jackie Lansley, *I Giselle* (1980), an evening-length feminist reworking of the revered nineteenth-century classic. Early was one of the group who produced the controversial Men's Issue of *New Dance* in 1980.[3] Shortly after this Early created an evening-length solo show *Are You Right There Michael? Are You Right?* (1982) based on his father's life.

Are You Right . . . combines theatre, dance and tape slide presentation to tell the story of Noel Early, who was born and brought up in Ireland and became a doctor who served in the Indian Medical Service. In the war in Korea he received wounds resulting in the amputation of a leg, and the piece concludes with his decline into alcoholism and subsequent death from cancer. The story is told through taped reminiscences about Noel Early made by members of the family, and accompanied by back-projected slides of family photographs and general pictures that establish the *mise en scène* as India, Ireland or the south of England. Often these are shown while Fergus[4] is changing from one costume into another in full view of the audience. There is one moment where the staging draws attention to the striking resemblance between Fergus and a photograph of Noel projected on screen; there are the same clothes, moustache, facial expression and posture. Fergus himself was 8 when his father died and during most of Fergus's life until then his father had been absent overseas. The soundtrack therefore reproduces the process through which Fergus would initially have found out about his father's life. The father is a crucial figure in the psychological development of the male child. The boy's (all too often absent) father is a primary figure for identification in the process of creating his own sense of identity. *Are You Right. . .* can be seen as the acting out publicly of a private and psychologically charged process of assessing his ties with the memory of his father.

Michael Huxley, in his analysis of *Are You Right* . . . , has given a very useful description of Early's movement style.

Despite the use of steps from different styles and periods, the overall range of movement styles is not great and they are executed within a modest spatial and dynamic range. Jumps and turns appear close to the body because their lines are never extended to the full.

(1988: 166)

The extent to which Early's anti-virtuosity contradicted conventional expectations can be gauged in a review by Nadine Meisner (who subsequently wrote for *The Times*). 'Part of the trouble' for her in Early's *Are You Right . . .,*

lies in an incongruous combination of choreography and costume: it is difficult to take seriously a small, stocky man moving poetically in, for example, unflatteringly chunky army shorts and jacket, thick knee socks and sandals.

(Meisner 1983: 28)

But why should she think he is trying to move poetically, or presume that Early should as a matter of course try to conform to conventional notions of ideal body type? Meisner presumes this must be the case as Early is using a vocabulary derived from ballet. She is a sufficiently sensitive critic to pick up on the references to ballet and to the fact that these are being used in a way that contradicts conventional expectations of ballet dancing. She allows that the piece 'pleases by its measured, unsentimental tone, its careful structure, its thoughtful, disciplined originality' (*ibid.*). But for her the incongruities in the way the male dancing body is presented through the vocabulary of ballet are a problem.

What does not occur to her, but is implicit in what she writes, is the implication that the traditional uses of ballet movement are inappropriate for expressing the sorts of ideas about masculinity Early sets out to explore in this piece. It doesn't occur to her that Early might, on the level of body politics, intentionally want to make trouble, through disassociating ballet-derived movement from conservative, metaphysical ideas about dance as art, and sexual difference.

The dance component of *Are You Right . . .* is in the form of short numbers interspersed with bits of acting and the costume changes. It is Early's belief that dance is (or should be available to be) a valued part of everyone's life;[5] many of the dances in *Are You Right . . .* clearly refer to the sorts of social or folk dances that Noel would have done at that time in his life. They affirm that dancing is a significant part of an individual's life and contradict the low status that dance and non-verbal communication have in western society, particularly for men. *Are You Right . . .* amounts to a history of Noel Early's experience of embodiment.

In the first dance, Fergus uses a life-size two-dimensional prop made to resemble a photograph of Noel Early's brothers and sisters all lined up in

165

order of descending height – the photograph itself is recognizable from having been previously back-projected. It is loosely based on traditional Irish step dancing, and is performed to a recording of an Irish jig. Through bright, fast steps and jumps, this dance signifies Noel's youth, and the Irish culture in which he grew up, and, by showing his interaction with members of his family, the dance functions as an expression of community and shared cultural values.

Later, to the crackly strains of an old recording by Peter Dawson of 'Pale hands I loved beside the Shalimar', Fergus presents an animated version of his parents' wedding photograph, standing beside a cut-out figure of his mother in her bridal dress. Taking the words literally, Fergus choreographed, for the first verse of the song, movements for his hand and arm only. The choreography here develops a motif based on a yoga exercise in which the hand is rotated so that the palm faces outwards, and the arm is then raised up to the side. The exercise is designed to stretch the arm muscles in a particular way. In the second verse of the song he uses a motif from another yoga exercise which stretches the leg muscles. During this Fergus holds the toe of his knee length army boot as he straightens the whole leg. Because he is wearing army uniform and a solar topee, the effect of straightening the leg in this way looks strongly militaristic and hence masculine, reminiscent of a goose step. But at the same time it is based on yoga movement, ironically appropriate to the Indian *mise en scène* of the story and of the song.

In a key section towards the end of the piece, the disabled Noel falls on the floor and is at first unable, because he has only one leg, to get himself up again. Through most of the sequence he rolls and turns himself about on the floor, with his face generally hidden from the audience. Within this movement material there are references to earlier dance sections – for example from the 'Pale hands I loved' dance sequence, the tight yoga stretch with the hand and the image of the leg being extended with the hand grasping the toe. On one level this suggests that Noel is checking and testing his body out, comparing what he can do in his disabled state of health with what he had been able to do in his prime. It also suggests a process of reflection on his life.

Overall it is by parodying ballet and referring to folk and social dance and music hall traditions that Fergus Early creates representations of aspects of masculinity that could not have been created within conventional ballet usage. Through his unconventional uses of the body and of dance vocabularies, Early challenges the spectator to reassess aspects of masculine identity and experience that are generally denied or rendered invisible in mainstream cultural forms.

One consequence of the pluralism of postmodern practice is that there is no longer a hierarchy between different dance styles or subjects and ideas, as *Are You Right . . .* demonstrates. Introducing methods of representation

Figure 10 Fergus Early uses a motif from a yoga exercise in the 'Pale hands I loved beside the Shalimar' section of *Are You Right There Michael? Are You Right?* (1982). (Photo: Dee Conway)

from forms other than dance has the consequence of bringing in a wider range of ways of representing masculinity – and the last three chapters have surely proved how limited that range has been in theatre dance for most of the last hundred years. One dance artist who has been particularly concerned with images of men in the rock music world and in film and advertising media is Lea Anderson. Anderson choreographs for and directs two companies, The Cholmondeleys – her original all-female company which she founded in 1984 – and The Featherstonehaughs, formed in 1988 and in which all the dancers are men.

The Featherstonehaughs, Anderson has revealed, currently receive four times as many requests for performances, tours, residencies and other work as The Cholmondeleys. Anderson says that her starting point for the men's company was the observation that all the women she knew were dancers while all the men she knew were in bands. She decided, in her words, to get a load of these band men and take their mannerisms, along with the sorts of expectations which audiences have for a performance by a music group (these being different from those for a dance performance) and try playing around with these.[6] In both The Featherstonehaughs' shows the stage has been set up with a microphone on a stand at one side which each dancer uses to introduce himself (first names only) and give the title of the next dance. Both programmes consist of a series of about a dozen short dances. The dancers stay on stage throughout the evening; between numbers, or when they are not performing in a piece, they rest at each side of the performing area drinking bottled spring water.

The Featherstonehaughs' appearance is very cool and sharp – identical cheap dark suits, Doc Marten shoes, short and stylish haircuts. Carl Smith (who was not actually a trained dancer but used to be a singer in a band called Goat) usually sings a Frank Sinatra song while the others dance – in the first show 'Strangers in the night' and in the second show 'Come fly with me'. Both songs are ground out in a very confidently bad manner, awful enough to be a delight. One feature of The Featherstonehaughs' style is an expansively clumsy or literally pedestrian way of moving. Sophie Constanti (1990) has called this their 'buoyant, tripping pedestrianism and off-balance stumbling'. But this is put very clearly in inverted commas by the use of unison and what Constanti calls the tight groupings and Escher-like floor patterns. Allen Robertson (1990) describes them 'cantering across the stage in closely harmonized moves'.

A good example of this is *My Flip Flop Got Eaten by a Camel* (1991). In order to recreate this 'sand dance' nostalgically, Anderson and three of The Featherstonehaughs closely studied on film the style of the old music hall male speciality dance act Wilson Kepple and Betty. Anderson also quotes from acting or lighting conventions used in film and television. *Rauschleider* (1991) is an essay in the style of film noir, while *Ibli Knibli Boulevard* (1990) and the video version of *Jesus Baby Heater* (1993) draw on the conventions of violent gangster films. The Featherstonehaughs' stage shows carefully foster the appearance of a bunch of cool young men. But once this has been established within the show, Anderson goes on to find ways of showing The Featherstonehaughs doing things which don't quite fit in with, or strain the credibility of, their buddy, buddy appearance: 'Just get everyone all buddy buddy, get everyone all nice and relaxed, you know – the Featherstonehaughs, all nice and accessible – and then just start to make them uncomfortable.'

Jeux Sans Frontière (1991) demonstrates how she does this. It explores the way men interact with other men, and presents physical contact between men in ways which are, from the dominant homosocial, hetero-sexual point of view, problematic. It is in three sections. The first starts with the three dancers wearing cloth caps and sitting on a park bench up stage. To begin with, little bursts of activity are interspersed with long pauses: all three stretch out their arms in a shape like a fan; pause; all three stick up an arm with fingers wriggling. The two on the outside pile their legs onto the lap of the person sitting in the middle, then everyone shifts round like a game of musical chairs and Carl sits on Frank's lap. This bizarre game-playing sets the pattern for the piece as a whole. In the second part they are joined by the three more dancers and there is a petulant, game-like structure which rings the changes of a sequence: the three in front throw their caps on the ground and the three behind retrieve them and put them back on the heads of the three in front. Whereas the effect in the first section is slightly surrealistic, the second section verges on the comic. The last part, however, has a melancholy feeling to it. Two dancers sit on the bench at the back, seemingly unaware or ignoring the other two couples in front of them dancing. Side by side, each of the two couples perform identical supported duets that involve very heavy lifting, holding and catching movements. In contrast to the graceful way in which male ballet dancers lift their female partners, The Featherstonehaughs not only do not disguise the effort involved in lifting partners but make the result look like manual labour (in western countries an exclusively masculine occupation). They lift their partners with the clumsiness of men lifting awkward inanimate objects: too much initial attack resulting in the application of slightly too much energy and a jerky flow of movement.

What is also strange about these final duets is the way the dancers involved never look at their partner or appear to be co-operating with him. All through the piece as a whole the men act in an isolated and unco-operative way – like children, petulantly and selfishly. Put together with the fact that despite close physical contact the men ignore each other, what might ordinarily appear 'ordinary' male behaviour is made to look decidedly odd. It is clearly an example of Anderson using 'normal' male behaviour to make the audience feel uncomfortable. Anderson is know-ingly presenting male behaviour that may be approved in certain contexts but censured in others. This is because there is no clear dividing line between on the one hand an approved and necessary ability for men to work closely with, and be interested in, other men, and, on the other hand, gay desire for other men. *Jeux Sans Frontière* purposely blurs and makes ambiguous the distinction between what is acceptable and what is unacceptable in male behaviour. The dancers involved in the duets are po-faced because (like the soldiers that Theweleit has written about – see Chapter 3) they feel insecure about the maintenance of their physical boundaries. The awkwardness of their partnering, clearly signalled in the contrast with the classical *pas de deux*, denies the sensuous materiality of the body, a denial which it has been argued is a precondition of the maintenance of dominant male homosocial, heterosexual bonding. This is all there in *Jeux Sans Frontière* but never explicit, always subtly hinted at. Underlying this is a deconstructive use of stylistic, theatrical and dance conventions, which problematizes social attitudes towards the male body and constitutes a radical and critical practice.

Both Early and Anderson are examples of highly articulate and well-informed choreographers from different generations of British dance, who approach gender representation with the deliberate intention of resisting dominant norms. Active debates about dance and sexual politics have been informing experimental British dance since the early 1970s, emerging in the United States somewhat more recently. Ralph Lemon, who started presenting his own work around the same time as Anderson, is older than her but younger than Early. Along with other American choreographers who emerged in the 1980s, Lemon came to dance after a university education. Initially he wanted to be a painter, but studied theatre arts and literature at the University of Minnesota before discovering dance. Most articles about him stress that he is a 'private man' and the word most often used to describe his choreography is 'contemplative'. His handling of themes and imagery is clearly informed by a deliberation on ways of resisting dominant norms that begs comparison with the work of Anderson. Both had a background in the visual arts before coming to dance and both are highly eclectic in their use of dance elements. Just as Anderson frequently turns to the media for imagery, Lemon has used the visual and gestural clichés of the Wild West in *Happy Trails* (1988) as a starting point to explore quietly what appears to be one of his recurring preoccupations: the dynamics of community and relationship between couples.

Like Early, Lemon choreographs material which demands light, precise execution and he combines a balletic vocabulary with the bright, spontaneous energy of folk dance. Lemon too gives his male dancers movements that are not fully extended, thus refusing to make them conform to expectations of male bravura display. He is also one of those choreographers who purposely show men lifting men or women lifting men so as to break explicitly with the heterosexual balletic conventions of the *pas de deux*. What characterizes the way Lemon presents himself and the male dancers in his company is that he finds theatrical ways of showing male dancers as unexceptional, vulnerable and full of ordinary inadequacies. All his dancers perform lots of everyday gestures that suggest feelings. In the duet in *Folk Dances* (1991), Lemon starts off sitting isolated on a plain wooden chair back stage with his foot twitching. Lemon's pieces are full of these sorts of naturalistic gestures. He uses them to create a context for the dance movement which seems to continue quite 'naturally' the image they have suggested of 'real' personalities on stage. Eventually in this duet, Lemon's partner has to drag him into the middle of the floor and make him dance with her. Several times she throws herself down on top of him, as if in frustration with his inability or unwillingness to be more forthcoming. Lemon is creating an image of the way men and women relate to one another in the 1990s that seems psychologically true. But in doing so he is consciously contradicting the rules which dictate how men should appear as dancers.

Lemon's *Solo* in *Folk Dances* addresses the fact that he is black. Much of his choreography has succeeded in ignoring this subject, and this has been helped by the fact that he has used only white dancers in his company.[7] *Solo* starts with the image of Lemon dancing barefoot but dressed in a suit and a grotesque mask with distorted 'African' lips and nose and pendulous ear lobes. The mask is then taken off and Lemon repeats the movement sequence – stamping, staying around one spot, falling to the floor, and using minimal, slightly involuntary arm movements. He then takes off his jacket and switches on a small cassette recorder which plays a tape of an interview with LaVaughn Robinson about the hierarchy among tap dancers. While this runs he dances a typical 'Lemon' sequence of fast, stretchy balletically derived movement, again around a fixed spot but with more spatial freedom, and turns. He takes off his red T-shirt and, still barefoot, starts to pat out a tentative tapping rhythm with his hands locked behind his back. This builds up and becomes more energetic. He places a harmonica between his lips, blows and then starts to clap rhythmically as the lights fade.

Solo provides a sequence of discrete and carefully selected images that invites a series of dialectic readings – suit and mask; balletic (western) movement with discussion of black dance history; tentativeness and excitement. These are presented in such a way as to suggest that Lemon himself is assessing his relationship to white stereotypes of the black dancer, and this has the effect of stopping the audience from objectifying him as black, mysterious, 'Other'. It is as if he is saying, do you really see me as this grotesquely distorted savage? but watch how the same sequence looks in a western suit. The mask loses its primitive power and becomes the sort of souvenir that tourists bring back from trips to Africa, including

171

middle-class black Americans in search of their roots. The black American dance tradition of jazz and tap is presented as oral history – a subject for sociological enquiry. Lemon then acknowledges his admiration for the achievements of the old hoofers but, though his stamping footwork is fast and rhythmically complex, it is also quirky, original, very 'Lemon'. He is definitely not presenting the type of easily accessible jazzy display that black performers have danced in Broadway musicals, or that Alvin Ailey choreographs for what were described, in Chapter 5, as his celestial jazzy acrobats. Lemon is not giving his audience a display of supposedly 'innate' black ability in dance which white audiences generally take for granted. Nor is he responding to the challenge of the audience's objectifying gaze that Bill T. Jones described (at the beginning of Chapter 3) and which Jones said made him feel compelled to put on a dynamic display of masculine energy. The pleasures that Lemon's dancing offers spectators are those of recognizing that he is one jump ahead of their expectations, finding something fresh in a potential minefield of stereotypes and clichés. Above all, Lemon is coming down on the positive side with a burst of energy at the end. He has also made visible a positive image of an individual who is black and male that could never be presented within the mainstream conventions which he so deftly denaturalizes and destabilizes.

POST DUETS: REVEALING DESIRABLE MALES

The conventions of the duet and of partnering that were considered in Chapter 3 generally ensure that the male dancer does not embarrass any male spectator: the male dancer should not appear sexually desirable and should direct the audience's gaze towards his female partner; if noticed at all he should be tested and must prove himself through bravura display.

Partnering or doublework is a basic component of theatre dance which generally presents and explores the relationship between a man and a woman. Quite a distance separates social dances concerned with courtship from the grand *pas de deux* of one of Petipa's ballets: the former explore the possibility of a relationship, the latter are an idealized abstraction of the summation of Romantic love. The seasoned dance spectator will consciously or unconsciously compare each new duet with the many, many other ways in which they have seen a male and a female dancer moving together. The duet form has taken on a life of its own. It need no longer necessarily be about heterosexual love: Ashton's *Enigma Variations* (1968) for example contains a series of duets that explore the composer Elgar's various friendships, including a male–male duet between the dancers playing Elgar and Nimrod. Considerable freedom and lassitude therefore already surrounds the form. The following examples of partnering in recent choreography show the radical and disruptive ways in which male dancers have been made subject to a desiring gaze – when they are looked at by other men (where men partner men) or are presented as the object of female desire in the work of female choreographers.

The kissing section of Lea Anderson's *Birthday* (1992), exemplifies new pluralist attitudes towards desire. It starts with Alexandra Reynolds (who is tall with blonde hair) standing nervously, and on-stage comes the tall, good-looking Frank Bock who is also looking sheepish. With an embarrassed laugh they start to kiss and then exit together. Then three identically dressed pairs of dancers come on in a long, horizontal line from the side: a male–female, male–male and female–female couple. Their actions and gestures have been carefully observed, and reproduce ways in which couples kiss and embrace one another. The dancers make eye contact. Each tilts their head the opposite way, they slowly bring their mouths together and their arms enfold one another. But each couple is doing exactly the same movements at the same time – turning in space while mouth to mouth, or caressing the same part of their partner's shoulders in perfect unison. The style is seemingly naturalistic. They seem to be acting out just how they might actually behave with their chosen partner, but at the same time the fact that these actions are mirrored across the stage makes the whole section signify that heterosexuality is clearly only one of other options, no better and no worse.

Birthday was made by bringing together Anderson's two companies the all female Cholmondeleys and the all-male Featherstonehaughs. *Surabaya Johnny* (1990), an earlier piece for The Featherstonehaughs, also took as its starting point the behaviour involved in a sexual embrace, but focused the audience's attention on the way men kiss and cuddle by having them caress an invisible partner. (From a pedantic point of view this therefore barely qualifies as an example of partnering.)

Surabaya Johnny is the title of a song by Brecht and Weill, and Anderson's piece is accompanied by a recording of this, sung by Dagmar Krauss. Four of The Featherstonehaughs lie separately on their backs on the ground through the piece miming the caressing of an imaginary partner on top of them. Their gestures are choreographed to fit the music and, as in *Birthday,* are performed in unison. The song comes from the 'opera' *Happy End* in which it is sung by a night club singer to a gangster who is being chased by the police; it can, however, be read as a biting denunciation of the way men mistreat women:

> You said so much, Johnny
> Not a word was true Johnny
> You deceived me, Johnny
> From the very first moment
> I hate you so, Johnny
> As you stand there grinning
> Take that pipe out of your kisser – you dog.

Jann Parry describes the four men as 'four impassive figures who move without being moved themselves' (1990). If they look impassive this is perhaps an effect of the use of unison. The mood is introspective because the loving partner is absent. The words of the song elicit a sympathetic identification with the point of view of the singer as she complains about how badly Surabaya Johnny (or men in general) treat their lovers. The dancers therefore seem to represent several Surabaya Johnnies, each calmly but faithlessly caressing the hard-done-by, complaining female singer.

Surabaya Johnny therefore sets up its disturbing atmosphere through showing men as desirable in ways that are not generally presented. It creates a context that signals they are being looked at as objects of sexual desire by women and they are thus also available to a gay male gaze.[8] Because the piece breaches the institutionalized conventions that defend the way the male body appears in representations, the dancers look vulnerable. Here I disagree with Parry's suggestion that the men are impassive, and would argue that they in fact use an intimate expressive range of movements and gestures. The gentleness of The Featherstonehaughs' movements is within the marginal 'feminine' area of bodily experience which, as was argued in Chapter 3, has the potential to disrupt and expose repressed memories of male developmental conflicts. There is a disruptive tension both in the words of the song and in the dance between the idea that Surabaya Johnny is a typical manip-ulative male bastard, and the fact that he is nevertheless desirable (and perhaps wouldn't be desirable if he wasn't a bastard). Men never appear (or are looked at) like this in ballet or mainstream modern dance.

Using somewhat similar devices, Anne Teresa de Keersmaeker presents the male partner in the duet that forms the opening section of the dance film *Hoppla!* (1989)[9] as similarly brutal but nevertheless desirable. This duet is untitled and I shall call it 'Mikrokosmos' because it is performed to Bartók's *Mikrokosmos: Seven Pieces for Two Pianos*.

'Mikrokosmos' presents a male and a female performer – Jean-Luc Ducourt and Johanne Saumier – who on the face of it seem slightly mismatched. The way Ducourt pushes Saumier around would appear as brutal as the male–female relationships one finds in, for example, the work of Pina Bausch or Lloyd Newson, except that Saumier appears not to be bothered by it. Generally the two of them have been given fairly similar movements and gestures in terms of space, speed and weight – almost like a Bournonville duet or one from the pre-Romantic ballet in its use of symmetry and mirroring. De Keersmaeker's dancers do not pursue a balletic ideal of effortless and unearthly grace. Their dancing is graceful with fast, light steps and turns, but there is no attempt to hide the spontaneous adjustments they have to make when they become or are pushed off balance, or the sound of their footfalls on the marble flooring.

The two dancers are mismatched in size – Ducourt is big, solid and slightly balding (though deft and nimble when the choreography requires this), while Saumier is rather small and adolescent in appearance. Ducourt's baggy pullover gives the impression of slightly bowed shoulders, while his trousers muffle the liveliness which he is occasionally allowed to exhibit. A lot of the slower movement he seems almost to mark out, but in the faster movement his mobility and flexibility belie the carefully constructed stolid awkwardness of his role.

Saumier portrays the typical Rosas clone: young, flirtatious, capricious, but nervous and unsure of herself. If you have seen de Keersmaeker or the other members of Rosas off the stage, you might have been surprised to find that they are not the young, naive girls they appear when performing. Their appearance is constructed through costume and makeup, by qualities of movement that suggest youth and gaucheness, and in the little 'personalized' gestures that are such a prominent feature of all of de Keersmaeker's work. For Judith Mackrell 'the way they childishly lift a skirt, the way they display their bodies' is narcissistic behaviour and, she says, makes her as a spectator feel uncomfortably voyeuristic:

> As extraordinary technicians, as totally committed performers, I felt nothing but admiration for them. But because they were not given clear roles to perform, yet at the same time were not dancing themselves, I felt I had no point of contact with them.
>
> (Mackrell 1988: 6)

But perhaps there is not supposed to be such a point of contact. The 'little girl' role, the heterosexual image of femininity, is itself a male-determined fiction that has no reality for women. The artificiality of its presentation, which makes Mackrell uncomfortable, has the effect of denaturalizing and destabilizing the heterosexual male discourse of the duet.

The way in which de Keersmaeker plays with the conventions surrounding the spectator's gaze is disruptive. In the opening sequence of the piece both Saumier and Ducourt compete with one another for the camera's/spectator's attention. She tentatively walks up and stands directly between her partner and the camera. He moves her out of the way, and then she does the same to him in an accelerating sequence which culminates in her suddenly jumping up into his arms, precipitating an embrace.

In focusing attention upon their female partner, male dancers are supposed to avoid the full glare of the spectator's gaze. At the beginning of the second dance in 'Mikrokosmos' the camera stays on Ducourt as he waits for the cue to come on, and one gradually becomes aware that he is watching his partner already dancing off-camera. Just as Dolin says he should, he is watching his partner and he is unaware that he is being looked at. But the constructed appearance of his awkwardness here as elsewhere in the piece has the effect of drawing attention to him without catching him up in that remorseless glare of attention which, as Bill T. Jones suggests, forces the male dancer to prove himself.

Finally, de Keersmaeker disrupts expectations of a conventional climax. It is through embraces, like the one at the start of the piece, rather than through more conventional climactic lifts that a summation of the couple's courtship is signified. Elsewhere, when Ducourt lifts his partner in the middle of a hectic dance sequence, he takes her weight into his body, momentarily uniting their momentums as they speed across the floor. Thus 'Mikrokosmos' refuses to build up gradually to one climactic moment but diffuses several little 'high spots' in a generally unexpected way throughout the piece. Saumier herself is in control of these. It is she who initiates the embraces, and in the lifts there is no sense of the male partner showing off the female body to the audience. Irigaray's description of woman's sexuality offers a useful point of reference for this deconstructive distribution. She suggests that the geography of woman's pleasure is 'much more diversified, more multiple in its differences, more complex, more subtle than is imagined' (Irigaray 1981: 103). Thus 'Mikrokosmos' problematizes and destabilizes the heterosexual male gaze while addressing aspects of feminine desire both in terms of the way the male dancer is made visible and the subject of an investigative gaze and through the pattern of an alternative feminine pleasure.

If the way Ducourt is displayed in 'Mikrokosmos' addressed feminine desire, then the David Dorfman and Dan Froot duet *Horn* (1990) was driven by masculine desire for unequivocally masculine bodies. In *Horn*, male bodies were unashamedly revealed since the performers wore only plain kilts and black lace-up shoes, and each had a soprano saxophone slung around his neck. Both performers are of a similar build and, as Iris M. Fanger points out, Dorfman is not a male dancer of the graceful and effete mould: 'The thickness of his body has slipped a bit towards the belt-line, the crew cut over his assertive features could satisfy a Marine Corps inspection, and his stocky legs are well suited for a football field' (Fanger 1992: 60). If there is nothing effeminate about this sort of body, nor was there anything effeminate about the choreography. It was very muscular, with powerful lifts and risky balances made more exciting by the fact that one or other of the dancers kept playing a saxophone throughout. Part of the impact of *Horn* was the ingenuity with which this was achieved. *Horn* was rather baldly described by the English critic John Percival as 'playing, manipulating, lifting and carrying [which] seemed to symbolize a gay seduction' (1991: 28). Sex was indeed cunningly implied through the saxophones: the action of moistening lips before blowing on the instrument's mouth piece can be highly suggestive. At one moment one dancer pulled the saxophone out of the other's mouth, and, at another, each played the other's instrument. *Horn* explored an outrageous subject – athletic All-American male bodies doing things that no 'real' man should do. The piece boldly and positively defied the homophobic taboos that render men's relationships with men fraught and problematic.

One of the stronger themes in the first half of Jean-Claude Gallotta's *Mammame* (1985–7) is the relationship between two men – Pascal Gravat and Christophe Delachaux – which is expressed in a long duet. I may be wrong but I interpret their relationship as a heterosexual one, and their duet provides a strong contrast with *Horn*. *Mammame* was initially choreographed in, and presented at, Gallotta's home base in Grenoble in 1985. Then Gallotta persuaded the director of the Avignon Festival to commission a second half which was premièred with the first half in a three-hour-long performance in Avignon in July 1986. This is the version I saw.[10] A subsequent version titled *Mammame Montréal* was presented at the 1987 Festival International de Nouvelle Danse in Montreal. Each version had different set and costumes as also did the two videos of the piece. The first version was filmed by Raoul Ruiz, while for a second, Claude Mouriéras took the dancers to the Gare de L'Est in Paris to make a free adaptation and partial restructuring of some of *Mammame* that was called *Un chant presque étient* (A song almost extinguished). This latter includes much of the material performed by the two men.

While the women in *Mammame* should not be seen as blameworthy, there are moments when they give the men a hard time, making it hardly surprising that Gravat and Delachaux are left to console one another. Near the beginning of *Mammame* Gravat and Delachaux ceremoniously approach Mathilde Altaraz and Viviane Serry who link their arms around them and you expect them to start dancing together. Next thing you know the two men have slipped down on to the floor in front of the women who dance on without them. At the start of the second half, all the men strip off all their clothes and tuck their penises between their legs. Mathilde Altaraz however catches hold of Gravat's penis and forces him to run in circles around her across the stage while she shouts 'the prince charming . . . the prince charming'.

Linde Howe-Beck describes Gravat and Delachaux as 'a Mutt and Jeff couple, one man balding and chubby, the other tall, thin, and crooked-legged' (1988: 70). Gravat jumps up and is caught upside down by the other, head to groin. The catcher promptly purses his lips and makes a farting noise. The dancers part and then have a series of collisions accompanied by loud groans and ending in a long, poetic, anguished stare into the audience. Later one rushes into the other's arms and seems to die, as if shot in the back.

The overall effect is one of humour laced with sadness. What have they got to be so melancholic about? Modern psychoanalytic accounts of melancholia (as opposed to the medieval definition) suggest that it is the result of repression and disavowal.[11] The male dancers are melancholy because that is part of the nature of the close relationships between men in modern western society. They are, in Sarah Kent's phrase, witnesses to the crumbling of (male) certainty. Indeed the vast melancholy scale of Gallotta's piece fits her description of male postmodern painting: Gallotta and his dancers seem to mourn for lost power, lost belief and lost confidence, in a spectacle which irritated some British critics for its over-blown self-importance and inflated scale. As far as the two men are concerned, they are drawn to each other, but, lest this acceptable attraction be mistaken for forbidden homosexual interest, their affection is severely restrained. What is being disavowed in this duet is what Sedgwick calls male homosocial desire, a disavowal made more urgent by the need for acceptable comradeship in the face of crumbling certainties. The men in *Horn* were bright, positive and courageous because they dared to challenge the social attitudes which produce the melancholic humour of the men's duet in *Mammame*.

DV8's piece *My Sex, Our Dance* (1987) also challenges homophobia, but in the process presents a bleak and chilling view of male–male relationships. *My Sex, Our Dance* was made and performed by Charnock and Newson, founding members of the British company DV8 Physical Theatre. It explores the dynamics of a relationship between two men. The programme included the following poem by Newson.

In the beginning there were the men who told me how to be a man.
Then there were the women of the men who told me how to be a
man.
Then there were the feminists who told me how to be a man.
Then there were the critics.
Then came Nigel.
Then came My Sex, Our Dance.

Newson says that Charnock and he, while developing material for the piece, looked at situations in their own lives where they had been physically violent. These were combined with situations where they had to really trust one another. It starts with Newson shaking hands with Charnock and then reaching out to touch him. Charnock flinches away from him and their interactions develop into a fight followed by a brooding truce and then more combat. Charnock says he reacts violently in real life when he feels hemmed in or held.[12] In *My Sex, Our Dance* one dancer hurls himself through the air backwards for the other to catch. Sometimes he is caught, sometimes not. They also trip one another up; one hurls himself on to a mattress where the other is lying so that the latter has to roll out of the way. Lesley Ann Thom, writing about a performance at the Brooklyn Academy of Music in New York, suggested that: 'The intimacy of their developing relationship was heightened by daredevil physicality that demanded trust at one moment and implied denial at another' (1989: 69–70). Alys Daines in London observed: 'He [Newson] hurls himself at Charnock as if to say "You want my body, OK here it is but don't ask for more"' (1987: 27). *My Sex, Our Dance* introduced a high-energy, risky dance style which became something of a trademark of DV8's work. As both Thom and Daines suggest, it was used to convey the fraught and dangerous nature of male–male relationships.

Newson recalls a moment while they were rehearsing the piece when he and Charnock had collapsed, worn out, lying one on top of the other on the mattress.[13] At this moment someone came into the rehearsal room and, seeing them lying there, was very embarrassed, excused themselves and quickly left. Newson reproduced this moment in the finished piece. Throughout the piece as it was performed in Britain, a heterosexual couple sit at a table in the front, far left corner of the performance space chatting quietly and drinking wine throughout, apparently oblivious of the performance behind them. Stephanie Jordan described them as 'the man and woman who canoodle and giggle at the cafe table on the stage's edge and openly express their lighter attachment' (1987: 23). At the moment when Newson collapses exhausted on top of Charnock lying on the mattress, the woman at the table laughs (although she is apparently laughing at something unrelated to what Charnock and Newson are doing). Newson says his intention was to draw attention by this to the fact that public physical contact between men in our society is not allowed. The presence of the couple at the table is a continual reminder to the audience of the intimate and 'deviant' nature of what Charnock and Newson are performing. Thom's description of the New York perform-ance doesn't mention this couple but describes two men in business suits who walk on stage at the end of the piece and shake hands, the same social ritual with which the piece had begun. Clearly these 'extra' performers were used to present 'normal', acceptable social behaviour that ironically highlighted the taboo nature of the social behaviour that Newson and Charnock were presenting.

MASCULINITY AT THE LIMITS

The dancers in *Horn* and *My Sex, Our Dance* have taken up certain positions in relation to masculinity that are right on the edge of, or outside and beyond, the bounds of accepted societal norms. Mary Douglas (1966) has argued that there is a homology between the socially constructed image of the body and the idea of society. There is power and danger at the boundaries of each, power to reward conformity and repulse attack but also energy in its margins and unstructured, chaotic areas. The rest of this chapter considers the question: what are the limits of acceptable repres-entations of masculinity in theatre dance and what powers and dangers are unleashed when these are purposely transgressed? It does this by looking at two ways in which recent theatre dance has challenged or

transgressed the limits of acceptability where representations of masculinity are concerned: through the manipulations of style and parody in the
work of Michael Clark and Mark Morris, and through presenting abject
and horrifying imagery in Pina Bausch's *Bluebeard* and DV8's *Dead Dreams
of Monochrome Men*.

Pina Bausch's Tanztheater deals with imagery and situations that push
to the limits ideas about gendered behaviour. Her work has provoked
mixed reactions from North American critics. Kelly and Stuart sum up an
attitude towards her influence on dance in the 1980s that is respectful but
suspicious: 'Pina Bausch began things in Europe with the radical realities
of her dance theatre, its circus-of-horrors imagery drawn with sado-
masochistic attention to the details of disintegrating humanity' (1989: 36).
Bausch's work certainly represents horrific and despairing behaviour, the
performance of which imposes on her dancers considerable hardship of
both an emotional and a physical nature. Her dancers may do sadistic
things on stage in some of her works but there is no indication that the
recipients have either asked for it or masochistically enjoy the resulting
pain. There are nevertheless parallels between the theatricality of sado-
masochism (s/m) and elements in the work of other dance companies in
the 1980s and 1990s. DV8's *Dead Dreams of Monochrome Men*, while not
being a piece about s/m, nevertheless explores power relations in some
scenes in ways that are reminiscent of s/m sessions. Michael Clark's
performances present sado-masochistic imagery, particularly through the
contribution of Leigh Bowery as designer and performer. These are
performers who are working on the edge. They are also gay men, and s/m
has become an issue within the gay communities. Debates about s/m frame
useful questions that can be applied to examples of theatre dance that go
to or push beyond the limits through either abjection or camp parody.

S/m is theatrical in its ritualized exploration of power relations. As
Jeffrey Weeks has put it, s/m depends upon consensual situations between equals, who take up oppressive or oppressed positions in a
theatrical eroticization of the wish for suffering and pain. It is about
'pleasure as the realization of forbidden fantasies, and about power
differences as a signifier of desire' (Weeks 1985: 237). S/m itself is a tiny
minority activity at the extreme fringe of acceptable sexuality, but since
the 1970s there has developed a debate about its political nature. It has
been argued that s/m, through its preoccupation with power differences,

> shows the way in which repressed sexuality lies behind the formal
> front of oppressive forces. . . . By tearing away the veil from the face
> of authority, s/m reveals the hypocrisy at the heart of our sexual
> culture – the bulge under the uniform – and therefore contributes to
> its exposure and to the dissolution of its effects.
>
> (*ibid.*: 238)

Some have argued that camp also has the effect of revealing and destabilizing hypocrisy.[14] The term 'camp' refers to forms of gay style, language and culture which are a type of clever, witty self-protection that runs rings of logic and subversive humour around pedestrian, 'straight' ideas and attitudes. There is a long tradition of gay dance performers cross-dressing to present camp parodies of masculinity – think of Ashton and Helpmann's party piece as the Ugly Sisters in *Cinderella*, or the Trocaderos, or some of Lindsay Kemp's work. Mark Morris and Michael Clark have both choreographed drag roles. The question is: what effect on notions of gendered identity do such parodic representations have?

If to be a gay man is, from some points of view, not to be a 'real' man, then the camp imitation of femininity is on one level a facetious repetition of that judgement. Judith Butler (1990: 138–9) argues that a defiant statement that the performer is not a 'real' man destabilizes the notion that there is anything 'real' about 'real' men in the first place. The trope here is the same as Jameson's account of pastiche as blank parody. Butler argues that this sort of parodic performance has the effect of compelling a reconsideration of the stability of masculinity and femininity. Not everyone is so optimistic about the effectivity of camp. The camping process is one that trivializes indiscriminately through its 'droney, knowing, nudge-nudge, flat, Aren't-We-Bitches, fourth form, in-house, messing about chat' (this is Alastair Macaulay's description of some dialogue in Michael Clark's *Because We Must* (1988)). Through indiscriminately parodying and trivializing its subjects, camp seems to present no actual threat to hetero-sexual norms. As Richard Dyer points out,

> The emphasis on surface and style can become obsessive – nothing can be taken seriously, anything deep or problematic or heavy is shimmied away from in a flurry of chic. Camp seems unable to discriminate between those things that need to be treated for laughs and style, and those that are genuinely serious and important.
>
> (1992: 145)

Dyer also points out that camp style has been adopted by straight men and women, although they aren't so good at it. Would camp humour be quite so acceptable and entertaining to straight audiences if it constituted a threat to the stability of patriarchy?

Both camp and s/m are excessive – going too far, doing too much, being too extreme etc. – in relation to 'normal' values. Critics of s/m question whether it is 'really necessary to go to the limits of physical possibilities simply because we think we want it' (Weeks 1985: 239). One could similarly ask whether it is necessary to cause dancers the pain that Bausch and Newson do, or to be as gratuitously shocking as Clark and Bowery. Do the shocks that derive from camp parody, or the horrors and despairs of Tanztheater and the degrading sado-masochistic exchanges in DV8's work, have a revelatory power that challenges audience's cosier pre-suppositions about the coherence and stability of social norms and values? Or are these dance artists, as some argue, merely dealing in sensationalism? What are the powers and dangers that occupy the boundaries of the presentation of the male body in their work?

Clark, Morris and subversion

Most critical writing about Michael Clark's work balances derogatory or despairing remarks about his shock tactics with eulogies about his abilities as dancer and as creator of classical movement material. Clement Crisp, for example, dismissed most of Clark's *Mmm* (1992) (initially called *Modern Masterpiece*) as 'gimmicks and what might best be known as dirty tricks', but said of Clark himself: 'Every gift is his, from purity of line to the most delicate and precise shaping of steps' (1992). Alastair Macaulay gives a typical list of Clark's 'dirty tricks' in *Because We Must* (1988).

> Clark is an anything goes anarchist. Nudity, obscenity, fancy dress, the chain saw, dancing to the National Anthem, Knees Up Mother Brown, Elvis singing 'Silent Night'. Loud rock-music accompanying the quaint woodland scenery of La Sylphide (La La La Sylphide) . . . all of that and more, all to give you one frisson or another.
>
> (1988: 440)

Previous works had included bare bottoms, dangling dildos, goose-stepping, Nazi salutes and various other obscenities. In *Mmm* Clark's own 68-year-old mother appeared, bare-breasted, to re-enact giving birth to her son with Bowery acting the part of the midwife. Bowery's influence on Clark, according to Judith Mackrell, 'has made critics (including me) grind their teeth'.[15]

What then do the critics find so special about Clark as a dancer and choreographer? Jann Parry, writing about *Mmm*, says 'He has always been beautiful, but now at 30, he has an elegiac quality that makes the angle of his head or the slow extension of a leg almost unbearably moving' (1992). Clark trained at the Royal Ballet School where he was a star pupil of Richard Glasstone who teaches the Cecchetti tradition of ballet. What is admired in Clark's dancing is the pure, classical quality of his 'line', not just a succession of beautifully presented positions but an internal understanding of a flow that links them together. It is this which the British critics invariably praise. Also appreciated are the ways in which Clark choreographs extremely difficult and demanding material for himself and his dancers that exemplify this quality.

In other words, in a time when traditional ballet companies are having difficulties in finding worthwhile new choreography – American companies for example turning to postmodern choreographers for new rep – Clark represents someone for whom the Cecchetti tradition of training (on which Pavlova and the artists of the Ballets Russes flourished) is still alive. Those who have grown up watching ballet will seemingly put up with anything for a sight of Clark's pure, classical *port de bras*.

Interviewing Clark in 1984, Alastair Macaulay put the question: how important are the shocks in Clark's work? Clark's initial answer – that he really liked it that people appreciate different aspects of his work – is a typical cop-out. When pushed, he acknowledged that they were 'a reflection of his mentality' and that the good dancing and shocking trimmings are not totally separate but made sense to him as a whole. What is being signified therefore through the ambiguities of Clark's shocking classicism? In Norris's terms, what lies in the difference between the logic and the rhetoric that creates this ambiguity?

As a high-profile gay man and dance star, Clark's body has probably achieved the status of a gay icon.[16] He has revealed it in various ways throughout his career like an adolescent tease. This exposure is an outrageously unequivocal statement of his sexuality. For example in *Hetrospective* (1989) Clark wore a costume by Bowery consisting of two fur muffs which he held in front to hide his genitals. The rest of his body was entirely naked. In a similar solo in *Mmm* Clark danced naked with his hands holding in place one big fur muff. Of the *Hetrospective* solo, Judith Mackrell said 'I defy anyone not to be moved by seeing that beautiful body, that play of muscles and effortless line close up' (1989: 14). But it goes further than just self-expression. Clark uses subversive or parodic strategies to present what is, from a 'normal' point of view, completely unacceptable male behaviour – (homosexual) sex, drugs and (ear-splitting punk) rock and roll. *Hetrospective* was perhaps the most extreme and explicit theatrical statement Clark has made about the unacceptability of his sexual and other practices. A solo was danced in a leotard 'bristling with discarded syringes' and there was a bedroom scene called 'Bed Peace' with his then partner the American dance artist Stephen Petronio. Mackrell found Clark's long embrace with Petronio briefly intriguing. 'Its naked tonguing explorations are the frankest I have seen in the theatre and give pause for thought about sex on stage, narcissism and display. But, at about 15 minutes, the whole scene feels a tedious imposition' (*ibid.*). But this performance wasn't actually in a theatre but in the upstairs premises of the Anthony D'Offay Gallery, London.[17] Clark is following in the tradition of gay artists and writers like Genet who use shocking and degrading imagery intentionally to debase their highly valued art.[18] Clark's manipulation of symbols of degradation can be read as a defiant theatrical gesture of identification with the debased status which social prejudice allots to ordinary gay men. It has the effect of degrading highly rarefied, ballet-derived movement.

Ballet is not degraded in Clark's work just through what Macaulay calls 'silly trimmings'. It is degraded through the use of punk and new wave rock music resulting in a 'breakneck force with which the dancers whip their bodies, stamp, spiral and fly' (Mackrell 1992). Furthermore the new ways Clark has found of exploring classical line themselves contain references to unacceptable behaviour. In *New Puritans* he used sequined platform soled and heeled boots (designed by Bowery) to put a new twist on the idea of dancing on pointe, wearing them himself (and thus dancing as a ballerina) in a duet with Ellen van Schuylenburch. (Platform soles were a feature in the early 1970s of the costume of glam rock pop performers, many of whom were gay.) For *Mmm* Clark devised a strangely contorted variation of ballet movement by flexing the pelvis so that, as Jann Parry describes 'the movement ripples outwards from the body's sexual centre' (*ibid.*). On a mechanical level ballet technique is based on a fixed pelvis: 'Unless our hip girdle is held in a strong muscular grip we have not the central stability to rise and sink on our feet with ease and control' (Quirey 1976: 89). It is not just ballet but also the social dances of what Belinda Quirey calls 'polite society' which, until the advent of dancing to jazz music, have treated the chest and pelvis as one unbroken unit. Pelvic movement in the West has inevitable sexual connotations. Thus in *Mmm*, Clark and his male dancers (as well as the female ones) danced balletically derived movements that 'look wrong' because they refer inescapably to sex. Furthermore, when Clark dances in this way, it is a display of male homosexual eroticism. Suzanne Moore suggests that it is through the codification of the gay male body that a female pleasurable gaze is permitted which is otherwise denied by the patriarchal, heterosexual point of view (see Chapter 3). This is surely why Judith Mackrell says she defies 'anyone not to be moved by seeing . . . that effortless line close up'; but she is expressing her delight using the vocabulary of traditional formalist ballet criticism. Does his work challenge his audience's cosier presuppositions about the coherence and stability of social norms and values? Surely rather than being shocked by Clark into reassessing their attitudes towards gender and sexuality, straight spectators are more likely to be titillated by his sensationalism while securely feeling that it confirms their sense that gay men are just not like 'us' at all.

The same ambiguous relationship between traditionally valued choreographic and dancing skills and parodic manipulations of style can be detected in the work of that other young gay dance superstar, Mark Morris. The mainstream critics who praise Morris do so principally by stressing his abilities in the areas of musicality and mime, thus enlisting him within an ahistorical tradition of 'great' choreographers. In praising Morris, they generally turn a blind eye to or play down the camp, parodic element in his work. For Arlene Croce, for example, 'Morris turns the transsexual chic and the frivolous passions of his generation into pretexts for dances . . . he doesn't try to be more than a good choreographer and a completely sincere theatre artist' (1987: 157). Morris may be a completely sincere theatre artist, but he nevertheless also has great skills as a parodist – he likes playing. He plays around with the traditional forms and conventions of European high culture – Virgil, Purcell, Vivaldi, Blake, Handel, Milton, etc. – and in so doing gives his many supporters much pleasure. He also plays around with signifiers of gender and sexuality that are socially contentious and on the margins of acceptability. In *Lovey* (1985) his dancers simulated various sexual acts with children's dolls. As the witch Belinda in *Dido and Aeneas* (1989) Morris acted out a woman masturbating and then wiping her hand clean on her/his tunic. *One Charming Night* (1985) presented a romantic heterosexual duet which turns into a vampire piece as Teri Weksler sucks blood from Morris's wrist. To share blood is of course to risk HIV transmission. 'I won't live that long' Morris told an interviewer, and when asked why replied 'AIDS. I wasn't celibate all the time I lived in New York' (quoted in Acocella 1993: 115).

Joan Acocella, in her admirable biography of Morris, suggests that AIDS is one theme of the dance set to 'Nicht Wandel' (do not stray, dear love) in *Love Song Waltzes* (1989). Here Jon Mensinger, who had been diagnosed as HIV-positive, dances wanderingly in the middle of a ring of dancers who keep catching him and bringing him back into the middle of the circle. It is, Acocella suggests, as if they were saying 'don't go, your place is here with us' (1993: 113). *Dogtown* (1983) is surely another piece about AIDS. Why else would the dancers be wearing the surgical rubber gloves of (AIDS-aware) safe sex? The dog-like crawling movement causes the dancers to waggle their bottoms provocatively inviting other dogs/dancers to lift a leg in an unmistakable but unerotic gesture of mounting and copulating. What is being signified in this display is penetrative anal sex, one of the main homosexual male sexual practices through which bodily fluids, which may contain the HIV virus, are exchanged. The dance is performed by a mixed company of men and women. Men and women are both in danger from AIDS. During the section danced to Yoko Ono's song 'Dogtown', a woman repeatedly lifts a man, spins round with him and then vigorously throws him on the ground. In most of the pieces male and female dancers do exactly the same moves, and who mounts whom is not determined by heterosexual norms.

When Croce wrote about *Dogtown* she enjoyed its skilful play of signifiers. She didn't speculate on what these might signify, but praised Morris's choreographic skills in crafting them. 'The dogginess of it all is a continual, shadowy implication in movement as finely drawn and cunningly interlocked as the patterns on an ancient Greek jar' (1987: 159). To be fair it all depends what Croce meant by 'dogginess'. But what ancient Greek jar do you think she had in mind? No doubt the type of which Keats wrote 'a thing of beauty is a joy for ever'.

But joy is surely not the most appropriate way to describe one's response to a piece that is disturbing in its allusion to 'unacceptable' and 'un-

185

mentionable' sexual acts. The piece presents a parody of the more unsympathetic heterosexual view of gay men – they're like dogs, animals, less than human, not like 'us'. Such parody is pretty despairing. Another way of looking at *Dogtown* is that it is an expression of complete revulsion with sex as a whole regardless of sexuality.

> I don't have a lot of time for sex. [Sex is] hormones, probably like rutting. . . . It's like a mandrill's genitals turning red. People go into heat, and that's wonderful, but it's not love.
> (interview with Tobias Schneebaum quoted in Acocella 1993: 94)

The piece which goes furthest in expressing Morris's revulsion with the idea of sex was 'Striptease' from the suite *Mythologies* (1986) inspired by the collection of Roland Barthes's early essays. From descriptions, the revelation of male and female bodies in 'Striptease' amounted to the opposite of Michael Clark's displays with fur muffs: instead of titillation, Morris had intentionally set out to choreograph acts that didn't work theatrically and thus deglamorized and demystified the process of erotic display.

The way that, particularly in his early work, men lift men, women lift women and women lift or as in *Dogtown* throw men is all very politically correct. In *New Love Song Waltzes* (1982), as Acocella describes it, 'dancers crawl in and out of various pairs of arms . . . without regard to the sex of the other person' (1993: 90) and the same could be said of *Dogtown*. Near the end of *L'Allegro, Il Penseroso et il Moderato* (1988), there is a group circle dance for men which has been nicknamed 'the stupid men's dance' in which they punch one another like sparring boxers, kiss and make up then change partners and go through it all over again. As an outer circle of men runs round them, those in the inner circle slap each passing man on the bottom, but the men also slap themselves on the bottom, and bounce up and down in powerful jumps all cleverly set to the slightly plodding 4/4 rhythm of the tenor air 'I'll to the well-trod stage anon' in Handel's *L'Allegro* (1740).

In 'the stupid men's dance', as in 'Striptease', Morris is using the sorts of steps and movement qualities that exemplify 'male energy' – jumps, punches – and should therefore be exciting; but he presents them in such a way that they become deflated and demonstrably fail to impress. There is nothing particularly sympathetic about the way Morris presents men in this section. They look stupid, particularly in comparison with the next dance, for women only, which is set to the soprano air 'And ever, against eating cares' in which the key words are 'the hidden soul of harmony'. This is, in conventional terms, a very beautiful piece of music interpreted straight. The two dances one after the other suggest a very traditional view of gendered difference. Morris has commented on the fact that one can ask a woman in rehearsal to act like a 65-year-old man but that a straight man would be too embarrassed to act like a 13-year-old girl. 'Women', he added, 'have a richer and more varied emotional life than men' (Acocella 1993: 92). By the late 1980s Morris seems to have lost interest in male dance and turned to female roles as a vehicle for his most serious choreographic statements.

Morris had already explored the presentation of emotional depths in female roles, for example his drag role in 'Say it's not you' in *Deck of Cards* (1983). In the roles of Dido and Belinda in *Dido and Aeneas* (1989) he gave what is widely said to be his greatest performance. What comes across from descriptions of these pieces is Morris's seriousness. Judith Butler's argument that camp parody destabilizes and denaturalizes heterosexual norms by means of its shock value seems inappropriate here. Surely rather than being shocked into recognition of the contingent nature of sexual identities, straight spectators are more likely to feel that Morris's performance as a woman confirms their sense that gay men are just not like 'us' at all. It is only within the community of his dance company that gay and straight are unproblematically equal, and with this community Morris has sought increasingly to represent things of beauty that are a joy for ever.

I have come to more or less the same conclusion about the subversive representations of masculinity in both Clark's and Morris's work. Judith Butler suggested that some parodic performances are disruptive while others 'become domesticated and recirculated as instruments of cultural hegemony' (1990: 139). If Clark and Morris are in danger of domestification this is surely because, apart from the parodic element, they use and give new life to traditional dance vocabularies and skills – Clark's sense of line, Morris's brilliant interpretation of the roles of Dido and Belinda, his much-praised musicality. The accepted view seems to be that they have now got over their youthful indiscretions. Neither choreographer apparently sees anything wrong with good old-fashioned dance. But in sticking with it they are in a position from which they are unable to stop their work from being viewed from the dominant heterosexual point of view which judges and punishes gay men for going beyond the prescribed limits.

Dances of despair: DV8 and Pina Bausch

When *Dead Dreams of Monochrome Men* was first performed at the Institute of Contemporary Arts in London in October 1988, it came at a time when gay men were under considerable public pressure on three fronts: from the threat of AIDS, from hostile press coverage of AIDS and from Clause 28 of the 1988 Local Government Bill which made it illegal for local authorities in Great Britain to intentionally promote homosexuality or publish material with the intention of promoting homosexuality. At a time when there was concern among gay people and social progressives about a resurgence of deeply rooted and age-old prejudices against homosexuality, DV8 presented an uncompromising exploration of controversial ideas. Although *Dead Dreams . . .* wasn't 'about' the life of the homosexual mass murderer Dennis Nilsen, it was based on improvisations that explored the dancers' reactions to reading Brian Masters's book *Killing for Company* about Nilsen. Newson himself, interviewed by Sophie Constanti, said that *Dead Dreams . . .* could not 'be hauled up under Section 28 as a promotion or glamorisation of homosexuality' (1989: 6). John Percival in *The Times* said it showed a 'bleak, angry, almost hopeless homosexual world' (1988) and that 'to use the word gay in this context would be ludicrous'. Nadine Meisner said the four characters in the piece are 'drained of normal emotional colour, their urges twisted into fetishism, sadism and self-loathing' (1989). From a dominant heterosexual point of view, this is not an unacceptable picture of homosexuality.

Nigel Charnock recalls that, after the first performances of *Dead Dreams . . .*, the company had expected the audience to be made up largely of gay men; they were therefore surprised when they got feedback from straight men who said that they could identify with some of the situations in the piece. Newson, however, told William Pierce of *Square Peg* magazine about some very negative and anti-gay responses to the piece (Pierce 1988). Newson argued later that the piece was not exclusively aimed at gay audiences.

> I don't think it matters whether the men are gay or straight. A gay man is still a man and has those same emotional blockages. For all sorts of reasons, most men want to protect themselves. I wonder why so many men – gay or straight – have problems relating to people.
>
> (Constanti 1989: 6)

Dead Dreams . . . presents the loneliness and hollowness that results when gay or straight men are unable to form meaningful relationships, and uses the presentation of sado-masochist situations as a way in which to explore this. For example Douglas Wright does a series of s/m-like actions to Russell Maliphant. The latter is blindfolded; at first his wrists are bound and he is undressed and teasingly caressed and then slapped; then he is made to lean against the wall in a vulnerable position and submit to slaps and to being pulled off balance by tugs on the elastic waist-band of his underpants.

In some of these encounters, whose fantasy is being acted out is not always straightforwardly apparent. In one of the central encounters in *Dead Dreams . . .*, Maliphant faces Charnock and slowly reaches out to touch and then embrace him. Charnock remains passive and withdraws himself. Maliphant then repeatedly reaches out to touch him but each time Charnock recoils, sometimes hitting him back, until Maliphant eventually catches him and holds him tight. Charnock then again withdraws himself until he is holding Maliphant's wrists and draws him towards a ladder.

188

This he climbs up a little way and then lets himself fall so that he is caught by Maliphant; in catching him they both fall to the ground. Charnock then gets away from him as quickly as he can and climbs up again, this time a little higher and jumps again. Charnock says the inspiration for this section was the idea of asking 'how much do you love me? Do you love me this much? or this much?' as he gradually goes further and further up until finally Maliphant walks away and Charnock almost crashes to the ground on his own. At first it appears that Charnock is being unwillingly approached by Maliphant, but as the section develops it becomes apparent that Charnock is forcing Maliphant to go through this 'session' to feed his own fears of being held and constrained, together with his submissive fantasy of being rejected.

Part of the theatrical power of this section derives from the fact that the situation is to some extent a 'true' one for Charnock. The discomfort that the audience is made to feel in this and similar scenes is further exacerbated by the way voyeurism is used in the piece. In some sections either Newson or Charnock is shown to be actively watching intimate scenes performed by other dancers. When Charnock watches the action between Wright and Maliphant described above, his reactions are so extreme that he gets down on all fours on the floor with his face contorted as if in a silent scream.

The presence of a watcher within the performance can have the effect of making the individual audience member shift their point of view, and make them aware that they too are outside the action and watching it, thus denaturalizing the conventional role of the spectator's gaze. This challenges the audience to recognize that they are looking at men who are looking at other men in a way motivated by sexual tastes conventionally judged to be deviant. *Dead Dreams . . .* prompts the audience to consider whether or not they accept that the behaviour presented in the piece is totally alien to them. It thus questions and problematizes the criteria behind the distinction between what is and is not considered acceptable masculine behaviour.

The most disturbing images are at the end of the piece. Reproduced in Masters's book *Killing for Company* is a notebook titled 'Monochrome Man, sad sketches' which Nilsen, while he was on remand in Brixton prison in 1983, filled with drawings and writing about his crimes. It includes a drawing of Nilsen, dressed in a suit, looking down at a dead male body, clothed in underpants and socks laid out on a mattress. He kept the bodies of some of his victims for several months under the floorboards of his flat and sometimes got them up, washed them in the bath and acted out ordinary everyday activities with them. Each of the four dancers takes it in turns to be the Nilsen figure looking at and manipulating the prone body of one or more dancers, recalling Nilsen's strange rituals. Charnock, in the role of victim and dressed only in underpants, crawls out of the bath up to and along the ceiling, and then down a rope from which Maliphant is hanging upside down. He crawls over Maliphant's prone body and then flops around in hideous spasms on the floor before finally lying still at Newson's feet.

The physical risks, the emotional pitch of the piece and the horrifying nature of Nilsen's crimes (like the Fascist German soldiers' fantasies which Theweleit has studied) present an image of male violence that is so abject and grotesque as to be beneath humanity. To present such an image obviously subverts the idea that masculinity is an unproblematic, unquestioned norm. Theweleit and Chodorow both locate the male body as a key site of repressed developmental conflicts, Theweleit suggesting that it has potential for modifying norms of masculine behaviour. As dance or 'physical theatre', *Dead Dreams . . .* focuses attention uncomfortably on the male body and uncompromisingly highlights taboo areas of masculine behaviour through channels of nonverbal bodily communication that, as was argued in Chapter 3, are marginalized in western society. The same could be said of Pina Bausch's work.

Bausch deals with gender issues the way she deals with most things in her work by pushing them to and beyond the limits. On a superficial level, in one piece after another Bausch's dancers bash and hurl themselves against the walls of the set, as if trying to get beyond the stage's limits. On a more abstract level Bausch questions conceptual limits. In reply to a question about the use of existing and recognizable dance movement in her piece she told Jochem Schmidt: 'It is a question of when is it dance, when is it not? Where does it start? When do we call it dance?' (Servos 1984: 230). Just as she questions the limits of dance, so she also questions the limits of social behaviour. For example there is an incident towards the end of *Kontakthof* (1978) where the eleven men in the piece come up and surround one woman (originally Meryl Tankard) and touch her. Raimund Hoghe says that a central theme of *Kontakthof* is tenderness, and that throughout the piece different situations explore the limits of tenderness. In this instance

> They cover her body with touches. Hands stroke across hair, eyes, brow, mouth, nose, chin, ears, neck, arms, legs, breast, stomach, back – until the woman collapses underneath what is understood (by men) as 'tenderness'.
>
> (Hoghe 1980: 66)

Norbert Servos summed up what I myself felt watching this sequence – that the men were either raping or clinging helplessly to the woman (1984: 120). Both alternatives are excessive and extreme, and this is in itself a challenge to the notion that masculinity is an unquestionable and unproblematic norm.

It is the point where the audience begin to feel uncomfortable or provoked that Bausch says interests her because 'there I try to understand how it is as it is' (Hoghe 1980: 72). Bausch was not alone among Germans in the 1970s in deciding to face up to the unpalatable. This is the time when Klaus Theweleit was working on his study of the psychology of fascist soldiers. It is a time when German visual artists were rediscovering the figurative painterly expressionism that characterized German expressionist art in the first decades of the twentieth century. Bausch, like them, can be seen to be returning to 'German' artistic and philosophical themes and concerns that had been tainted by association with the Nazism.[19] As Alice Yaeger Kaplan said of the context of Theweleit's study:

> postwar German society was caught up in a massive social project where reconstruction and forgetting were intertwined. Theweleit's context is, as he states it, 'the injunction prevailing in Germany against learning about fascism and its antecedents'.
>
> (Kaplan 1989: 167)

The men in Bausch's work could fit in with Theweleit's broad definition of fascists. Particularly in her earlier pieces, men act out brutally violent, aggressive, controlling and raping roles, the most obvious example being Jan Minarik's part in *Bluebeard* (1977). In later works men sometimes wear unisex shifts – for example in *Nelken* (1982) – or dresses – as in the film *Lament for the Empress* (1989) (though there are also violent and oppressive male roles in this piece). Clothes do not just signify gender but are used to give the dancers particular feelings. Louise Brooks recalls in her memoirs (1982) how when filming *Lulu* (1928) the German expressionist film director Pabst wanted her to project feelings of a tramp's utter dejection and despair. So he took from her room the suit of clothes that Brooks was most fond of and had it systematically destroyed so that it looked like a tramp's dress. When she came to perform the scene in question he gave her the now ruined suit to wear and, she says, she felt so low wearing it that she didn't have to act at all. Bausch frequently uses costumes to give her performers this sort of real feeling. For example the Chosen One's dress for the sacrificial solo at the end of *The Rite of Spring* (1975) is so skimpy, transparent and loose-fitting that it keeps falling off her torso to reveal her naked breasts as she dances her tortured solo. The male suits and heavy overcoats male dancers wear in other pieces give them feelings of power and security, while female dresses give their performances a quality of insecurity and vulnerability even when their gestures are identifiably masculine.

Bausch's work shows the spectator what exists outside the boundaries. Her pieces often become seemingly chaotic or meaningless, or seemingly random behaviour is arbitrarily structured through loops and repeats. The effect is to force spectators to find some sense in it,

191

or to consider actively the nature of their own responses. Her work does not present pre-digested conclusions. It is not about making points – hence her unwillingness to accept that her work has anything to do with feminism. She has acknowledged that the way she sees gender roles 'certainly has to do with myself – with the fact of me being a woman'.

> But 'Feminism' – perhaps because it has become such a fashionable word – and I retreat into my snail shell. Perhaps also because they very often draw such a funny borderline that I don't really like. Sometimes it sounds like 'against each other' instead of 'together'.
>
> (Hoghe 1980: 73)

What she disagrees with is 'single-stranded thinking' with which some interpret her work. This, she says, simply isn't right because 'you can always watch the other way' (ibid.). Ways of thinking that have multiple strands are open both to non-verbal channels of communications as well as to spoken language. Bausch is aware of the marginality of the non-verbal in relation to language. Of the difficulty she finds talking about her work, she says, 'I suddenly get the feeling that if I talk about it too much then I've dirtied it already' (Servos 1984: 230). On the other hand Bausch is highly sensitive to non-verbal bodily communication.

> Somehow we are very transparent . . . the way somebody walks or the way people carry their necks tells you something about the way they live or about the things that have happened to them. Somehow everything is visible – even when we cling to certain things. You really can see where something is suppressed. There are spots where people don't think about controlling themselves.[20]

In seeking to counteract suppressed conflicts and to reveal the ways in which people are controlling themselves, Bausch is on the same wave-length as Theweleit. While he advocates radical therapy as a method of breaking down the rigidity of physical boundaries, she makes spectators watch representations of social, gendered behaviour which question and destabilize the edges of permissible masculine behaviour.

Most of Bausch's pieces consist of collections of cameo-like incidents in which the behaviour of individuals is set against the behaviour of the group as a whole. *Bluebeard* is different in that it has a central male character who is the dominant figure almost continually on stage through-out the piece. His role is thus more developed or more intensely explored than male roles in her other pieces, and, of all her work, *Bluebeard* presents some of the most violent and abject representations of masculinity.

The full title of this piece (in English) is 'Bluebeard – while listening to a tape recording of Béla Bartók's Opera "Duke Bluebeard's Castle"'. The tape is played by Bluebeard (Jan Minarik) on a tape-recorder mounted on a wheeled table with wires running up to the lighting grid above the stage. Bluebeard switches this on and off, sometimes repeating short excerpts several times. The setting is a big room like that of a large country house with white walls and a white floor thinly covered in dried leaves. The opera is about Duke Bluebeard and his new wife Judith. It tells how she is given the keys to seven doors in his castle. The first six are opened to reveal a torture chamber, an armoury, a treasure chamber, a garden of blood, a huge kingdom and a sea of tears. The seventh door contains the bodies of the Duke's previous wives, all of them murdered. The opera ends with Judith's aria accepting her fate. In Bausch's piece the roles of Bluebeard and Judith are represented, but the action on stage doesn't follow this story literally, presenting instead a commentary on it. Norbert Servos suggests that 'Bausch transposes the symbolism in Bartok's opera into a world of concrete and immediate images centering on the conflict between partners' (1984: 54).

A bald summary of the conflict between Judith and Bluebeard is that when he wants her sexually he is violent and she a passive victim; but, when she acts in a sensual and affectionate way towards him, he rejects her, again in a violent way. The women in the cast sometimes represent Bluebeard's previous wives, while subsidiary couples of men and women act out variations on Bluebeard and Judith's dire relationship. There is one scene which presents a reversal of the scene in *Kontakthof* described above in which the men touch a woman until she collapses underneath their 'tenderness'. In *Bluebeard* the roles are reversed. All the women come up and adoringly stroke Bluebeard monotonously repeating 'Thank you', while he remains impassively seated. Staring steadfastly in an elevated manner he seems unable to respond, keeping himself tightly under control, like the fascist soldiers Klaus Theweleit wrote about.

If Bluebeard's violence is one signifier of his masculinity, the way he controls both Judith and the action on stage is another. He keeps control through the tape-recorder. When the tape stops so do the dancers, as in a party game, and their movement activities restart or go back to repeat themselves when the tape is switched on again. In the final section of the piece, Bluebeard has dressed Judith up in all the other women's long, loose dresses so that she can hardly move. She is lying on top of him, pinning him to the floor, and he, with great difficulty, pushes the two of them around the room with his legs. He is thus unable to reach the tape which plays on to the end of opera. He still continues to control the action however, clapping to make the dancers move or freeze in a reprise of moments earlier in the piece.

Through all this controlling, Bluebeard repeats things he finds pleasurable. When on the tape the Duke sings 'This is my torture chamber' Judith on stage screams and acts out fainting. The excerpt is frantically rewound

n again a few times so that he can enjoy watching her doing
so uses the tape to maintain his own limits, stopping things
m feel uncomfortable. Either way he controls women. He is
en the women act spontaneously: for example the giggles and
/ make as they play in his magic garden eventually drive him
off the tape and turn round sharply as if to reprimand them if
e not stopped. Spontaneous expressions of female sexuality are
worse. As he sits by the tape-recorder, Judith kneels between his knees
and reaches up to caress his chin and cheek. Bluebeard puts his hands on
top of her head and violently thrusts her down on to the floor; but of course
she tries again in endless repeats. But earlier Bluebeard had buried his
head in an infantile way against Judith's belly and she leans her upper
body right over him as if hiding him. He is hiding from sexually explicit
behaviour. All around him on the floor, the women in the company
clamber crab-like above the men, planting their legs wide apart to show
their vulvas. Judith, on the tape, sings (about the seven doors) 'open them,
open them for me'.

The most extraordinary image of masculinity in *Bluebeard* is the body-
building sequence. This comes when the Duke on the tape sings 'This is
my armoury'. The men line up back stage and walk forward in a line
grinning and swaggering, showing off their muscles. Judith dances in front
of them as if unaware of them in a sequence of anguished reaching arms
and pliant, folding spine reminiscent of expressionistic early German
modern dance. The men run to the back of the stage, take off jackets and
shirts and come forward performing the same gestures bare chested. The
tape rewinds and they repeat the sequence wearing only briefs, and the
women in the cast follow close behind them admiringly caressing their
arms and chests. The poses that the men take up derive from circus strong
man acts, and use tension to make their muscles bulge, showing the
tendons and veins beneath the skin. These signify male strength, but
tightness and tension point to an unwillingness to let go and be free. These
macho men who turn their bodies into hard phallic forms surely do so
because they feel insecure about their bodies' limits, and need to repel any
pleasurable intrusion. Later Bluebeard himself, alone in the centre of the
stage with a doll, repeats these strong man poses. The doll has previously
been petted by a woman who brings it on, billing and cooing gently to it
as if it were an infant. It must be his child, and thus a sign of his virility,
his ability to become erect. Bluebeard's display, pumping his muscles
narcissistically in front of the doll, is almost like masturbation.

At the heart of Bluebeard's problem is his inability to give or accept
affection. Without this ability, everything he does is too violent, too
narcissistic, too clinging, too frigid, too far. There is something abject and
inhuman about him. Like the fascist soldiers in Theweleit's study, his
assertion of physical and phallic strength is a defence against the threat

Figure 11 Jan Minarik as Bluebeard, pumping his muscles narcissistically in front of a doll in Pina Bausch's *Bluebeard* (1977).
(Photo: Gert Weigelt)

posed by the women, their boundarylessness. To give in to them is to bring back repressed memories of the developmental traumas which necessitate the need to disavow feminine nurture. Whereas Bartók's opera is about Judith's submission, Bausch's Tanztheater piece is about Bluebeard's hopelessness and despair, as he ends up pinned to the ground by the dead weight of what is presumably his latest dead victim. In terms of its representations of masculinity, *Bluebeard* challenges the spectators to reassess their idea of what constitutes acceptable masculine behaviour by making disturbingly visible repressed aspects of the construction of masculine identity.

Bluebeard and *Dead Dreams* ... create subversive presentations of the body, through physical and emotional risks and through the uncompromisingly extreme tone of their work; these prompt the spectator into a heightened awareness of the relationship between the male dancer's body and the social and ethical issues that surround the unacceptable masculine behaviour which the pieces represent. These works force the spectator to see the male dancer differently. Michael Clark and Mark Morris in his 'stupid men's dance' fail to make the spectator see differently because they are unable or unwilling to question the conservative premises that are implicit within the rhetoric of inherited cultural traditions.

POST WHAT?

The slightly facetious title of this chapter is *Post Men*. The word 'post' is intended first to refer to postmodern culture and second to the idea that society might be able to move on and leave behind definitions of masculinity that are both oppressive and repressive. The evidence of the examples of representations of post men considered above does not appear, on the face of it, very hopeful on this second count.

From a female point of view, the men that the women get to dance with in recent theatre dance have not been exactly ideal partners in the Fred Astaire mould. Male dancers push their female partners around in 'Mikrokosmos', beat them up in *Bluebeard*, or women have to make do with what they've got as in Anderson's *Surabaya Johnny*. Women collapse underneath what is understood (by men) as 'tenderness' in *Kontakthof*, or they find men to be unwilling, awkward partners as in Lemon's *Folk Dances*.

From a gay male point of view the prospect is pretty despairing too. Only Dorfman's *Horn* puts a brave face on male–male relationships. Otherwise, to be gay is to be a shockingly disturbing outsider in Clark and Morris's work, or to be problematically lonely and violently abused or abusive in DV8's work.

From my own heterosexual, male point of view I find myself having to face up to the idea that men in many ways hate and fear women, as in

Bluebeard, and other men, as in *My Sex, Our Dance* and *Dead Dreams . . .*; and the realization, in general, of how gay men and feminists view masculinity is a disturbing one. These recent works present a powerful and uncomfortable critique of prevalent norms of masculine social behaviour. Nevertheless, by critically dismantling mainstream dance conventions and problematizing technical virtuosity in male dance, all these artists have brought about a situation in which a new relationship has been defined between the dancer's body and the meaning of dance movement. The resulting work has had the potential to challenge the spectator to reassess aspects of masculine identity and experience that are generally denied or rendered invisible in mainstream cultural forms.

In some ways, the recent works considered in this chapter do not appear to have made the decisive break with previous ideologies and practices that the prefix 'post' suggests. Michael Clark's *Mmm* ostensibly looked back to Nijinsky's *Sacre*. Clark's teasing revelations of his much-admired body probably have more in common with similar glimpses of Nijinsky's body in ballets like *Schéhérazade* and *Narcisse* – with Fokine's rather than Nijinsky's choreography (see Chapter 4). Moreover Clark's degrading uses of much-valued, virtuoso ballet movement find a precedent in Fokine's own attitudes towards ballet technique as exemplified in the roles of the ballerina doll and the two street dancers in *Petrouchka*. The abject, inhuman men in Nijinsky's *Sacre* have more in common with Pina Bausch's male dancers than they have with Clark's. One more parallel can be drawn between a work discussed in this chapter and an early modernist ballet: Nijinska's detached, critical presentation of dynamic male dancing in the athlete's entry in *Les Biches* (see Chapter 4) finds an echo in Mark Morris's treatment of similarly rumbustious male dancing in 'The stupid men's dance'. Both choreographers are using what Tim Clark calls practices of negation (see Chapter 6) to denaturalize the conventions and traditions of male dance.

Rather than constituting a radical break, the deconstructive strategies used by recent choreographers can thus be seen as the latest manifestation of an avant-garde tradition that questions art's institutionalized status. What recent works have decisively rejected are the ideologies of modernist art – modernism's assertion of its autonomy and its concentration on exclusively formal, aesthetic concerns. There is, in general, a greater gap between the works discussed in this chapter and those created in the 1940s and 1950s than between experimental work now and the more radical works created between 1910 and 1930. The gulf that separates Bausch's *Bluebeard* from Graham's *Cave of the Heart* (1946) (see Chapter 5) is perhaps clearest in the effects of the ways in which each represents masculinity. Graham, ultimately, celebrates and glorifies precisely those traditional male qualities of violence and aggression which Bausch problematizes and destabilizes. Limón's *The Moor's Pavane* (1949) and DV8's *My Sex, Our*

Dance (1987) both explore the problematic potential of the anxieties surrounding male–male relationships; but Othello's tragedy is a private one whereas DV8 reveal structures that constitute a widespread social problem.

By drawing attention to areas of men's subjective experiences of embodiment, many of these works have revealed otherwise hidden aspects of the construction of masculine identity. Chodorow has suggested that some of the conflictual and contradictory aspects of masculine identity have roots in repressed memories of developmental stages that are linked with the early, developing awareness of the integrity of the body (see Chapter 1). Recent experimental dance, through contradicting the metaphysical view of the dancer's body observed in relation to André Levinson's dance theory (discussed in Chapter 2), has the potential to emphasize the materiality of the male body in ways that draw attention to these conflictual and contradictory areas. Theweleit has argued that western male identity is dependent on the maintenance of tight physical and psychological boundaries (see Chapter 3). The various ways in which the works discussed in this chapter (and others) present men's subjective experiences of embodiment constitute a challenge to these boundaries. The hidden dependence upon the maintenance of these boundaries is revealed when movement qualities associated with bravura male dancing are problematized (in Cunningham's and Paxton's work, discussed in Chapter 6, and in DV8's works) or when anxieties are aroused through showing male bodies moving into close proximity or contact with one another (for example in *Jeux Sans Frontière* and *My Sex, Our Dance*). The freer, released and anti-virtuosic movement style presented by Fergus Early and Ralph Lemon represents a challenge to the tighter ways in which men dance in Graham-based modern dance pieces or Russian-influenced ballet productions. The necessity of maintaining tightness is also undermined where intimate expressions of male behaviour are revealed (for example blowing in *Horn*, caressing in *Surabaya Johnny*), or where men appear out of control (the loser in *Blues Suite*) or less than whole (exploring disability in *Are You Right . . .*) or so abject and grotesque as to appear almost beneath humanity (*Dead Dreams . . .*, *Bluebeard*).

Overall the effects of denaturalizing and demystifying masculinity in recent works seem to have been to show up some of the more unsatisfactory aspects of what it is to be a man in western society today. Nevertheless there are sometimes glimpses of possible alternatives where the rules are ignored and conventions and traditions destabilized and denaturalized. Where these works challenge homophobic, heterosexual conditioning, restrictive logocentric ways of thinking and communicating, or tightly bound aspects of male identity, they give glimpses of possible alternatives. They suggest that there are ways in which some men are surely, albeit with great difficulty and in slow motion, responding to recent debates about the nature of gendered identity, and dancing and working towards more acceptable ways of being masculine.

NOTES

INTRODUCTION

1 E.g. Sofonisba Anguissola, Maria Tintoretto, Artemisia Gentilleschi: see Parker and Pollock (1981) and Nochlin (1971).
2 See Bland and Percival (1984), Clark and Crisp (1984), Swinson (1964) and Terry (1979).
3 For example a report in 1969 by the Arts Council of Great Britain on opera and ballet in the United Kingdom stated that 75 per cent of audiences for ballet were female.
4 I do not mean that there may not be inspiring ballet performances but only that I have never seen any. Never having lived in or near London I have not been in a position to see those ballet performances which the London critics value.

1 THE TROUBLE WITH THE MALE DANCER . . .

1 Illustrated in Guest (1966), plate 12.
2 See Heller (1982) and Allen and Haccoun (1976).
3 Writers such as Andy Metcalf, Victor Seidler and Paul Ryan along with other similar writers in Metcalf and Humphries (eds) (1985).
4 This is one of the themes of the Men's Issue of *New Dance* magazine, no. 40 (spring 1980).
5 Editorial, *Achilles Heel*, 3 (undated: probably 1979 as no. 2 is dated 1979).
6 But Victorian women were stuck within this notion of purity, so that if they didn't conform absolutely to it they were in danger of becoming fallen women. This dichotomy of virgin/whore allowed female ballet dancers to be considered to be sexually available.
7 For example the brush strokes of Romantic painters like Delacroix, Constable or Géricault might be seen as expressive of emotional struggle, while the touch of impressionist painters like Manet, Monet and Renoir could be seen as a sign of their extreme sensitivity. Were they not considered 'great artists', such expressiveness would have been considered inappropriate behaviour for men.
8 Sedgwick refers to work on structures of kinship by Lévi-Strauss and Gayle Rubin's critique of the former's work on kinship systems (1978). Rubin argues that women have been used as an object of exchange which she characterizes as traffic in women.
9 A different view could be taken of the male dancer in Bournonville's work. One could argue that Bournonville's ballets – particularly his later ones like

Life Guards on Amager (1871) – kept apace with new ideas and developments in the theatre in a way that ballet did not do elsewhere during the nineteenth century. It is surely more than a coincidence for example that when Ibsen's *A Doll's House* was premièred at The Royal Danish Theatre in 1879, the lead role of Nora was played by Betty Hennings (née Schnell), an ex-ballerina who had danced roles in several Bournonville ballets including Hilde in *A Folk Tale* and Sigyn in *The Lay of Thrym*. Despite Royal patronage, Bournonville's ballets might therefore be said to have created a contemporary bourgeois world-view. See Aschengreen (1979) and Hallar and Scavenius (1992).

2 DANCE, MASCULINITY AND REPRESENTATIONS

1 It is an abbreviated version of a chapter of my thesis (Burt 1994).
2 In his *Poetics*: Aristotle (1934).
3 Janet Wolff has pointed out that most accounts of modernism in the arts either overlook or exclude women writers and artists from the modernist canon (1990: 3).
4 Noel Carroll has argued that Rainer, in pursuing the intention of eradicating expression in the narrowest sense in *Trio A*, introduces expressive qualities at other levels. See Carroll (1981).
5 One could point out here that although some of Balanchine's works like *Agon* (along with some of his later restagings of his earlier ballets) did dispense with decor, narrative and costume, Balanchine did go on using period costume and decor in new ballets more or less to the end of his life. One could also point out that Rainer's minimalism was of exactly the sort that Fried would have condemned as theatrical. In her essay about *Trio A*, 'A quasi-survey of some minimalist tendencies in the quantitatively minimalist dance activity amidst the plethora', Rainer explicitly compares pedestrianism in her work and in that of Steve Paxton with minimalist sculpture. She herself is a close friend of the sculptor Robert Morris and in the 1960s produced collaborative works with him.
6 This is the notion of power developed in Foucault's *Discipline and Punish* (1979) and *History of Sexuality*, vol. 1 (1981), especially pp. 92–102. See also the interview 'Power/body' in *Power/Knowledge* (1980). With Michael Huxley I have applied Foucault's notion of the investment of power in the body to an analysis of the teaching of dance classes in Burt and Huxley (1986).

3 LOOKING AT THE MALE

1 Camille Paglia has suggested something quite similar: 'A women simply is, but a man must become. Masculinity is risky and elusive. It is achieved by a revolt from woman, and it is confirmed only by other men. Feminist fantasies about the ideal "sensitive" male have failed. Manhood coerced into sensitivity is no manhood at all.' (1992: 82).
2 Rose English, who trained in fine art and has subsequently worked in the area of performance and live art, was involved in the mid-1970s in developing feminist dance works with Jacky Lansley and Sally Potter. The central argument of her article concerns the way images of the ballerina are determined by male desire, and has been taken up by Valerie Briginshaw (forthcoming). It is worth saying, however, that there is perhaps an element of humour and exaggeration in parts of 'Alas Alack': the image of the ballerina as a giant phallus crowned with a pink tiara is surely wildly over the top.

3 See Marks and de Courtivron (1981) and American writers associated with *October* magazine published from MIT such as Rosalind Krauss, Jane Gallop, Hollis Frampton, Annette Michelson. There are problems over the use of the word 'feminism' in France, and Kristeva, Cixous, Irigaray and other French writers working along similar lines do not necessarily use it to describe themselves. Nevertheless they have been called feminists in most English-language writing about them: for example Marks and de Courtivron's anthology is titled *New French Feminisms*.

4 Claid mentioned this in unpublished parts of an interview with myself for an article in *Artscene*, February 1992. The article was about her choreography but she was also at the time writing about Cixous and other French feminist theorists as part of her master's degree.

4 NIJINSKY: MODERNISM AND HETERODOX REPRESENTATIONS OF MASCULINITY

1 It was not of course the supported adagio on its own that was new to western European audiences at the time but the far greater formal and technical complexity which Petipa had developed in St Petersburg.

For this performance, the 'Blue Bird' *pas de deux* was renamed 'L'Oiseau de feu', and was variously retitled in later programmes. In 1921 Diaghilev nearly bankrupted himself when he presented his full-length version of *Sleeping Beauty* in London. The 'Blue Bird' *pas de deux* was not the only classical extract on the programme: see Garafola (1989), appendix C.

2 For example, see Nijinska's account of Fokine choreographing the role of Papillon in *Le Carnaval* (1910): Nijinska (1981): 284–9. Nijinsky himself heard Stravinsky play the music for *Petrouchka* some time before Fokine did, which suggests that he was very largely responsible for the creation of that role: Buckle (1975): 180.

3 While the Ballets Russes appeared in opera houses they also when in need of money appeared in music halls, and in the American tours in vaudeville theatres. Nijinsky performed in a music hall in London when he formed his own company in 1914.

4 Lady Juliet, in Richard Buckle's words, established a kind of record in having seen Nijinsky dance *Le Spectre de la rose* in three cities in the first nine months of its existence. Buckle (1975): 259.

5 Quoted in Chadd and Gage (1979): 22. They ascribe the passage to *Vogue* in 1911 or 1912 but give no reference. *Vogue* was not published in the UK until 1916. The quotation may therefore refer to the interest of New Yorkers not Londoners.

6 Of course Rambert was writing over half a century later and might well have been thinking of Cocteau's drawing when she wrote this. Richard Buckle suggests that the drawing depicts an occasion when Nijinksy and Karsavina repeated the whole of *Faune* a second time. Rambert (1972): 57; Buckle (1975): 259.

7 See Dyer (1990): 17–20 for further information on late-nineteenth-century and early-twentieth-century ideas about the third sex.

8 Nevertheless, when *Narcisse* was performed in New York in 1916, the reviews specifically mention Nijinsky's 'effeminacy', though this may have been a reflection of the extraordinary impression left by Mordkin. Buckle (1975): 434.

9 In 1912 it was planned for the Ballets Russes to appear at the Narodny Dom Theatre in St Petersburg. Diaghilev had even signed contracts but the season

had to be cancelled when the theatre unfortunately burnt down. See Buckle (1975): 262. For details of Diaghilev's dismissal from the Imperial Theatres in 1901 and Nijinsky's dismissal in 1911 see Buckle (1979): 60–3 and (1975): 191–3.

10 The most interesting example of this point of view is Buchloh 1981, but it can also be found in Lyotard (1984) and Jameson (1985).

11 Though during most of his life Stravinsky denied liking Nijinsky's choreography for *Sacre*, he reaffirmed his original opinion in 1967 when a piano score he had marked for Nijinsky during rehearsals was rediscovered. For Stravinsky's retraction see Stravinsky (1969), appendix 3. He had given the score to Misia Sert after the first night of the ballet. She had subsequently given it to Diaghilev who had given it to Anton Dolin. Robert Craft points out that, while the first performance of the ballet must have been a painful experience for Stravinsky, when *Sacre* was performed in a concert in Paris in 1914 the result was a triumph. It is understandable therefore for Stravinsky to have suppressed the memory of the ballet. At the end of his life, however, he said that Nijinsky's was the best ballet version he had seen. Craft (1976): 37 and Dolin (1985): 133–4.

12 Nijinska mentions that he had a book of Gauguin's paintings at the time (1981: 442) and told Richard Buckle that he actually had it open during rehearsals (Chadd and Gage 1979: 21).

13 For more on connections between the poètes maudits and homosexual identity see Stamboulian and Marks (1979).

14 But extremely difficult to perform because of the way the body is always presented in profile, and, as Lydia Sokolova put it, because of the ingenious way it fitted with the music: Sokolova (1960): 40.

15 Recently reconstructed at San Francisco for the Oakland Ballet by Frank Ries.

16 Nijinska was half-deaf, having being caught in the shelling of Kiev during the civil war, and spoke little French: Baer sums it up best (1987: 42–4).

5 MEN, MODERNISM AND MODERN AMERICAN DANCE

1 See Kendall (1979), Jowitt (1988): 78–81, Siegel (1987), and Shawn (1968), his own book on Delsarte.

2 Not just through the example of his dancing and that of his company of male dancers but also through his writing and lecturing on men and dance: see Shawn (1916, 1933, 1936, 1946, 1966).

3 See Terry (1976): 109. Animating a classical sculpture in this way was also a recognized Delsarte exercise.

4 Given this chronology, Shawn might well have actually thought of the Husbandman when he was writing, but it is also likely that Graham and/or Hawkins may have had Shawn and his work at the back of her mind when she was choreographing the piece.

5 Dance in America TV film *Martha Graham Dance Company* directed by Merrill Brockway (1976) with Yuriko Kimura as the Bride and David Hatch Walker as the Revivalist.

6 *Appalachian Spring*, a film by Peter Glushanok for WQED-TV (1959).

7 Of course not all Graham's pieces are situated outside history in this way. *Episodes: Part 1* (1959) about Mary Queen of Scots looks in photographs like a historical costume drama. Usually, where a historical reference is indicated it is less specific: the design of *Time of Snow* (1968) about Héloïse and Abelard seems a strange mixture of Japanese decor and medieval European costume.

8 Cohan interviewed by Selma Jeanne Cohen (1973), tape in archive of Dance Perspectives Foundation.

9 See Fanon (1968) and Homi Bhabha (1983).

10 Marcia Siegel wrote: 'What had always been José's greatest asset, his virile style' (1987: 263). See also John Martin's comments on Limón in 1936 (1968: 281–4) and Deborah Jowitt's tribute to Limón written in 1972 at the time he was dying (1977: 90–4).

11 Apart from Barbara Pollack's short biographical sketch (1993) and sections in Marcia Siegel's *Days on Earth* (1987) and Pauline Koner's *Solitary Song* (1989), there is little information on Limón. More research could usefully be done through examination of Limón's autobiography in manuscript in New York Public Library Dance Collection.

12 Limón choreographed several pieces on Mexican themes throughout his career, of which one of the earliest was *Danzas Mexicanas* (1939).

13 In 1950 and 1951 The José Limón Dance Company visited Mexico by invitation from Miguel Covarrubias of the the Palacio de Bellas Artes, Mexico City. In 1954 the US State Department in collaboration with ANTA sent them on a tour of South America and again in 1960. In 1957 they went on a European tour, again arranged by the State Department. See Koner (1989): 191–236, especially the section where Koner and Limón decide to visit Spain after consultation with 'embassy officials' (1989: 227).

14 Limón's *The Traitor* (1954), however, came at the height of the McCarthy era.

15 Humphrey wrote a long letter to John Martin in response to his grudging review of a programme of pieces by Humphrey and Limón that were choreographed to music by Bach. Martin didn't think 'modern' dance should use 'classical' music. Part of the letter was printed in the *New York Times*, the full text in Cohen (1972): 255.

16 Limón doesn't say where this quotation from Humphrey comes from.

17 Limón's essay 'The virile dance' was initially written for *Dance Magazine* in December 1948, around the time that Limón was planning *The Moor's Pavane*, and subsequently printed in Sorrell (1966): 82–6.

18 Could Limón have been alluding to the Duke of Windsor?

19 Originally the dancers' roles were called 'The Moor', 'The Moor's Wife', 'The Moor's Friend' and 'His Friend's Wife'; this was presumably to distance it from the revered original, but for convenience and clarity the roles here are referred to as Othello, Desdemona, Iago and Emilia.

20 Pavanes were stately court dances during the sixteenth and seventeenth centuries. The composer and dance writer Louis Horst taught a series of composition classes on 'pre-classical forms' for modern dance artists, and the pavane was one of the forms examined. There is no evidence that Limón ever went to these, although Lucas Hoving did. Hoving says that Limón picked and chose from the various pre-classical forms what he wanted to make the 'emotional texture' for particular scenes (Mindlin 1992: 17).

21 Hoving actually floated this idea while referring to the film by Laurence Olivier of *Othello* (Mindlin 1992: 15).

22 Hilary Carty has written an intriguing examination of the make up of AAADT's audience in London in 1992: see Carty (1992).

23 This is not to imply that all black dancers in the United States are from working-class backgrounds. In the UK, at least, ballet as opposed to modern dance is not really a viable option for most young black people from lower-income families. There is still a much smaller black middle class in Britain than in the United States.

24 As Iain Chambers has put it: 'From plantation to ghetto, black culture, and especially black music, has provided one of the strongest means of survival – a secret language of solidarity, a way of articulating oppression, a means of cultural resistance, a cry of hope' (Chambers 1976: 161).

25 Introducing a British television screening of a video of *Blues Suite*, Robert Cohan said that this duet preceded the rest of the piece.

26 This was the costume worn on the video referred to, and in performance at the Alhambra Theatre, Bradford, in October 1991 and worn in a photograph in the programme there, but not in the photos in Mazo (1978).

6 AVANT-GARDE STRATEGIES

1 Sally Banes (1980) has applied the term 'postmodern' to the work of dancers like Paxton in the 1960s. I shall be applying this term in Chapter 7 only to dance work since the late 1970s. Cunningham's work sits uneasily in definitions of either modern or postmodern dance.

2 Cunningham is actually recalling an anecdote from an introductory talk before performances by the Cunningham Company which John Cage gave to college audiences in the mid-1950s. Cage (1961): 94–5.

3 One would expect Cunningham to come out well from the test Rubidge proposed, as she is a Cunningham fan, and was working for Ballet Rambert at the time that *Septet* was in their repertoire.

4 Carolyn Brown suggests that some earlier defenders of Cunningham who later said he had sold out probably weren't interested in the work itself, only in the revolution. But then can the one be surgically detached from the other? (Klosty 1975: 31).

5 One could almost make a subversive, homoerotic reading of the piece as one male energy rubbing against another. Although De Kooning's artistic philosophy was antithetical to that of Rauschenberg, Willem and Elaine De Kooning were on the faculty at Black Mountain College where Rauschenberg was a student and when Cage and Cunningham were in residence there. The De Koonings designed the set for a performance there in 1948 of Erik Satie's *Ruse of the Medusa* organized by Cage with Cunningham, Buckminster Fuller and others taking part. Incidentally Edwin Denby, in his article on photographs of Nijinsky, mentions discussing them with Willem De Kooning.

6 Nevertheless the Trustees of the Museum of Modern Art in New York did not purchase it in 1958, fearing 'it would offend patriotic sensibilities': see Orton (1988): 13 note 22.

7 These are not the titles Satie gave to the piano pieces, which are 'Manière de commencement', 'Prolongation du même', 'I', 'II', 'III', 'En plus', 'Redite'. See Orledge 1990: 55–6 for discussion of the music.

8 The pages in *Changes* are unnumbered.

9 More pull is discernible in the *Event for Television* version than in that of Rambert Dance Company. This image could be a reference to Apollo riding a chariot with muses for horses in Balanchine's *Apollon Musagète*.

10 This section of *Antic Hay* is performed as part of Cunningham's *Event for Television*.

11 Cunningham's *Second Hand* was to have been set to Satie's *Socrate* in a piano duet adaptation which Cage had written. The publishers of Satie's music wouldn't allow this to be performed so Cage developed his own solo piano piece which used Satie's accompaniment but had a new melody devised using chance procedures hence its title *Cheap Imitation*. Cunningham therefore

decided to call his own piece *Second Hand* as it reused an earlier solo of his, *Idyllic Song* (1944) which was set to part of Satie's *Socrate*.

12 For another example of associative meanings in Cunningham's work see David Vaughan's article on the way *Walkaround Time* refers to aspects of Duchamp's work and to his *Large Glass* which is silk-screened on transparent plastic boxes for the set: 'Then I thought about Marcel. . .' reprinted in Kostelanetz (ed.) (1992).

13 For example Vaughan *et al*. 1987: 30, King 1992.

14 See, for example, Stephanie Jordan's review of Cunningham and Cage's Dialogues in Liverpool in 1980: Jordan (1980).

15 The following description comes from my own experience of practising contact improvisation since 1979, and is supported by remarks made by Steve Paxton especially in two interviews published by Dartington College, in the UK. See Paxton (1977 and 1982).

16 See Novack (1990): 74, 87, 166–70 for other examples. These specifically British instances are given in order to put on record non-American examples to extend the examples given in Novack's book: they also of course deal with masculinity.

17 Weld (1979): 30–1. Laurieston Hall was, and at the time of writing still is, a large old sanatorium building in south-west Scotland which is occupied by a group of people who are committed to living communally and to a variety of counter-cultural beliefs. They have produced for many years a 'Communes Newsletter' and hold a regular programme of 'alternative' weekends and conferences. Another example is a contact improvisation workshop during the Bristol Men Against Sexism Conference, April 1980 (which I myself attended) reported on in *New Dance*, 15 (Men's Issue). Significant in this context is the fact that the first formally acknowledged instance of a contact workshop was one which Paxton held with a group of male students at Oberlin College, Ohio in 1972: see Novack (1990): 60.

18 For information on Mangrove see item in *New Dance*, 14 (spring 1980), pp. 5–6 and Novack (1990): 88 and *passim*. Novack also mentions Men Working (1990: 100).

19 I'm thinking here of choreographers like Kevin Finnan and Louise Richards of Motionhouse and Mark Murphy of Vtol in the UK or Bill T. Jones in the USA. Cynthia Novack gives an interesting example of the differences between the 1978 performance of Jones's *Shared Distance* and its revival in 1985: Novack (1990): 149.

20 Trisha Brown, during discussion after a performance at Riverside Studios, London, 11 November 1983.

7 POST MEN

1 Two exceptions being Owens (1985) and Lee (1987).

2 In a way that is what I have been doing in some of the readings I have made of representations of masculinity in the last three chapters.

3 *New Dance*, 14 (spring 1980). This provoked caustic comments by women and gay men in the letters pages of the following Women's Issue of *New Dance*, 15 (summer 1980).

4 For clarity I am referring to them by their first names only.

5 This is most clearly exemplified in his work with Green Candle Community Dance Company.

6 This and subsequent comments by Anderson comes from an interview with myself, December 1991.

7 Interviewed in 1991, Lemon said that he intended the next dancer who joined his company would be black (Fanger 1991: 40).

8 Anderson stressed to me in December 1991 that some spectators might either know or suspect that some members of The Featherstonehaughs are gay and that this would affect the way they watched *Surabaya Johnny*: a gay Featherstonehaugh in this piece might therefore be caressing a faithless Surabaya Johnny.

9 In the film by Wolfgang Kolb broadcast on British TV Channel 4 on 7 May 1989.

10 See my review in *New Dance*, 38 (autumn 1986).

11 As Judith Butler puts it 'As opposed to grief or mourning, in which separation is recognized and the libido attached to the original object is successfully displaced onto a new substitute object, melancholy designates a failure to grieve to which the loss is simply internalized and, in that sense, refused' (1990: 84).

12 This and subsequent comments come from an interview with Nigel Charnock at Yorkshire Dance Centre, Leeds, 21 October 1991.

13 Lloyd Newson, interview with Julie Tolley and Ramsay Burt at Yorkshire Dance Centre, 3 April 1987.

14 See Meyer (1993) for full discussion of the history of, and different attitudes towards, camp.

15 Mackrell (1989). For more on Bowery before he started working with Clark see Lesley White, 'The new glitterati 2', *The Face* 48 (April 1984), pp. 56–7.

16 See for example David Buckland's photograph of Clark in the National Portrait Gallery, London.

17 On 14–24 October 1989. The next exhibition in the gallery was of Jasper Johns's Dancers on a Plane series. D'Offay also deals in Beuys, Gilbert and George, Clemente, Schnabel, Baselitz, etc. – the bestsellers of the 1980s. Beuys did at least one performance there.

18 For discussion of degrading imagery in Genet's work see Dyer (1990).

19 On Wigman, Laban and the Nazis see Burt (1990) and Preston-Dunlop (1988).

20 Hoghe (1980): 65. Here Bausch sounds like someone trained in Laban Movement Analysis, which is almost true. She trained initially at the Folkwangschule in Essen under Kurt Joos where she will have come in touch with Laban's ideas.

BIBLIOGRAPHY

Acocella, J. (1993) *Mark Morris*, New York: Farrar Straus Giroux.

Adair, C. (1992) *Women and Dance: Sylphs and Sirens*, London: Macmillan.

Adshead, J. (ed.) (1988) *Dance Analysis*, London: Dance Books.

Aldrich, R. (1994) *The Seduction of the Mediterranean*, London: Routledge.

Allen J. G. and Haccoun D. M. (1976) 'Sex differences in emotionality: a multidimensional approach', *Human Relations*, 29.

Aristotle (1934) *Poetics* (translated by Twining, Thomas, 1789), London: J. M. Dent.

Asaf'yev, B. (1982) *A Book about Stravinsky*, Ann Arbor, Michigan: UMI Research Press.

Aschenbrenner, J. (1980a) 'Black dance and dancers', *Dance Research Annual*, 12 (New York): 33–9.

—— (1980b) 'The critical response', *Dance Research Journal*, 12 (New York): 41–7.

Aschengreen, E. (1974) 'The beautiful danger: facets of the Romantic ballet', *Dance Perspectives*, 58 (summer).

—— (1979) 'Bournonville and male dancing', *Danish Journal*, special issue, 'The Royal Danish Ballet and Bournonville': 24–7.

Auslander, P. (1987) 'Towards a concept of the political in postmodern theatre', *Theatre Journal*, 39 (1) 20–34.

Baden-Powell, R. (1922) *Rovering to Success: A Guide for Young Manhood*, London: Herbert Jenkins.

Baer, N. Van N. (1987) *Bronislava Nijinska: A Dancer's Legacy*, San Francisco: The Fine Arts Museums of San Francisco.

Bailey, D. A. (1988) 'Re-thinking black representations', *Ten-8*, 31 (winter): 36–49.

Banes, S. (1980) *Terpsichore in Sneakers: Post-modern Dance*, Boston, Mass.: Houghton Mifflin.

—— (1984) 'Judson Dance Theatre: democracy's body 1962–1964', unpublished Ph.D thesis, New York University (University Microfilms, Ann Arbor).

—— (1987) 'Vital signs: Steve Paxton's *Flat* in perspective', *Cord Dance Research Annual*, 16: 120–34

Baron (1950) *Baron at the Ballet*, London: Collins.

Barthes, R. (1983) 'Inaugural lecture, Collège de France', in *Barthes: Selected Writings*, London: Fontana.

Battersby, C. (1989) *Gender and Genius*, London: The Women's Press.

Benjamin, A. and Osborne, P. (eds) (1991) *Thinking Art: Beyond Traditional Aesthetics*, London: ICA.

Benois, A. (1936) 'The decor and costume', in C. Brahms (ed.), *Footnotes to the Ballet*, London: Lovat Dickinson.

—— (1941) *Reminiscences of the Russian Ballet*, London: Putnam.

Berger, J. (1972) *Ways of Seeing*, Harmondsworth: Penguin.

Bhabha, H, K. (1983) 'The other question . . .', *Screen*, 24 (6): 18–36.

Bland, A. and Percival, J. (1984) *Men Dancing: Performers and Performances*, London: Weidenfeld.

Boyce, J., Daly, A., Jones, B. T. and Martin, C. (1988) 'Movement and gender: a roundtable discussion', *TDR*, 32 (4): 82–101.

Brahms, C. (ed.) (1936) *Footnotes to the Ballet*, London: Lovat Dickinson.

Bratton, J. S. (1990) 'Dancing a hornpipe in fetters', *Folk Music Journal*, 6 (1): 65–82.

Briginshaw, V. (forthcoming) 'Dancing dicks – a case in point(e)'.

Brinson, P. (1966) *Background to European Ballet*, Leyden: A. W. Sithoff.

Bristow, J. (1988) 'How men are', *New Formations*, 6 (winter): 119–31.

—— (1991) *Empire Boys*, London: HarperCollins.

Brod, H. (ed.) (1987) *The Making of Masculinities*. London: Allen & Unwin.

Brooks, L. (1982) *Loulou in Hollywood*, London: Hamish Hamilton.

Brown, C. (1975) Untitled contribution to J. Klosty (ed.), *Merce Cunningham*, New York: E. P. Dutton.

Buchloh, B. (1981) 'Figures of authority, ciphers of regression', *October*, 16 (spring): 39–68.

Buckle, R. (1975) *Nijinsky*, Harmondsworth: Penguin.

—— (1979) *Diaghilev*, London: Weidenfeld & Nicolson.

Bürger, P. (1984) *Theory of the Avant-garde*, Minneapolis: University of Minnesota Press, and Manchester: Manchester University Press.

Burgin, V. (ed.) (1986) *Formations of Fantasy*, London: Methuen.

Burt, R. (1986) 'Avignon festival', *New Dance*, 38 (autumn): 22–5.

—— (1990) 'Zarathustra's dancers: the influence of Nietzsche's philosophy on Jacques-Dalcroze, Rudolph Steiner, Laban and Wigman', *M T D* (2 July): 24–30.

—— (1994) 'Representations of masculinity in theatre dance with special reference to British new dance', unpublished Ph.D. thesis, West Sussex Institute of Higher Education, Chichester.

Burt, R. and Huxley, M. (1986) 'La nouvelle danse: Comment ne pas jouer le jeu de l'establishment' in M. Febvre (ed.), *La Danse au defi*, Montreal: Parachute; and 'Not quite cricket: how British new dance doesn't quite play the establishment's game', *International Working Papers in Dance*, vol 2, London: Laban Centre (forthcoming).

Butler, J. (1990) *Gender Trouble*, London: Routledge.

Cage, J. (1961) *Silence*, Cambridge, Mass.: MIT Press.

Carroll, N. (1981) 'Post-modern dance and expression', in G. Fancher and G. Myers (eds), *Post-modern Dance and Expression in Philosophical Essays on Dance*, New York: Dance Horizons.

Carty, H. (1992) 'Alvin Ailey – a voice for today', *Dance Now*, 3(1) (Autumn): 5–7.

Chadd, D. and Gage, J. (1979) *The Diaghilev Ballet in England*, Norwich: The Sainsbury Centre for Visual Arts.

Chaikin, J. (1972) *The Presence of the Actor*, New York: Atheneum.

Chambers, I. (1976) 'A strategy for living', in S. Hall and T. Jefferson (eds), *Resistance through Rituals* London: Hutchinson.

Chapman, R. and Rutherford, J. (eds) (1988) *Male Order*, London: Lawrence & Wishart.

Chipp, H. B. (ed.) (1968) *Theories of Modern Art*, Berkeley: University of California Press.

Chodorow, N. (1980) 'Gender, relation, and difference in psychoanalytic perspective', in H. Eisenstein and A. Jardine (eds), *The Future of Difference* Boston: G. K. Hall.

Clark, M. and Crisp, C. (1984) *Dancer: Men in Dance*, London: British Broadcasting Corporation.

Clark, T. J. (1990) 'Jackson Pollock's abstraction', in S. Gilbaut (ed.) *Reconstructing Modernism*, Boston, Mass.: MIT Press.

Cobbett Steinberg, S. (ed.) (1980) *The Dance Anthology*, New York: New American Library.

Cockcroft, E. (1985) 'Abstract expressionism, weapon of the cold war', in F. Frascina (ed.), *Pollock and After: The Critical Debate*. London: Harper & Row.

Cohen, M. (1983) 'Primitivism, modernism and dance theory', in R. Copeland and M. Cohen (eds), *What is Dance?* Oxford: Oxford University Press.

Cohen, S. J. (ed.) (1967) *The Modern Dance: Seven Statements of Belief*, Middletown, Conn.: Wesleyan University Press.

—— (ed.) (1972) *Doris Humphrey – An Artist First*, Middletown, Conn.: Wesleyan University Press.

—— (1982) *Next Week Swan Lake*, Middletown, Conn.: Wesleyan University Press.

Constanti, S. (1989) 'Giving birth to *Dead Dreams*: interview with Lloyd Newson', *Dance Theatre Journal*, 6 (4) (spring): 5, 6, 30.

—— (1990) review of The Featherstonehaughs, *The Guardian*, 14 April.

Cooper, E. (1986) *The Sexual Perspective: Homosexuality and Art in the Last Hundred Years in the West*, London: Routledge & Kegan Paul.

Copeland, R. (1983) 'Merce Cunningham and the politics of perception', in R. Copeland and M. Cohen (eds), *What is Dance?*, Oxford: Oxford University Press.

—— (1986) 'Theatrical dance: how do we know it when we see it if we can't define it?' *Performing Arts Journal*, 26/27: 174–84.

Copeland, R. and Cohen, M. (eds) (1983) *What is Dance?*, Oxford: Oxford University Press.

Corbin, A. (1986) *The Fragrant and the Foul: Odour and the French Social Imagination*, Cambridge, Mass.: Harvard University Press.

Cosgrove, S. (1989) 'The zoot suit and style warfare', in A. McRobbie (ed.), *Zoot Suits and Second-hand Dresses*, London: Macmillan.

Coward, R. (1984) *Female Desire*, London: Paladin.

Craft, R. (1976) 'Nijinsky and *Le Sacre*', *New York Review of Books*, 15 April.

Craven, D. (1985) 'The disappropriation of abstract expressionism', *Art History*, 8 (4) (December).

Crisp, C. (1992) review of Michael Clark's *Mmm*, *Financial Times*, 23 June.

Croce, A. (1987) *Sight Lines*, New York: Knopf.

Cunningham, M. (1968) *Changes*, New York: Something Else Press.

Daines, A. (1987) 'DV8', review, *New Dance Magazine*, 40, Easter.

Dalva, N. (1992) 'The way of Merce', in R. Kostelanetz (ed.), *Merce Cunningham: Dancing in Time and Space*, London: Dance Books.

Daly, A. (1986) 'The Balanchine woman', *TDR*, 31 (2) (T110) (summer): 8–21.

—— (1988) 'Movement analysis: piecing together the puzzle', *TDR*, 32 (4): 40–52.

—— (1989) 'To dance is "female"', *TDR*, 34 (4) (T124) (winter): 23–7.

Davidoff, L. and Hall, C. (1987) *Family Fortunes: Men and Women of the English Middle Class 1780–1850*, London: Hutchison.

D'Emilio, J. (1983) *Sexual Politics, Sexual Communities: The Making of a Homosexual Minority in the United States*, Chicago: University of Chicago Press.

Deleuze, G. and Guattari, F. (1983) *Anti-Oedipus*, Minneapolis: University of Minnesota Press.

Denby, E. (1986) *Dance Writings*, London: Dance Books.

Dolin, A. (1969) *Pas de Deux*, London: Dover.

—— (1985) *Last Words*, London: Century.

Douglas, A. (1977) *The Feminization of American Culture*, New York: Knopf.

Douglas, M. (1966) *Purity and Danger*, London: Ark.

—— (1970) *Natural Symbols*, London: Barrie & Jenkins.

Duchamp, M. (1973) 'The creative act', in G. Battcock, (ed.), *The New Art*, New York: E. P. Dutton & Co. Ltd.

Dyer, R. (1982) 'Don't look now', *Screen*, 23 (Sept./Oct.).

—— (1987) *Heavenly Bodies*, London: Routledge.

—— (1990) *Now You See It*, London: Routledge.

—— (1992) *Only Entertainment*, London: Routledge.

Early, T. (1977) 'What Balletmakers was', *New Dance*, 2 (spring): 16–17.

Ehrenreich, B. (1983) *The Hearts of Men*, London: Pluto.

Eisenstein H. and Jardine, A. (eds) (1980) *The Future of Difference*, Boston, Mass.: G. K. Hall.

Ellis, J. (1982) *Visible Fictions*, London, Routledge & Kegan Paul.

Emery, L. F. (1972) *Black Dance in the U.S. 1619 to the Present Day*, London: Princeton Book Co.

English, R. (1980) 'Alas, alack', *New Dance*, 15: 18–19.

Fancher, G. and Myers, G. (eds) (1981). *Post-modern Dance and Expression in Philosophical Essays on Dance*, New York: Dance Horizons.

Fanger, I. M. (1991) 'Ralph Lemon: private man in the public arena', *Dance Magazine* (August): 39–42.

—— M. (1992) 'Looking up: David Dorfman's ascending boundaries', *Dance Magazine* (April).

Fanon, F. (1968) *Black Skin, White Masks*, London: MacGibbon & Kee.

Febvre, M. (ed.) (1986) *La Danse au défi*, Montreal: Parachute.

Flugel, J. C. (1930) *The Psychology of Clothes*, London: Hogarth Press.

Fokine, M. (1961) *Memoirs of a Ballet Master*, London: Constable.

Foster, H. (ed.) (1985) *Post Modern Culture*, London: Pluto.

Foster, S. L. (1985) 'The signifying body', *Theatre Journal*, 37 (1): 44–64 (March).

—— (1986) *Reading Dancing*, Berkeley: University of California Press.

Foucault, M. (1979) *Discipline and Punish*, Harmondsworth: Penguin.

—— (1980) *Power/Knowledge*, Brighton: Harvester.

—— (1981) *History of Sexuality*, vol 1, Harmondsworth: Penguin.

Frascina, F. (ed.) (1985) *Pollock and After: The Critical Debate*, London: Harper & Row.

Freud, S. (1963) *Leonardo*, Harmondsworth: Penguin.

Fried, M. (1968) 'Art and objecthood' (1967) in G. Batcock (ed.), *Minimal Art: A Critical Anthology*, New York: E. P. Dutton & Co.

Fulkerson, M. (1982) 'The move to stillness', *Theatre Papers*, fourth series, 1981–2, no. 10, Dartington: Dartington College of Arts.

Fuller, P. (1978) 'Jasper Johns interviewed part 2', *Art Monthly* (London), 19 (September): 5–7.

Gadamer, H. (1975) *Truth and Method*, London: Sheed & Ward.

—— (1976) *Philosophical Hermeneutics*, London: University of California Press.

Gallagher, C. (1987) 'The body versus the social body in the works of Thomas Malthus and Henry Mayhew', in C. Gallagher and T. Lacquer (eds), *The Making of the Modern Body*, Berkeley: University of California Press.

Gallagher, C. and Lacqueur, T. (eds) (1987) *The Making of the Modern Body*, Berkeley: University of California Press.

Gamman, L. and Marshment, M. (1988) *The Female Gaze*, London: The Women's Press.

Garafola, L. (1985–6) 'The travestie dancer in the nineteenth century', *Dance Research Journal*, 17(2) and 18(1): 35–40.

—— (1989) *Diaghilev's Ballets Russes*, Oxford: Oxford University Press.

—— (1992) 'Choreography by Nijinska', *Ballet Review*, 20 (4) (winter): 64–71.

—— (1993) book review article in *The Drama Review*, 37 (1) (T137) (spring): 167–72.

Gautier, T. (1947) *The Romantic Ballet*, London: C. W. Beaumont.

—— (1983) 'A ballet called Giselle', in R. Copeland and M. Cohen (eds), *What is Dance?*, Oxford: Oxford University Press.

Gilbaut, S. (1985) 'The new adventures of the avant-garde in America', in F. Frascina (ed.), *Pollock and After: The Critical Debate*, London: Harper & Row.

—— (ed.) (1990a) *Reconstructing Modernism*, Boston, Mass.: MIT Press.

—— (1990b) 'Postwar painting games, the rough and the slick', in S. Gilbaut (ed.), *Reconstructing Modernism*, Boston, Mass.: MIT Press.

Gilman, S. L. (1988) *Disease and Representation*, Ithaca: Cornell University Press.

Gledhill, C. (1980) 'Klute 1: a contemporary film noir and feminist criticism', in E. A. Kaplan (ed.), *Women in Film Noir*, London: BFI.

Goodman, N. (1976) *Languages of Art*, Indianapolis: Hackett.

—— (1983) 'Afterword to languages of art', in R. Copeland and M. Cohen (eds), *What is Dance?*, Oxford: Oxford University Press.

Gottlieb, B. (1951) 'The theatre of José Limón', *Theatre Arts Monthly* (November): 27, 94–5.

Graham, M. (1973) *Notebooks of Martha Graham*, New York: Harcourt Brace.

Greenberg, C. (1965) 'Modernist painting', in C. Harrison, *Modern Art & Modernism: A Critical Anthology*, London: Harper & Row.

Guest, I. (1966) *Romantic Ballet in Paris*, London: Dance Books.

Hall, S. and Jefferson, T. (eds) (1977) *Resistance through Rituals*, London: Hutchinson.

Hallar, M. and Scavenius, A. (1992) *Bournonvilleana*, London: Dance Books.

Hanna, J. L. (1988) *Dance, Sex and Gender*, Austin: University of Texas.

Harrison, C. (1983) *Modern Art and Modernism: A Critical Anthology*, London: Harper & Row.

Haskell, A. (1928) *Some Studies in Ballet*, London: Lamley & Co.

—— (1934) *Balletomania*, London: Victor Gollancz.

Hearn, J. (1987) *The Gender of Oppression: Men, Masculinity and the Critique of Marxism*, Brighton: Wheatsheaf.

Hearn, J. and Morgan, D. (eds) 1990 *Men, Masculinity and Social Theory*, London: Unwin Hyman.

Heller, A. (1982) 'The emotional division of labour between the sexes', *Thesis Eleven*, 5/6: 54–71.

Hoch, P. (1979) *White Hero, Black Beast*, London: Pluto.

Hodson, M. (1985) 'Ritual design in the New Dance: Nijinsky's *Le Sacre du printemps*', *Dance Research*, 3 (2) (summer): 35–45.

—— (1986) 'Ritual design in the new dance: Nijinsky's choreographic method', *Dance Research*, 4 (1) (spring): 63–77.

Hoghe, R. (1980) 'The theatre of Pina Bausch', *The Drama Review*, 24 (1) (March): 63–74.

Howe-Beck, L. (1988) review of *Mammame*, *Dance Magazine* (January): 27–8, 70.

Huxley, M. (1988) 'Are you right there Michael? Are you right?', in J. Adshead, (ed.), *Dance Analysis*, London: Dance Books.

Irigaray, L. (1981) 'This sex which is not one', in E. Marks and I. de Courtivron (eds), *New French Feminisms*, Brighton: Harvester.

Jackson, G. (1978) *Dance as Dance*, Toronto: Catalyst.

Jameson, F. (1985) 'Postmodernism and consumer society', in H. Foster, (ed.), *Post Modern Culture*, London: Pluto.

Johnston, J. (1971) *Marmalade Me*, New York: E. P. Dutton.

—— (1987) 'Jigs, Japes and Joyce', *Art in America* (January): 103–5.

—— (1992) 'Two reviews (1960, 1963)', in R. Kostalenetz (ed.), *Merce Cunningham: Dancing in Time and Space*, London: Dance Books.

Jones, A, R. (1984) 'Julia Kristeva on femininity', *Feminist Review*, 18 (November): 56–73.

Jordan, S. (1980) 'Merce Cunningham and John Cage in dialogue', *New Dance*, 16 (autumn): 16–17.

—— (1987) review of DV8, *New Statesman*, 27 February.

Jowitt, D. (1977) *Dance Beat*, New York: Marcel Dekker.

—— (1985) *The Dance in Mind*, Boston, Mass.: David R. Godine.

—— (1988) *Time and the Dancing Image*, New York: William Morrow & Company, Inc.

Kaplan, A. Y. (1989) 'Theweleit and Speigelman', in B. Kruger and P. Mariani (eds), *Remaking History*, Seattle: Bay Press.

Kaplan, E. A. (ed.) (1980) *Women in Film Noir*. London: BFI.

Karlinsky, S. (1983) 'Stravinsky and Russian pre-literate theatre', *Nineteenth Century Music*, 6 (3) (spring): 232–40.

Karsavina, T. (1930) *Theatre Street*, London: Heinemann.

Kelly, P. and Stuart, O. (1989) 'Dancing the difference: neoromanticism, men and the eighties', *Dance Magazine* (January): 34–8.

Kendall, E. (1979) *Where She Danced*, New York: Knopf.

Kent, S. (1984) 'Feminism and decadence', *Artscribe* 44.

Kent, S. and Morreau, J. (eds) (1985) *Women's Images of Men*, London: Writers & Readers.

Kimmel, Michael S. (1987) 'The contemporary "crisis" of masculinity in historical perspective', in H. Brod (ed.), *The Making of Masculinities*, London: Allen & Unwin.

King, K. (1992) 'Space dance and the galactic matrix', in R. Kostelanetz (eds), *Merce Cunningham: Dancing in Time and Space*, London: Dance Books.

Klosty, J. (ed.) (1975) *Merce Cunningham*, New York: E. P. Dutton.

Koner, P. (1989) *Solitary Song*, Durham, NC and London: Duke University Press.

Kostelanetz, R. (ed.) (1992) *Merce Cunningham: Dancing in Time and Space*, London: Dance Books.

Kristeva, J. (1980) *Desire in Language*, London: Blackwood.

Kruger, B. and Mariani, P. (eds) (1989) *Remaking History*, Seattle: Bay Press.

Lacqueur, T. (1987) 'Orgasm, generation and the politics of reproductive biology', in C. Gallagher and T. Lacqueur (eds), *The Making of the Modern Body*, Berkeley: University of California Press.

Langer, S. (1953) *Feeling and Form*, London: Routledge & Kegan Paul.

Lee, R. (1987) 'Resisting amnesia: feminism, painting and postmodernism', *Feminist Review*, 26 (summer): 5–28.

Lesschaeve, J. (1985) *The Dancer and the Dance: Merce Cunningham in Conversation with Jacqueline Lesschaeve*, New York: Marion Boyars.

Levin, D. M. (1983) 'Balanchine's formalism', in R. Copeland and M. Cohen (eds), *What is Dance?*, Oxford: Oxford University Press.

Levinson (1980) 'The spirit of the classic dance', in S. Cobbett Steinberg (ed.), *The Dance Anthology*, New York: New American Library.

—— (1983) 'The idea of dance from Aristotle to Mallarmé' (1927), in R. Copeland and M. Cohen (eds), *What is Dance?*, Oxford: Oxford University Press.

Lieven, Prince P. (1980) 'Vaslav Nijinsky', in S. Cobbett Steinberg (ed.), *The Dance Anthology*, New York: New American Library.

Limón, J. (1966) 'The virile dance' (1948), in W. Sorrell (ed.), *Dance Has Many Faces*, New York: Columbia University Press.

—— (1967) 'In an American accent' in S. J. Cohen (ed.), *The Modern Dance: Seven Statements of Belief*, Middletown, Conn.: Wesleyan University Press.

213

—— (1979) 'On dance', in J. Morrison Brown (ed.), *The Vision of Modern Dance*, London: Dance Books.

Lyotard, J.-F. (1984) *The Postmodern Condition: A Report on Knowledge*, Manchester and Minneapolis: Manchester University Press and University of Minnesota Press.

Macaulay, A. (1984) 'Michael Clark talks', *Dance Theatre Journal*, 2(3) (autumn): 16–28.

—— (1988) 'The addict of camp: Michael Clark's "Because We Must"', *Dancing Times* (February): 440–1.

MacDonald, N. (1975) *Diaghilev Observed*, London: Dance Books.

Mackrell, J. (1988) 'Umbrella dance and dancers', *Dance Theatre Journal*, 5(4) (spring): 5–8.

—— (1989) review of Michael Clark's *Hetrospective*, *The Independent*, 16 October.

—— (1992) 'Living up to his promise', review of Michael Clark's *Mmm*, *The Independent*, 22 June.

McRobbie, A. (ed.) (1989) *Zoot Suits and Second-hand Dresses*, London: Macmillan.

Manchester, P. W. (1950) 'English male dancers: a cautious prophecy', *The Ballet Annual*, 4: 98–9.

Mangan, J. A. (1981) *Athleticism in the Victorian and Edwardian Public School*, Cambridge: Cambridge University Press.

Mangan, J. A. and Walvin, J. (eds) (1987) *Manliness and Morality: Middle Class Masculinity in Britain and the United States 1800–1940*, Manchester: Manchester University Press.

Manor, G. (1980) *The Gospel According to Dance*, New York: St Martin's Press.

—— (ed.) (1992) 'The Bible in art', *Choreography and Dance*, 2 (3).

Marks, E. and Courtivron I. de (eds) (1981) *New French Feminisms*, Brighton: Harvester.

Martin, J. (1968) *America Dancing*, New York: Dance Horizons.

Mazo, J. (1978) *The Alvin Ailey American Dance Theatre*, New York: William Morrow.

—— (1991) 'Martha remembered', *Dance Magazine* (July): 34–45.

Meisner, N. (1983) 'Fergus Early', *Dance and Dancers* (April): 27–8.

—— (1989) review of DV8's *Dead Dreams of Monochrome Men*, *Dance and Dancers* (March): 19–20.

Mercer, K. (1988) 'Racism and the politics of masculinity', in R. Chapman and J. Rutherford (eds), *Male Order*. London: Lawrence & Wishart.

Metcalf, A. and Humphries, M. (eds) (1985) *The Sexuality of Men*, London: Pluto.

Meyer, M. (1992) 'Unveiling the word: science and narrative in transsexual striptease', in L. Senelick (ed.), *Gender in Performance*, Hanover and London: Tufts University Press.

—— (ed.) (1993) *The Politics and Poetics of Camp*, London: Routledge.

Mindlin, N. (1992) 'José Limón's The Moor's Pavane: an interview with Lucas Hoving', *Dance Research Journal*, 24(1) (spring): 13–26.

Moi, T. (1985) *Sexual/Textual Politics*, London: Methuen.

Moore, S. (1988) 'Here's looking at you, kid!', in L. Gamman and M. Marshment (eds), *The Female Gaze*, London: The Women's Press.

Morrison Brown, J. (1980) *The Vision of Modern Dance*, London: Dance Books.

Mort, F. (1988) 'Boys' own? Masculinity, style and popular culture', in R. Chapman and J. Rutherford (eds), *Male Order*, London: Lawrence & Wishart.

Mulvey, L. (1975) 'Visual pleasure and narrative cinema', *Screen* 16 (3): 6–18.

—— (1981) 'Duel in the sun', *Framework*, 15/16/17 (summer): 12–15.

—— (1989) *The Visual and Other Pleasures*, London: Macmillan.

Neale, S. (1983) 'Masculinity as spectacle', *Screen*, 24 (6): 2–19.

214

—— (1986) 'Sexual difference in cinema', *Oxford Literary Review*, special issue 'Sexual Difference', 8: 123–32.

Nijinska, B. (1981) *Early Memoirs*, London: Faber & Faber.

—— (1986) 'On movement and the school of movement', in N. Van N. Baer, *Bronislava Nijinsky: A Dancer's Legacy*, San Francisco: The Fine Arts Museums of San Francisco.

Nochlin, L. (1971) 'Why have there been no great women artists?', in T. B. Hess and E. C. Baker (eds), *Art and Sexual Politics*, New York: Collier Books.

Nochlin, L. (1991) *The Politics of Vision*, London: Thames & Hudson.

Norris, C. (1982) *Deconstruction: Theory and Practice*, London: Methuen.

—— (1992) *Uncritical Theory*, London: Lawrence & Wishart.

Novack, C. (1990) *Sharing the Dance*, Madison: University of Wisconsin Press.

Orledge, R. (1990) *Satie the Composer*, Cambridge: Cambridge University Press.

Orton, F. (1987–8) 'Present, the scene of . . . selves, the occasion of . . . ruses', *Block*, 13: 5–19.

Owens, C. (1985) 'The discourse of others: feminists and postmodernism', in H. Foster (ed.), *Post Modern Culture*, London: Pluto.

Paglia, C. (1992) *Sex Art and American Culture*, New York: Viking Penguin.

Parker, R and Pollock, G. (1981) *Old Mistresses*, London: Routledge & Kegan Paul.

Parry, J. (1990) review of The Featherstonehaughs, *Observer*, 18 February.

—— (1992) review of Michael Clark's *Mmm*, *Observer*, 28 June.

Paxton, S. (1972) 'The Grand Union', *TDR*, 16 (3) (September): 128–34.

—— (1977) 'In the midst of standing still something else is occurring and the name for that is the small dance' (interview with P. Hulton), *Theatre Papers*, first series, 4, Dartington: Dartington College of Arts.

—— (1982) 'Contact improvisation', (interview with F. Bents), *Theatre Papers*, fourth series, 5, Dartington: Dartington College of Arts.

Percival, J. (1988) review of DV8's *Dead Dreams of Monochrome Men*, *The Times*, 5 November.

—— (1991) review of David Dorfman's *Horn*, *Dance and Dancers* (December): 28.

Person, E. S. (1980) 'Sexuality as the mainstay of identity: psychoanalytic perspectives', *Signs*, 5(4): 605–30.

Pierce, W. (1988) 'Meat and murder', *Square Peg*, 22.

Poesio, G. (1990) 'The story of the fighting dancers', *Dance Research*, 8 (1) (spring): 25–36.

Pollack, B. (1993) *Dance is a Moment*, Princeton: Dance Horizons.

Praz, M. (1967) *The Romantic Agony*, London: Thames & Hudson.

Preston-Dunlop, V. (1988) 'Laban and the Nazis', *Dance Theatre Journal*, 6 (2) (fall): 4–7.

Prickett, S. (1989) 'From workers' dance to new dance', *Dance Research*, 7 (1): 47–64.

—— (1990) 'Dance and the workers' struggle', *Dance Research*, 8 (1) (spring): 47–61.

Pumphrey, M. (1989) 'Why do cowboys wear hats in the bath?', *Critical Quarterly*, 31 (3): 78–100.

Quirey, B. (1976) *May I Have the Pleasure? The Story of Popular Dance*, London: BBC.

Rainer, Y. (1981) 'Looking myself in the mouth' *October*, 17 (summer): 65–76.

Rambert, M. (1972) *Quicksilver*, London: Macmillan.

Richards, J. (1987) 'Passing the love of women: manly love and Victorian society', in J. A. Mangan and J. Walvin (eds), *Manliness and Morality: Middle Class Masculinity in Britain and the United States 1800–1940*, Manchester: Manchester University Press.

Riesman , D. (1950) *The Lonely Crowd*, New Haven: Yale University Press.

Rivière, J. (1983) 'Le Sacre du printemps', in R. Copeland and M. Cohen (eds), *What is Dance?*, Oxford: Oxford University Press.

Robertson, A. (1990) review of The Featherstonehaughs, *20/20 Magazine* (April).

Rosenberg, R. (1968) 'The American action painters', (1952), in H. B. Chipp (ed.), *Theories of Modern Art*, Berkeley: University of California Press.

Roth, M. (1977) 'The aesthetic of indifference', *Artforum* (November): 45–53.

Rubidge, S. (1989) 'Decoding dance', *Dance Theatre Journal*, 7 (2) (autumn): 2–5.

Rubin, G. (1978) 'The traffic in women: notes on the "political economy" of sex', in R. Reiter (ed.), *Towards an Anthropology of Women*, New York: Monthly Review Press.

Said, E. (1978) *Orientalism*, London: Routledge & Kegan Paul.

Sayre, H. M. (1992) *The Object of Performance: The American Avant-garde since 1970*, Chicago and London: Chicago University Press.

Schlundt, C. L. (1967) *Ted Shawn and his Men Dancers: A Chronology and an Index of his Dances 1933–1940*, New York: New York Public Library.

Sedgwick, E. K. (1985) *Between Men: English Literature and Male Homosocial Desire*, New York: Columbia University Press.

Seidler, V. (1990) 'Men, feminism and power', in J. Hearn, and D. Morgan (eds), *Men, Masculinity and Social Theory*, London: Unwin Hyman.

Senelick, L. (ed.) (1992) *Gender in Performance*, Hanover and London: Tufts University Press.

Servos, N. (1984) *Pina Bausch Wuppertal Dance Theatre: or The Art of Training a Goldfish*, Cologne: Ballett-Bühnen-Verlag.

Shawn, T. (1916) 'A defense of the male dancer: a talk with Ted Shawn', *New York Dramatic Mirror*, 13 May.

—— (1933) 'Principles of dancing for men', *Journal of Health and Physical Education* (November): 27–9, 60.

—— (1936) 'Men must dance', *Dance* (November): 10.

—— (1946) *Dance We Must*, London: Dennis Dobson.

—— (1966) 'Dancing for men', *Dance Magazine* (July): 16–17.

—— (1968) *Every Little Movement*, New York: Dance Horizons.

Sheets, M. (1966) *The Phenomenology of Dance*, Madison: University of Wisconsin.

Sherman, J. and B. Mumaw, (1986) *Barton Mumaw Dancer: From Denishawn to Jacob's Pillow and Beyond*, New York: Dance Horizons.

Siegel, M. (1979) *Shapes of Change*, New York: Avon Books.

—— (1987) *Days on Earth*, New Haven: Yale University Press.

Smoliar, S. (1992) 'Merce Cunningham in Brooklyn', in R. Kostelanetz (ed.), *Merce Cunningham: Dancing in Time and Space*, London: Dance Books.

Sokolova, L. (1960) *Dancing for Diaghilev*, London: John Murray.

Sorrell, W. (ed.) (1966) *The Dance Has Many Faces*, New York: Columbia University Press.

Stamboulian, G. and Marks, E. (eds) (1979) *Homosexualities and French Literature*, Ithaca and London: Cornell University Press.

Staples, R. (1982) *Black Masculinity: The Black Man's Role in American Society*, New York: Black Scholar Press.

Stern, D. (1985) *The Interpersonal World of the Infant*, New York: Basic Books.

Stokes, A. (1942) *Tonight the Ballet*, London: Faber & Faber.

Stravinsky, I. (1969) *The Rite of Spring: Sketches 1911–1913*, London: Boosey & Hawkes.

Swinson, C. (1964) *Great Male Dancers*, London: A & C Black.

Taylor, P. (1975) *Private Domain*, New York: Alfred A. Knopf.

Terry, W. (1976) *Ted Shawn: Father of American Dance*, New York: Dial.

—— (1979) *Great Male Dancers of the Ballet*, New York: Hale.

Theweleit, K. (1987) *Male Fantasies*, Minneapolis: University of Minnesota Press, and Oxford: Blackwell.

Thom, L. A. (1989) review of DV8, *Dance Magazine* (April): 69, 88.

Turner, C. and Carter, E. (1986) 'Political somatics', in V. Burgin (ed.), *Formations of Fantasy*, London: Methuen.

Vaughan, D. *et al.* (1987) 'Cunningham and his dancers', *Ballet Review*, 15 (3): 19–40.

Walters, M. (1979) *The Male Nude*, Harmondsworth: Penguin.

Weeks, J. (1977) *Coming Out*, London: Quartet.

—— (1985) *Sexuality and its Discontents*, London: Routledge & Kegan Paul.

—— (1986) 'Masculinity and the science of desire', *Oxford Literary Review*, 8, special issue 'Sexual difference': 22–7.

Weeks, M. (1987) 'Breaking the conspiracy of silence! Lesbianism and dance', *New Dance*, 41 (July).

Weld, T. (1979) 'Men's week at Laurieston Hall', *Achilles Heel*, 2: 30–1.

Wengerd, T. (1991) 'Martha's men', *Dance Magazine* (July): 48–52.

White, L. (1984) 'The new glitterati 2', *The Face*, 48 (April): 56–7.

Wilkie, W. (1943) *One World*, New York: Simon & Schuster.

Williams, R. (1989) *The Politics of Modernism*, London: Verso.

Wohl, R. (1979) *The Generation of 1914*, Cambridge, Mass.: Harvard University Press.

Wolff, J. (1975) *Hermeneutic Philosophy and the Sociology of Art*, London: Routledge & Kegan Paul.

—— (1982) *The Social Production of Art*, London: Macmillan.

—— (1990) *Feminine Sentences*, London: Polity.

Wolff, J. and Seed, J. (eds) (1987) *The Culture of Capital*, Manchester: Manchester University Press.

Wollen, P. (1987) 'Fashion/orientalism/the body', *New Formations*, 1: 5–33.

INDEX

Abbreviation: ch. choreographed. Titles of works in italics.